Explore the World
NELLES GUIDE

NEW ZEALAND

Authors:
Peter Hinze, Ainslie Talbot, Marc Marger,
Maureen Te Rangi Rere I Waho Waaka, John Berry,
Pat Hanning, Craig Potton, Peter Birkenmaier,
Peter Linden

*An Up-to-date travel guide with 128 color photos
and 21 maps*

**Third Revised Edition
1998**

Dear Reader,

Being up-to-date is the main goal of the Nelles series. To achieve it, we have a network of far-flung correspondents who keep us abreast of the latest developments in the travel scene, and our cartographers always make sure that maps and texts are adjusted to each other.

Each travel chapter ends with its own list of useful tips, accommodations, restaurants, tourist offices, sights. At the end of the book you will find practical information from A to Z. But the travel world is fast moving, and we cannot guarantee that all the contents are always valid. Should you come across a discrepancy, please write us at: Nelles Verlag GmbH, Schleissheimer Str. 371 b, D-80935 München, Germany, Tel: (089) 3571940, Fax: (089) 35719430.

LEGEND

✴	Place of Interest	♣	National Park, Nature Reserve	▦	Expressway
▦	Public or Significant Building	\25/	Distance in Kilometers	▬	Principal Highway (Paved/ Unpaved)
■	Hotel	Waiotapu	Place Mentioned in Text	▭	Main Road (Paved/ Unpaved)
✈	International Airport	■---■	Cable Car	───	Other Road
✈	National Airport	①⑩	Route numbers	----	Track
☂	Beach	**Mt. Cook** 3764	Mountain Summit (Height in Meters)	✕✕✕	Railway

NEW ZEALAND
© Nelles Verlag GmbH, D-80935 München
  All rights reserved

Third Revised Edition 1998
ISBN 3-88618-905-8
Printed in Slovenia

Publisher:	Günter Nelles	**Translation:**	Liz Goldmann, G'Ann Stratil
Project Editor:	Peter Hinze		
Editors:	Christine Grimm, Marton Radkai	**Color Separation:**	Priegnitz, München
Cartography:	Nelles Verlag GmbH	**Printed by:**	Gorenjski Tisk

- X07 -

TABLE OF CONTENTS

GUIDELINES

LIST OF MAPS

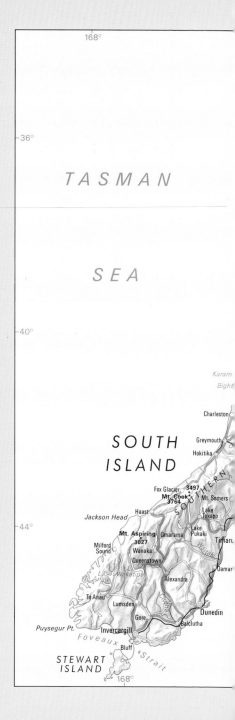

THREE KINGS IS.
176°
0°

Reinga   North Cape
Great
Exhibition
Bay

Awanui
Kaitaia

Rawene   Kawakawa

Whangarei

GREAT
BARRIER I.
Wellsford
C. Colville
36°
East Coast Bays
Kaipara   Takapuna   Coromandel
Harbour   AUCKLAND   Hauraki
MANUKAU   Gulf
Papakura   Thames

Waihi
Bay
Mt.   of
Maunganui   Plenty   East Cape
Hamilton   Tauranga
Cambridge   Whakatane   1753
Otorohanga   Rotorua
Tokoroa
Awakino   Wairakei
L.   Taupo
New Plymouth   Taupo)   Gisborne
C. Egmont   2517   2291   Turangi   Wairoa
Mt. Taranaki   Mt. Ruapehu   Hawke
2797   Bay
Hawera   Napier
1733   Hastings
Wanganui
Feilding

Farewell   Palmerston   Woodville
North   40°
D'URVILLE I.   Levin
Tasman   Poirua   Masterton
Bay   WELLINGTON   Upper Hutt
Nelson   Havelock Picton   Lower Hutt
1875   Blenheim   Wainuiomata
Kawatiri   C. Palliser
ton   Tapuaenuku
2338   2885

Kaikoura

Waipara
ffield   Pegasus Bay
CHRISTCHURCH

urton

nterbury
ght

NORTH ISLAND

PACIFIC

OCEAN

CHATHAM
ISLANDS
44°
PITT I.

4°

NEW ZEALAND
0   100km   200km

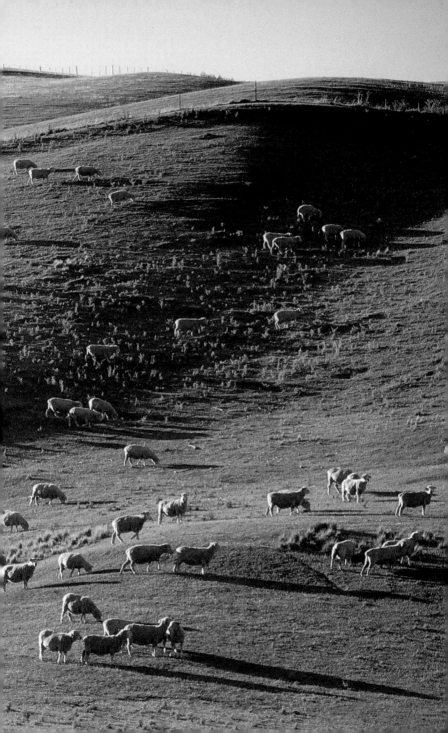

MAORI MYTHOLOGY

Maori first discovered the two islands in the South Pacific, now collectively called New Zealand, approximately 1000 years ago after sailing on uncharted water ways in their long seafaring canoes.

The Maori were the very first people to inhabit the region. Today they still refer to it as *Aotearoa*, meaning "land of the great, white clouds." Their own story of creation is strongly rooted in this land. It begins with the following words:

At the beginning was Te Kore, complete oblivion. And from Te Kore was born Te Poo, the night. In this utter darkness, the sky father Rangi lay in the arms of Papa, mother earth. Their children crawled around in the closeness of their parent's bodies. The children longed to be free, to feel the wind that swept the mountaintops and valleys, and to feel the light warming their pale bodies. What can we do?, they cried. We need a place to stretch our constrained limbs. We need light. We need space.

Tane Mahuta, the mighty god of the forests, and father of all living creatures who love light and freedom then rose up. In order to gather enough strength, Tane remained standing quietly, for as long as a man can hold his breath. He pressed his hands against his mother's body and placed both his feet firmly upon his father. He then stretched his back and pressed against Rangi. His parents continued to hold each other tightly, but Tane managed to gather all of his strength until at last the mighty bodies of heaven

Preceding pages: The jagged contour of Cape Reinga. Sheep, a mainstay of New Zealand's economy, graze peacefully near Queenstown. The artistic carving of the Maori. A portrait of two Maori by George French Angas (1822-1886).

and earth were separated. Rangi was blown away by the strong winds raging between heaven and earth.

Aotearoa was thus created. Compared to the island where the Maori came from, this country was much wilder. The sea was rougher, the cliffs more precipitous, the climate more changeable and the vegetation more lush. Volcanoes erupted, and in many places Mother Earth showed signs of unrest. Much of the inexplicable phenomena required a mythological explanation. The status of the gods changed with the new environment. The ocean, once the only source of nourishment, was no longer of such importance. The sea god, Tangaroa, lost his significance. The mainland was the perfect place to grow plants, and the wingless moa, which lived in the forests and reached a height of up to three meters, was easy game for the Maori hunters. And so it was that Tane Mahuta grew to be immensely important. Originally only the god of the forests, Tane became the creator of all things. Today there are over 1000 bird species in Aotearoa alone. According to Maori mythology, Tane is also responsible for their creation.

Tane – the Giver of Life

Tane and his brothers observed their mother's soft profile. As the light began to spread over the land, they saw that their mother's bare shoulders were enveloped in a silver veil of mist. It was a veil of mourning for the loss of her husband. Tears streamed from Rangi's eyes.

Although he had separated his parents with such brutal force, Tane loved them dearly. He began to clothe his mother in a robe of exquisite beauty. She could not have dreamed of wearing such a beautiful robe in the former dark world. First he brought the trees, his children, and he planted them in the fertile soil. But despite Tane's fame as one of the youngest gods, he still behaved like a child, since

names. According to Maori mythology, Tane also created the splendor of the moon, the sun, the stars and sky during a strenuous odyssey through the vast universe, as he described to the Maori upon their arrival on Aotearoa:

Mother earth lay there, quite still and beautiful, covered in a cloak of living green. The gods, whose skin had turned brown in the meantime, frolicked under the frondage of Tane's garden. Raango-maa-tane maintained the plants' fertility. Haumia-tiketike took care of the ferns' delicate roots. Tuu-matauenga was the god of war. Tangaroa held the relentless ocean in check. Only one of the 70 brothers left the protection of the mother in order to follow his father. It was Taaw-hirimaatea, god of all winds, which swept between heaven and earth.

Tane Mahuta glanced upwards to Rangi, who lay cold, gray and numb in the huge space above the earth, and had pity on his father's sense of despair. He took the bright sun and placed it on Rangis' back, and in front of the sun Tane placed the moon. He journeyed throughout the ten heavens until he found a bright red robe. Tane waited ten days before spreading the mantle over the sky from east to west and from north to south. But he wasn't satisfied. He decided it wasn't a worthy present for his father and removed it. A small fragment was left hanging, however, and this is what we still can see when the sun goes down.

Other than the gods and their children, nobody else fit on the earth. Everyone lived in harmony. Aotearoa, whose birds had almost lost their ability to fly since they had no natural enemies to contend with for over two million years, seemed like paradise on earth. It was a paradise void of rules and regulations, but also without knowledge and progress. Once again, it was Tane who paved the way for a life of creativity in this static paradise. He disappeared into the heavens, in search of the holy teachings:

wisdom was yet to be born. He planted the trees with their leaves facing downwards, so that they were buried under the ground, while the long white stiff roots stood motionless in mid-air. No room remained for his other children, the birds and insects. So he pulled a huge kauri tree out again, shook the soil from its branches and planted its roots firmly in the earth.

Maori believe that all trees are sacred plants, a conviction that is still upheld today. Kauri forests proliferated almost everywhere on the North Island of Aotearoa. Kauri trees grow to an enormous height, continually renewing their branches and bark. When the Maori had to fell a kauri tree in order to build one of their 50-meter long canoes, they asked Tane to forgive them. The tallest kauris, as the children of God, were given

Above: The Maori Pikau Teimana from Putaruru in traditional garb. Right: The first European settlers arrive in New Zealand in 1642 (Isaac Gilsemans).

In the eleventh heaven, Tane finally went to Puu-motomoto, the gateway to the uppermost heaven. There he was received by Rehua, the god of friendliness, with whom he was on very good terms. He presented Tane with the three coveted baskets containing the required knowledge for maakutu (witchcraft), tapu (religious laws) and karakia (magic). The evil Whiro stopped Tane on his way back to the ninth heaven. Accompanied by his followers, mosquitoes, sandflies, owls, bats and other nocturnal creatures, Whiro fiercely fought against Tane. But strengthened by his newly-acquired knowledge from the uppermost heaven, Tane was able to defeat him. Whiro and his followers were banished from the heavens, and forced to live on earth, where they became a menace to mankind.

Tane's second long journey taught him about the fundamental moral values necessary to develop a just and humane society. However, the price he had to pay for this was very high. In essence, it was the epitomy of all that is evil, in relation to Aotearoas's less harmful creatures like mosquitoes and sandflies. The *tapu* soon played an important role in Maori society. Carved wooden figures depicting warrior heads with their tongues sticking out indicate that the town or village is presided over by *tapu*. These figures are placed outside every Maori assembly building. They are also sometimes used as stakes to mark off the boundaries of property. Maori meet their potential foes with faces painted black and tongues sticking out in order to frighten them off. Along with acquiring the baskets of knowledge, the discovery of the female side of life also belongs among Tane's great and noble deeds.

Search for the Female Element

Papa and Rangi's children were male gods, and had a trace of the god-like element known as ira atua. At the same time, they were not able to create the human element known as ira tangata. This could only be derived from the female element,

17

known as uha. While searching for uha and mortal life, Tane gave numerous gifts to humanity. Papa had advised him to visit Mumuhango. Many trees, birds and insects were brought forth by this partnership. The union with other female beings brought forth stones, tides, mud and reptiles. Yet, the basic female element was still missing. Tane returned to Papa with a feeling of despair. She advised him to go to Kurawaka, where the feminine was still in its virginal state. The soil there is tapu, said Papa, for it contains the human seed. When you have reached the beach at Kurawaka, gather together the soil and form it into a human shape. Unwillingly, Tane did what Papa had asked him to do. On arriving in Kurawaka, he created a replica of mother earth as the first woman, who subsequently became known as Hineahuone. His brothers helped him with this task. While the older brothers formed her body, the younger ones filled it with muscle, fat, tissue and blood. Tane, the god of fertility, then laid himself upon this newly-created body, and breathed the breath of life into her mouth, ears and nose. And so it was that a daughter was created from this first union between a god and a woman. She was given the name of Hine-i-tauira.

Life had been created, but death was still missing.Two mighty oceans met at Cape Reinga, the Cape of the Leap, at the most northerly point of the North Island of Aotearoa – the Tasman Sea and the Pacific. The colors green and blue mingle in the relentless surf. The waters here are never calm, owing to the clashing tidal rythms. On a clear day, the three islands of Oohau can be seen in the distance. This is where the entrance to *Raroheenga*, the underworld, is located, according to Maori mythology. On their journey to the distant homeland of *ha

Right: The Maori meeting house Tamate Kapua in Ohinemutu.

waiki, the dead first arrive at the red *pohutukawa* tree at Cape Reinga. Continuing their journey on the tossing waves, they finally reach Oohau to bid a last farewell before heading for Irihia, towards the setting sun:

When Tane's daughter became a woman, he made her his wife. Whenever she tormented him with questions about her parents, Tane was evasive. But she was so persistent that Tane felt obliged to tell her the truth. Deeply saddened, Hinei-tauira left her homeland. "Where are you going?", Tane then asked her. ,,You can't possibly escape me. I am present everywhere in this world of light". "I refuse to remain in your world of light," she replied. "My mother Papa will protect me in the depths of her bosom." The way to the underworld was to be established forever. When she took her place in the shades, her name was changed to Hine-nui-tepoo. She became the goddess of death.

Myths and Legends Still Alive Today

An endless number of myths and legends not only refer to Tane's story of creation, but include all kinds of spirits and cannibals, and also tribal chieftains. The story of the giant Matau is a great favorite among the Maori. It tells how the giant, who lived in Central Otago on the South Island of Aotearoa, kidnapped a beautiful young girl called Manata. Her lover, Matakauri, immediately set out to look for her, and finally found her on the banks of a river. There she was tied up with rope made from the skin of Matau's twelve-headed dog. Matakauri was unable to free Manata. But her tears ultimately dissolved the magic bonds.

In order to prevent the giant from striking again, Matakauri went to him in the dead of night. Finding him fast asleep, Matakauri set a fire around him. Matau sensed too late that he was in danger. He burned to death in the flames, except for

his heart. His dead body sank a few hundred meters into the ground, leaving a great hollow in the surface of the earth. Heavy rain soon filled this hole, creating Lake Wakatipu, meaning the hollow of demons. The water level rises and sinks at regular intervals even today. The Maori believe this movement indicates that Matau's heart is still beating.

The climbing of mountains was also a Maori *tapu* for a long time. Mountains were regarded as god-like beings. The volcanoes on North Island, with their occasional, devastating eruptions, gave rise to many myths and legends. According to the Maori, these volcanoes are said to have lived together at the heart of the island to the south of Lake Taupo. All the male volcanoes fell passionately in love with Phihanga, who stood at their feet in the form of a soft ball of lush green. The volcano Tongariro, for whom New Zealand's first National Park was named, triumphed in the great battle to win Phihanga's love. The losers were Taranaki, Tauhara and Puutauaki. The latter left the

region, heading towards the coast. Tauhara constantly looked back in despair at what he had left behind him, traveling only a few kilometers. Puutauaki journeyed as far as the Bay of Plenty and now towers above it as Mount Edgecumbe. Feeling very sad, Taranaki followed the setting sun towards the west. Without stopping, he went on until he came to the sea, far away from Phihanga. On the way he left the Wanganui filled with his tears. It grew into a mighty river, and subsequently served the Maori as a main water route between the north and south of the island. Taranaki still growls at the victorious Tongariro from his new location at regular intervals. There is no plant, animal, or place anywhere in Aotearoa that doesn't have its place in Maori mythology.

1642: The Europeans Arrive

While clouds of Maori mythology engulf New Zealand's past, the beginnings of its "modern" history can be traced to a single, exact date – December 13, 1642.

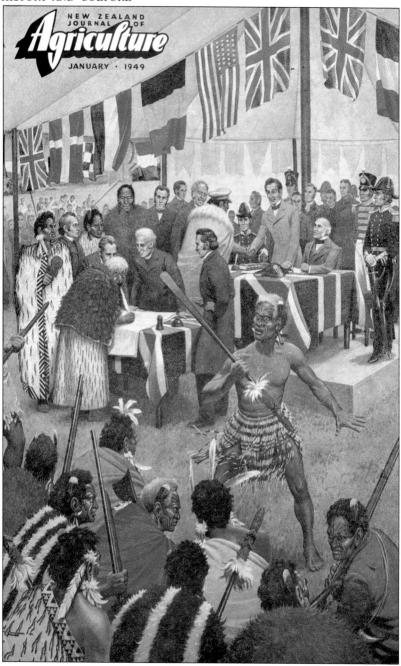

On this day, the Dutch seafarer, Abel Janszoon Tasman, came upon a new land after a strenuous journey through the Pacific. He suddenly spotted a snow-covered mountain range towering above the monotonous South Sea horizon.

Abel Tasman had set out with his two sailing ships *Heemskerk* and *Zeehaan* from the Indonesian port of Batavia, now known as Java, in order to seek new markets for the Dutch East India Company. What he found was a group of islands, which until that time had not been charted on any map in the world. The Dutchman believed what he saw was the coastline of a vast continent in the southern hemisphere. He had actually landed on the most northerly point of New Zealand's South Island, or to be more exact, in Golden Bay – an extensive bay cradled by beautiful sandy beaches.

Maori canoes went out to meet the visitors from another world and surrounded their sailing ships in the bay while sounding a shrill greeting from a wooden instrument. This was, in fact, a challenge to go to battle. Oblivious to this ethnographical wisdom, in a gesture of goodwill, Abel Tasman ordered a trumpet fanfare to return the greeting. By so doing, he had taken up the gauntlet. This misunderstanding was clarified in a brutal manner the very next morning: The crew from the Maori boat, which had disappeared overnight, attacked one of the *Zeehan's* dispatch boats, killing four of its men. This could well explain why Abel Tasman never set foot on land. With great haste, he ordered to set sail from *Murderer's Bay*, as he decided to call it, without attempting a landing. He called the newly-discovered land Staaten Landt, a name which was changed to Nieuw Zeeland in the following year. The Dutch, however, showed no more interest

Left: The 1840 Treaty of Waitangi, February 6, 1840 – prelude to further conflict between the Maori tribes and Europeans.

in this region. Tasman's name was later immortalized in many places throughout New Zealand, one of the most famous being the Abel Tasman National Park.

No less than 127 years passed before another European reached the group of islands, which had almost been forgotten by now. It was Captain James Cook, exploring the world on behalf of the British Crown in his ship *Endeavour*. He anchored for the first time on October 7, 1769, in Poverty Bay on the east coast of North Island, and claimed New Zealand for King George III.

Cook's encounter with the Maori was more amiable, due to the fact that he had a Tahitian interpreter on board. This enabled him to carry out extensive studies and explorations of the island. He drew up maps and wrote detailed reports about its plant and animal life and inhabitants. In the following decade, he undertook two more journeys to New Zealand, the second in the year 1799.

In Europe, the news of the islands in the South Pacific not only triggered interest among natural scientists. In the last years of the 18th century, the first whale and seal hunters, merchants and gamblers also set off to seek their fortune in New Zealand. The social conditions in the inchoate European settlements, mainly established in the sub-tropical regions of North Island, were probably as coarse as some of New Zealand's first white settlers. The dubious reputation of the notorious town of Kororareka, later called Russell, was known as far as Europe as the "hellhole of the South Pacific."

It was documented in acts of Parliament of 1817 and 1828 that New Zealand was subject to the authority of the British colonial rulers in Australia, and legally bound by decisions of the courts in New South Wales and Tasmania. The islands were regarded as part of New South Wales, and the governors in charge were far away from their additional spheres of responsibilty. They therefore appointed

British missionaries, active in New Zealand since 1814, as justices of the peace and their political representatives.

The bond between the British Crown and New Zealand became much stronger when King William IV sent a deputy, James Busby, there in 1833. Not only was he responsible for keeping law and order, but also to promote trade links and bargain with the Maoris regarding the necessary land acquisition. However, this soon proved too much of a responsibility for Busby, who had set up residence in the Bay of Islands. The problems increased at a rapid rate, and the conflict with the Maori became more intense.

A second envoy, Captain William Hobson, set out for New Zealand in 1837. He was successful in drawing up a treaty, which the Maori agreed to sign, and which subsequently became the

Above: Captain James Cook arrived in 1769. Right: Depiction of a battle between Europeans and Maori near Taranaki in 1863.

foundation stone of the New Zealand nation: The Treaty of Waitangi established the sovereignty of the British government, represented at that time by Queen Victoria, and the Maori committed themselves to selling their land exclusively to the British government and its representatives. In return, the Maori were guaranteed the unconditional rights to the use of their land, which included forests, fishing grounds and other resources, at all times, irregardless of whether the land was a collectively-owned property or belonged to one individual.

The Queen stipulated in another clause of the treaty that the Maori were to be guaranteed protection by the crown and endowed with the same rights and privileges as British citizens.

The Treaty of Waitangi was signed on February 6, 1840, by 46 Maori tribal chiefs. A few hundred more from all over New Zealand added their signatures to it during the following six months. Although the treaty was drawn up to serve as a basis for a peaceful co-existence between New Zealand's natives and the European immigrants, thus guaranteeing equal rights for everyone, it by no means solved all the problems prevalent in the country. On the contrary, it brought forth new conflicts – stemming from the disagreement as to how the treaty should be interpreted, and also because much of the Maori population felt the treaty had given them a bad deal. These conflicts flared up during the 1860s and the 1870s, almost to the point of a full-scale war.

It wasn't until 1975, 135 years after the signing of the treaty, that New Zealand established a special court of law for Maori legal issues regarding land rights and claims originating in the Treaty of Waitangi: the Waitangi Tribunal.

Following the final proclamation of British sovereignty, New Zealand was declared an independent colony on November 16, 1840, and its ties with New South Wales were severed. The small,

unruly town of Russell was the capital of New Zealand for a short period of time. William Hobson, architect of the nation, then transferred his governor's seat of residence from the Bay of Islands to Auckland in the year 1841.

As of 1840, large numbers of immigrants were brought to New Zealand at the cost of the British government, increasing the country's population at a rapid rate. Considerable groups of French immigrants had also started to settle on New Zealand's South Island, which was less under British influence at that time. The idyllic town of Akaroa, situated to the southeast of Christchurch, is reminiscent of the period when French colonialism attempted to establish itself here. British policy regarding the colonialization of New Zealand, which embraced the regions now known as Canterbury and Otago, made sure that South Island did not become French.

The Gold Rush in the middle of the 19th century, as well as the precious amber-like resin extracted from the in-digenous kauri tree, enticed prospectors and immigrants from all parts of the globe, from as far away as California and China. These groups were followed by people from India and Croatia, and a large number of Dutch after 1945. The Croatians played an essential role in establishing a wine industry.

New Zealand retained its status as a crown colony until, in the year 1852, it was granted restricted powers of self-government by the British Parliament. The islands were divided into six provinces, with a parliament elected in each of them. A National Assembly was planned and two years later, on May 24, 1854, it met for the first time. Two years after that, a cabinet under the leadership of Prime Minister Henry Sewell took over control of the executive government, which had been entirely in the hands of the governor until that time. The parliament continued to meet in Auckland until 1865, when the seat of the central government and of the parliament was transferred to New Zealand's new capital city of

Wellington. The six provinces lost their political powers a short time later and their governments were dissolved in 1876.

More than four decades passed before New Zealand made any progress in gaining independence. Its official status of colony was nominally replaced on September 26, 1907, by that of Dominion of New Zealand. A full 40 years later, on November 25, 1947, New Zealand accepted the Statute of Westminster and received its full sovereignty. Already 16 years previously, New Zealand had accepted the Statute of Westminster proclaimed by the British Parliament on an pathway to independence for all dominions. The New Zealanders had not found it easy to sever political ties to Great Britain, still regarded by many as their mother country. These strong feelings of patriotism were primarily ex-

Above: Auckland has all the trimmings of a modern metropolis. Right: Young New Zealanders just entering the market are faced with a stormy economic present.

pressed in their readiness to fight on the side of the British in the two world wars. An annual public holiday on the April 25, known as ANZAC Day, commemorates the many thousands of New Zealanders who lost their lives in these wars.

On the other hand, New Zealanders have always tended toward being independent. Over a century ago already, while child labor was still common in the mother country, New Zealand had already passed pioneering laws in the social security sector, granting free health care, pensions, worker compensation, maternity money, etc.... The new laws included a family allowance, free national health and education systems, social security and unemployment benefits. New Zealand also set an example to the rest of the world in matters of democracy as the first country anywhere to grant women the right to vote. Until 1950, the New Zealand parliament was modeled on its British counterpart in Westminster. It consisted of a lower and an upper house. The latter was soon dissolved, however, after the politicians reached the conclusion that an institution of this kind was much too archaic for a small country like New Zealand. The parliament of New Zealand now consists of only one House of Representatives, made up of 97 members and elected every three years. Four seats are exclusively reserved for Maori, whose representatives can be considered for the remaining parliamentary seats as well.

New Zealand, together with Great Britain, Australia and a further 45 nations, is a member of the Commonwealth. The British queen (still) presides over the Commonwealth, and is represented by a governor general. This island state in the middle of the South Pacific is one of the few countries in the world without a written constitution. For this reason, New Zealand's neighboring country Australia has kept a space free in its constitution: If the people of New Zealand choose to do so, it could quite easily become Aus-

tralia's seventh federal state. New Zealand, however, has long since chosen to remain independent. Only a tiny minority shows a degree of enthusiasm for the Australian idea, even though the ties concerning industrial and trade relations are very strong between the two countries. In comparison, New Zealand's trade links with the former mother country have weakened immensely since Britain became a full-fledged member of the European Community, which has its own economic interests and network. The close links with Britain were severed as a result. New Zealand was forced to partially reorient itself and look elsewhere for alternative markets. Agriculture, one of New Zealand's main sources of income for a great number of years, is gradually giving way to tourism.

With Great Britain's entry into the European Community, New Zealand lost one of its major export markets for agricultural goods. Together with the drastic drop in prices in the farming sector, the collapse of the stock market in 1987, and the high cost of the social services sector, this loss had a negative effect on New Zealand's economy and increased the unemployment rate drastically. The former welfare state was forced to abandon a large amount of its policies, leaving an increasing number of New Zealanders to fend for themselves in times of need. The Maori and Pakeha, the white New Zealanders, protested sometimes violently against the policies of the Labour Party, which ruled until the end of 1993. It had instituted a rigourous savings program. On November 6, 1993, the National Party took the reigns after a very close election. A month later, the government offered the Maori compensation amounting to 1 billion NZ$. They rejected the offer as outrageous and demanded some of their original land back instead. In February 1995, the Maori Queen and Präsident Bolger signed a treaty granting the largest Maori tribe a 16 000-hectare parcel of government land. Since 1993, New Zealand has also experienced an economic upswing that has restored its stability.

25

LINCOLN

RYELAND

BLACK ROM

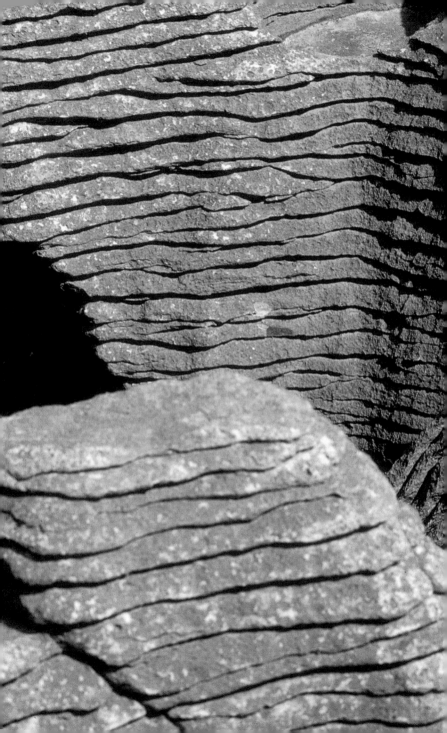

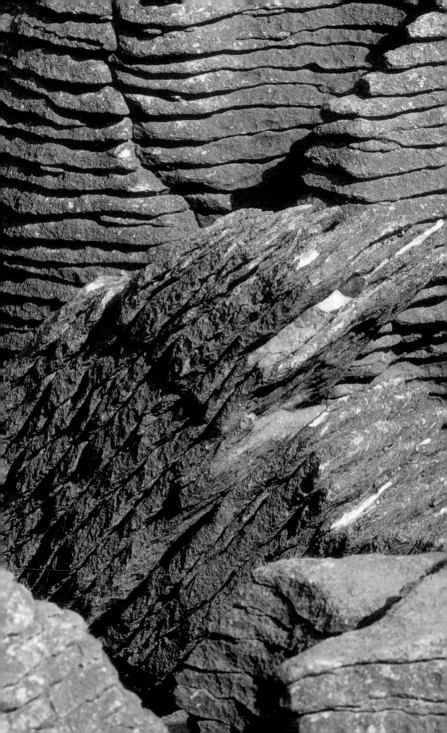

THE SECRET CAPITAL

AUCKLAND

City of Sails and Islands

Auckland, Ferry Building, 12 noon. There's no nicer place in Auckland than the **Harbourside Restaurant** at this time of day. Whether you have just arrived in New Zealand as a tourist after the 23-hour Air New Zealand flight from far-off Europe – 19,400 kilometers to be exact – or whether you are a businessman from one of the high-rise office blocks around the corner wanting to relax a little in the pleasant midday sunshine, perhaps with a fresh salad or cool glass of champagne, Ferry Building is the perfect place to go.

Ferry Building, built in 1912 and today a main thoroughfare for thousands of commuters who live on Auckland's north bank, is *the* lunch-time meeting place. Here you can pass the time of day observing and getting to know the New Zealanders, or *Kiwis* as they prefer to call themselves. You will mostly come across *townies* in Harbourside, people from the urban areas who like to distinguish themselves from the folk, otherwise known as *cockies*. The citizens of Auckland consider everything beyond the Bombay

Preceding pages: Sheering sheep in Rotorua. The so-called Pancake Rocks on South Island. Left: The great Harbour Bridge has become one of the hallmarks of Auckland.

Hills region on the southern outskirts of the city as "country." In addition, the people of Auckland regard themselves as representatives of a superior class. They also see Auckland as the true capital of New Zealand. They just turn up their noses at Wellington. A typical north – south conflict, just as in many other countries.

Auckland is also the "city of sails." This popular saying is certainly verified by a gaze at the magnificent **Waitemata Harbour** on a sunny summer weekend. According to statistics, every 15th person in New Zealand is a boat-owner, yet one in every five *Kiwis* in Auckland owns a boat. A view across the harbor also reveals that Auckland is the "city of islands" as well. Saying that New Zealand consists only of North and South Island, will engender strong disapproval from the people living on Stewart Island, who see their homeland as the "third island." Some Aucklander will also reply that a regular ferry service connects as many as 52 islands with the city, all within easy reach. This is precisely what makes Auckland such a charming place to live: its location on a narrow isthmus with a width of a mere nine kilometers, separating the waters of the Pacific from the Tasman Sea, and its natural surroundings make Auckland unique.

31

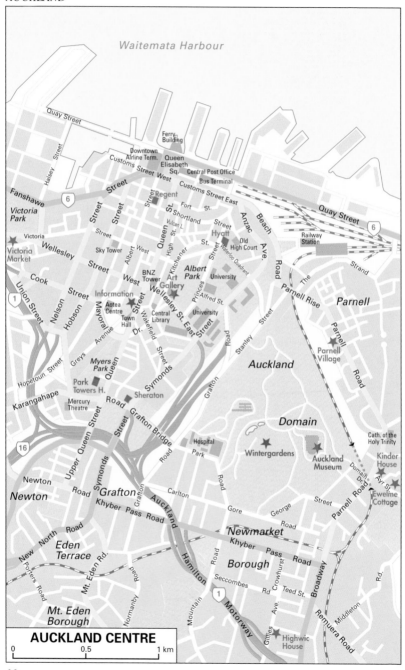

Waitemata Harbour

Quay Street

Ferry
Building

Halsey Street

Downtown
Airline Term.
Queen
Elisabeth
Sq.
Customs Street West
Central Post Office
Bus Terminal
Customs Street East

Fanshawe
Street

Quay Street

Victoria
Park

Regent
Street
Fort
St.
Shortland
Street

Anzac
Ave.

Beach
Road

Railway
Station

Strand

Victoria
Market

Wellesley
Street

Sky Tower

Albert
West

Queen
High
St.

Kitchener
St.
Hyatt
Waterloo Quadrant
Old
High Court

Parnell Rise

The

Parnell

Cook
Street
BNZ
Tower
Albert
Park

Street

University

Parnell Road

Union Street

Nelson
Street

Hobson
Street

West
Street

Wellesley St. East
Art
Gallery

Princes
St.
Alfred St.
University

Information
Aotea
Centre
Town
Hall

Mayoral
Dr.

Wakefield
Street

Central
Library

University
Street

Road

Stanley
Street

Street

Parnell
Village

Road

Auckland

Parnell
Road

Hopetoun Street

Greys
Ave.

Myers
Park

Queen

Symonds
Street

Grafton

Karangahape
Park
Towers H.

Road

Sheraton

Domain

Cath. of the
Holy Trinity

Mercury
Theatre

Grafton Bridge

Road

Kinder
House

Upper Queen Street

Symonds
Street

Grafton
Road

Hospital
Park

Wintergardens

Auckland
Museum

Domain Dr.

Ayr St.

Ewelme
Cottage

Newton

Newton
Road

Symonds
Road

Grafton

Auckland

Carlton
Road

Gore
Street

George
Road

Parnell Road

Eden
Terrace

North
Road

Khyber Pass Road

Newmarket

Khyber
Pass
Road

Borough

Broadway

Rd.

New
Road

Porters Road

Mt. Eden Rd.

Road

Normanby

Road

Road

Road
Seccombes
Rd
Teed St.
Crowhurst

Remuera Road

Middleton

Mt. Eden
Borough

Mountain

Hamilton

Motorway

Road

Giffies
Ave.

Highwic
House

AUCKLAND CENTRE

0   0.5   1 km

Since the majority of tourists visiting New Zealand want to experience nature rather than hectic city life, they are well-advised to begin their tour of Auckland with a trip to **Hauraki Maritime Park**. Most ferries leave from Queen's Wharf – and it is located directly at the Ferry Building.

Hauraki Maritime Park

Hauraki National Park, New Zealand's first national park, was opened in 1967 and stretches eastwards over a vast area of water off the shores of Auckland. It also includes 47 islands. Those closest to Auckland, like Rangitoto Island and Waiheke Island in the inner Gulf and Waitemata Harbour, are ideal destinations for day-trips. These islands are suitable for hiking tours all year round, and in the summer months perfect for diving and snorkeling. **Leigh Marine Reserve**, approximately an hour's drive north of Auckland, is an absolute must for all kinds of water-sport activities. This highly-protected marine reserve offers the visitor magnificent views of an unspoiled underwater world. As a result of commerical fishing, this opportunity has been destroyed to a very large extent elsewhere in New Zealand.

Although many of New Zealand's forests were cut down by the Europeans to make way for farming, each island has retained its own character and charm. Alongside the relics of early Maori settlements, there are also traces of ancient *pa* cities (former Maori fortifications) along the splendid white sandy beaches. The ocean most likely provided the early Maori tribes with a great variety of fish and sea-food.

On no account should you leave Auckland without visiting the two islands known as **Great Barrier** and **Little Barrier Island**. Great Barrier Island, also called The Barrier is quite easy to reach. A fast ferry will get you to the island in just under two hours, covering the distance of 80 kilometers. Great Barrier, largest of the islands situated along the coast, has many splendid beaches and protected bays, as well as good hiking routes. Those wishing to unwind in peace away from civilization have an ideal opportunity to get close to nature on The Barrier. Your search for a comfortable jet-set hotel will be in vain here.

There is an extensive federal bird conservation area on the smaller Little Barrier Island. If you wish to visit this area, make sure you first apply for a permit from the Department of Conservation.

The island of **Rangitoto**, a volcano which became dormant 800 years ago, can be reached from Auckland in half an hour by ferryboat. The top of the volcano offers a splendid panoramic view.

The **Mansion House**, residence of colonial governor George Grey, is located on the island of **Kawau**. It still contains fine exhibits of 19th century furniture and paintings.

The island of **Motuihe** is also ideal for day-excursions and a popular picnic destination among Aucklander. Mountain-bike tours are organized on the island of **Motutapu** by Ross Adventures with permission of the Department of Conservation.

The best time to visit **Rakino Island** is during the summer months, especially around Christmas time when the island is drenched in bright red blossoms from the *pohutukawa* trees. There are beautiful sandy beaches on **Waiheke Island**, especially at Oneroa Bay near Little Oneroa and at Rocky Bay in the vicinity of Omiha.

A Tour of the City from Past to Present

The Ferry Building on Quay Street is as good a place as any to start a tour of downtown Auckland. From this point the city is easily accessible on foot. How-

ever, if you want to include the outskirts of the city in your tour, you are advised to take a bus or car. After all, Auckland covers an area of more than 100,000 hectares, making it about the same size as Paris.

Over 600 years ago, a large number of Maori tribes settled on this narrow strip of land. The members of the Ngati Whatua tribe are regarded as Auckland's first inhabitants, the Tangata Whenua. Bloody battles between the various tribes were still common as late as the mid-18th century. The battles usually took place at strongholds, mostly built on volcanoes.

The city first made a name for itself when Captain William Hobson felt it necessary to transfer the capital from the small northerly town of Russell to Auckland in September of 1840. Under the strong influence of the New Zealand

Company, Auckland was forced to give up its status as capital city in the year 1865 and pass it on to Wellington.

During this century, Auckland has made the headlines on a number of occasions due to its harbor. **Harbour Bridge**, over 1000 meters in length, was opened on May 30, 1959. Even today, the bridge is one of New Zealand's most outstanding engineering feats and has long since become Auckland's most famous landmark. Ten years later, the road leading north had to be converted into an eight-lane freeway, with Japanese help. Since then, the bridge has had the nickname of *Nippon clip-on*. The harbor was also in the headlines on July 10, 1985. Not only did the bombing of the Greenpeace ship *Rainbow Warrior* shatter the Princess Wharf, it shook New Zealand's relationship to France as well.

There was tremendous joy and cheering from the hundreds of thousands of spectators who gathered at the harbor to welcome the skipper of the *Steinlager 2*, Peter Blake, in January 1990 when he an-

Above: A forest of masts in front of the West Haven Boat Harbour's skyline. Right: The Ferry Building at the harbor, a pleasant meeting place, recalls the old days.

chored at the same spot as the *Rainbow Warrior* had done years earlier. The *Steinlager 2* was the first yacht to reach Auckland's harbor during the grueling *Whitbread Round the World Regatta*, and it went on to win the race.

Queen Street

Queen Elizabeth Square, with the Central Post Office, is across from the Ferry Building. Not only is the square a popular place among street musicians and artists, but also a favorite lunch spot. From here the visitor has a a good view of **Queen Street**. With its numerous high-rise buildings and stores, it is one of New Zealand's busiest shopping streets.

Customs Street East leads off to the right of Queen Street towards the **Old Customs House**, built in 1889. Its beautiful Renaissance façade is contrasting sharply with the modern glass of the nearby high-rises. The **Regent of Auckland**, one of the best hotels in the city, is just around the corner on Albert Street.

Back to Queen Street for now. Those looking for a typical *Kiwi* souvenir will have a good opportunity to window-shop on Queen Street. Exploring some of the narrow streets leading off of Queen Street means avoiding all the hustle and bustle of the downtown area. Visitors to Auckland are often surprised by the large selection of elegant shops, bookstores, cafés and restaurants, imparting an international flair to the city. This is especially true of **Exchange Lane**, with its wonderful aroma of ground coffee. Not only is it freshly roasted on the premises of **Millers Café**, but also served over the counter as espresso or cappuccino.

It is advisable to leave Queen Street at **Vulcan Lane**, one of Auckland's most charming roads, turning to your left. This former "street of goldsmiths" has been closed to traffic since the 1960s. Vulcan Lane, the east end of which is formed by **Norfolk House**, built at the turn of the century with an elegant Art-Deco entrance, has been regarded as a trendy place by Auckland's younger generation

35

since the 1980s. Perhaps this is because one of the city's best cafés, **Kerouac's Coffee Bar**, is located here. Besides freshly-roasted coffee, there is a choice of Italian food, with a different menu each day. It's the perfect place to stop for a light lunch. Kerouac's Coffee Bar, like most places on Vulcan Lane, has a relaxed, Mediterranean-like atmosphere. It is usually fairly crowded. If you have problems finding a seat there, try the **Café Potter Blair** across the street, which will inevitably offer out-door seating in good weather.

Auckland's Expensive Landmark

This visit to Vulcan Lane now over, you can turn right at the end of the lane into **High Street**, finally returning to Queen Street via Victoria Street East. Or follow Kitchener Street to Albert Park

Above: Skyscrapers reflect the modern city.
Right: Enjoying jazz during lunch hour is part of the cultural experience of Auckland.

and the Auckland City Art Gallery via Wellesley Street East, which turns into Queen Street. Either way, you should arrive at **Aotea Square**.

The **Aotea Centre**, was was completed in November 1989 after a five-year construction period, for the considerable sum of NZ$ 128.5 million. The idea for the Centre was Dame Kiri Te Kanawa's, New Zealand's most famous opera singer. In 1984, she declared that she would not sing in New Zealand until an opera house of international stature had been constructed. She carried out her threat by staying away from New Zealand until the arts center had been completed, so that her return after the opening of the Aotea Centre also marked a triumphant reunion with her country.

Perhaps even more important to tourists is the **Auckland Visitor Centre**, located in Aotea Square. Its office is well-stocked with detailed information for those visiting New Zealand. **The Gateway**, a Maori archway made of wood by the artist Selwyn Muru, is close by, and Auckland's **Town Hall**, built of Oamaru limestone, towers in the background. Queen Street turns slightly uphill, meeting Karangahape Road and Grafton Bridge about 2000 ft (600 m) further.

Auckland has the reputation of being the largest city in Polynesia, and this is justified by **Karangahape Road**. Amid exotic food shops and colorful stores, the cacophony of island languages makes you feel as if you were on Apia, Nukualofa or Suva. Because of the increasing number of immigrants coming into New Zealand from the Polynesian Islands, there has been mounting ethnic conflict among the islanders, sometimes involving violence. Many Polynesian immigrants are unemployed and depend on the state for social security.

The best times to see the flea market on Newbury Street (off East Tamaki Rd.) is on Thursdays with longer business hours and Saturdays (6 am-noon).

The **Sky Tower**, which rises well over 1000 ft over the city, was completed in 1997 and is the country's tallest building. Besides a hotel with conference rooms, it harbors several lookout platforms, a revolving restaurant, a theater with 700 seats and the gigantic Harrah's Casino. (Victoria, corner Federal St., Tel: 912-6000).

Green City Center: Auckland Domain

While Karangahape Road leads to the vibrant part of Auckland, the more peaceful and greener sector of the city known as **Auckland Domain** can be accessed via the Grafton Bridge and Park Road. There are beautifully laid-out gardens, greenhouses, playgrounds and a cricket oval within this large verdant region, which covers an area of 80 hectares. The **Auckland War Memorial Museum**, erected after World War One on the Pukekawa, the "Sour Hill", is located in the park's east section. It is worth visiting the museum around lunchtime. At 11:15 a.m. and 1:30 p.m., the *Pounamu*, one of

New Zealand's most talented Maori groups, offers an insight into the music and culture of the natives. Furthermore, you can visit the **Maori Hall** located within the museum. It houses an extensive collection of Maori and Polynesian exhibits. Guided tours of the exhibition take place every day 45 minutes before the start of each concert, and are led by members of the *Pounamu* group.

The War Memorial Museum honors the memory of the soldiers from New Zealand who fought for Britain in the world wars. In another section, there is a model of an Auckland street as it appeared in the 19th century.

Parnell: From Oysters to Souvenirs

There are splendid views from the Auckland Domain, Auckland's most popular picnic spot, across the attractive Waitemata Harbour and Hauraki Gulf. The best approach to Parnell Road is via Domain Drive, situated on the eastern edge of the park. Opposite from it is Ayr

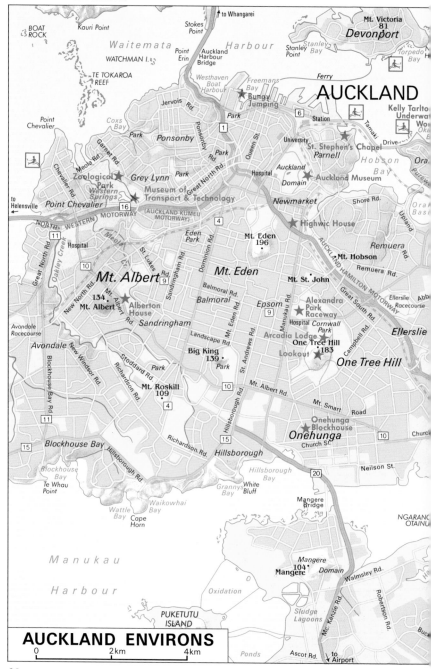

AUCKLAND ENVIRONS

0   2km   4km

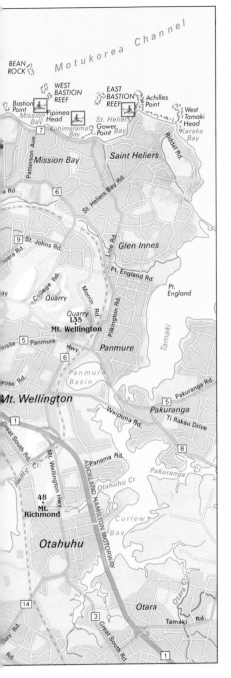

Street, leading to the **Kinder House**, a small museum in memory of its former owner, the Reverend John Kinder, and to a residence made of kauri wood known as the **Ewelme Cottage**, built in 1864. Both buildings, as well as Highwic House in Epsom and Alberton House in Mount Albert are under the protection of the New Zealand Historic Places Trust.

Before turning into Parnell Road, you can head right at St. Stephens Avenue and visit the **Cathedral of The Holy Trinity** (1888). **Selwyn Court**, the former Bishops's Library (1863), is a little farther down the road, along with **St Stephens Chapel** (1857) in a romantic setting close by on Judge Street.

The people of Auckland used to praise the suburb of Parnell because of the smoked oysters sold here. Today, tourists flock to Parnell for the large selection of souvenir stores, boutiques and cafés. Parnell is "in", and its highlight is **Parnell Village**. With shops and restaurants in Victorian style, it exudes a certain old-world charm. After a visit to the Auckland War Memorial Museum and other side-trips to the beginnings of the "new" Auckland, this is a pleasant place to stop for a lunch break. The locals who want to see and be seen generally frequent the **Metropole Café**.

Parnell Road gently winds its way downhill towards the harbor. Auckland University campus is situated on the southern edge of the **Old Reserve**. If you cut across the Old Reserve, it will take you to Customs Street and back to your starting point at the harbor.

Climbing a Volcano

As beautiful as the city of Auckland may seem around the harbor district, it's not until you climb one of the 60 volcanoes that you realize just how large it is. In the old days, they served the Maori as strongholds, who built their *pas* here. Nowadays, the Aucklander use the volca-

noes as nature parks or jogging paths. Tourists can go "volcano-hopping", with different views from each hill.

The very best panorama of Auckland is from the top of **Mount Eden.** At a height of 196 m, Mount Eden's volcanic crater remains intact as sheep graze on its grassy slopes. A little farther south, the volcano known as **One Tree Hill** is of historical significance. The Maori call it *Maungakiekie*, and a 183-m obelisk perches on its peak. The Maori erected a *pa* for 4000 people here at the end of the 17th century. John Logan Campbell, a Scotsman and one of New Zealand's first white residents, settled here in 1839. In 1901, ten years before his death, he bequeathed the region to the city of Auckland. Its name was later changed to Cornwall Park, in honor of the Duke and Duchess of Cornwall's state visit.

Above: The quaint look is part of the attraction of Parnell. Right: The singular silhouette of the appropriately named One Tree Hill, once the home of 4000 Maori.

The obelisk standing on the peak of the volcano commemorates Sir John Logan Campbell who, because of his strong sense of loyalty towards the city of Auckland and his great respect for the Maori people, won himself the title "Father of Auckland". The stone pine at the top was planted in place of a *totara* tree that once stood at the tip of the volcano and was considered sacred by the Maori, but unfortunately some of the first white settlers chopped it down, a thoughtless and coarse gesture.

Acacia Lodge stands at the foot of One Tree Hill and is certainly worth visiting. Constructed in the year 1839, it is the oldest building in Auckland. It was moved here from the city in 1920. Acadia Lodge bears witness to the fact that while Campbell came to New Zealand as a medical practioner, he changed his profession to become a successful businessman and politician, thus earning both wealth and fame.

One Tree Hill is especially worth visiting in the evening. Other "climbable"

volcanoes with splendid views are Mount Albert (up Mount Albert Road), Mount Wellington in the south, Mount Hobson and Mount St John, both situated in the district of Remuera, as well as Mount Victoria in Devonport.

Heading Eastwards on the Tamaki Drive

Auckland not only has volcanoes to offer, it also has some splendid coastal regions. In addition to Northshore Beach at **Takapuna** (north of Devonport), the coastal road known as **Tamaki Drive** on the eastern side of the city can be recommended. There are magnificent beaches and places of interest all along the route. At **Bastion Point** in Orakei, for example you will find a meeting house of the Ngati Whatua tribe.

The *Tangata Whenua*, the first Maori to come here, had lived in this area for hundreds of years. As time passed, the British crown deprived them of their land rights, which in turn led to a violent con-

flict lasting for decades. It wasn't until 1987 that the Waitangi Tribunal declared that the land should be returned to its rightful Maori owners, compensating them financially as well.

It's advisable to avoid visiting the Bastion Point section of the park on the 29th of January. This is the day that the *Auckland Regatta* takes place each year, and the park serves thousands of visitors as a picnic area and point from which to observe the Regatta. Don't forget to include the adjacent **Kelly Tarlton's Underwater World** in your visit. It presents over 15,000 fish and is one of Auckland's main tourist attractions. The Antarctic World exhibition has a replica of the hut Robert Scott built during his 1911 expedition. Live penguins are also kept here under artificial light and in extremely cold conditions. Visitors can wander through the plexiglass passages in the aquarium and examine sharks and electric rays close up. There is also a good terrace café in the complex, offering a splendid view of the Rangitoto Island.

Heading west from Ferry Building, there is only one destination: **Harbour Bridge**. Before coming to the harbor, you will pass the **Westhaven Boat Harbour**. Some of the most beautiful boats in Auckland are anchored here. The best place to enjoy the scenery is over breakfast at the café called **Sitting Ducks** which is conveniently situated beneath the harbor bridge .

Nocturnal Doings

Even if Auckland was built on top of volcanoes, the city's atmosphere hasn't exactly been explosive. But times are changing. In the past, shop shades were pulled down shortly after closing time and streets in the city center soon became deserted, in contrast to the vibrant nightlife in downtown Auckland today.

Those planning to paint the town red after sunset are advised to go to **Pon-**

Above: Seen from Devonport, the Auckland skyline glows in the evening sun.

sonby, with its numerous bars and restaurants. This part of Auckland is located above the Harbour Bridge. There is live music almost every evening and plenty of beer in the **Gluepot**, consisting of two bars and a concert hall. Mainly local groups perform here. Even *Split Enz* played here before they became famous in the international scene. As in Parnell, it's best to just stroll around.

There is a pleasant, casual atmosphere in the **Park in the Bar** (Fort Street, downtown) or at the elegant **Hammer-heads** (Tamaki Drive, Kelly Tarlton's). If you prefer to mix with yachtsmen, **Pier 21** at the Westhaven Boat Harbour is the place to go. Those preferring a bit of peace and quiet will enjoy taking the ferry to **Devonport**. Reminiscent of a British seaside resort at the turn of a century, it has retained its old-world charm and air of nostalgia. Numerous elegant restaurants flank Victoria Road, and from Mount Victoria there is a splendid view of the sunset and the brightly-illuminated skyline of Auckland.

AUCKLAND
AND ENVIRONS

Arrival

Auckland Airport is situated in Mangere, 23 km from the city center. The bus from the airport to the Downtown Airline Terminal in the city center runs from 6:45 a.m. to 8 p.m.

Several agencies operate additional shuttle-bus services between the airport and the majority of hotels, i.e. SuperShuttle, Tel: 09-3075210, fares are between 12 and 15 NZ$. A taxi-ride to and from the airport costs around 35 NZ$.

After passing the customs, visitors enter the arrival hall through a glass door. The Tourist Information Office (on the left) supplies hotel accommodation. The shuttle-bus stop is next to the Tourist Office.

The international Jean-Batten-Terminal and the close-by Domestic Terminal are connected by a pedestrian path.

An airport tax of 20 NZ$ is levied on all international departures. This tax is not contained in the ticket price.

Accommodation

LUXURY: **Hyatt Auckland**, corner Waterloo Quadrant and Princes St., P.O. Box 3938, Tel: 09-3661234. **The Pan Pacific Hotel**, Wellesley St., P.O. Box 5917, Tel: 09-3663000. **Sheraton Auckland Hotel and Towers**, 83 Symonds St., P.O. Box 2771, Tel: 09-3795132. **The Regent of Auckland**, Albert St., Tel: 09-3098882.

Airport Pacific Inn, 210 Kirkbride Rd., Tel: 09-2751129. **Ascot Motor Lodge**, 92 Great South Rd., Remuera, Tel: 09-5204833. **City Towers Serviced Apartments**, Maungawhau Rd., New Market, Tel: 09-5246512. **Mount Albert Lodge**, 201 Carrington Rd., Mt. Albert, Tel: 09-8462199.

MODERATE: **Alexandra Motor Inn**, 226 Green Lane Rd., Epsom, Tel: 09-6388145. **Ascot Parnell**, 36 St. Stephens Avenue, Tel: 09-3099012 (pleasant rooms, good service). **Bavaria Guest House**, 83 Valley Rd., Mount Eden, Tel: 09-6389641 (friendly, relaxed atmosphere, useful tourist-information is supplied by the German management). Badgers of Devonport, 30 Summer St., Devonport, Tel: 09-4452099. **Harbour Bridge Motel**, 6 Tweed St., Herne Bay, Tel: 09-3763489. **Onetangi Hotel**, The Strand, Waiheke Island, Tel: 09-3728028 (ideal spot for an island holiday). **Park Towers Hotel**, 3 Scotia Place, Tel: 09-3092800. **Ranfurly Court Motel**, 285 Manakau Rd., Epsom, Tel: 09-6389059. **St. Lukes Motor Lodge,** 697 New North Rd., Mount Albert, Tel: 09-8460086.

BUDGET: **Auckland Backpackers**, 10 Akiraho St., Mt. Eden, Tel: 09-604386. **Berlin Lodge**, 5a Oaklands Rd., Mt. Eden, Tel. 09-6386545. **Downtown City Backpackers and Bar**, corner Victoria and Hobson St., Tel: 09-3733737. **Auckland City Youth Hostel**, corner City Rd. and Liverpool St., Tel: 09-3092802.

Parnell Youth Hostel, 2 Churton St., Tel: 09-3790258. **Queen Street Backpackers**, corner Queen and Fort St. (Entrance at 4 Fort St., central), Tel: 09-3733471. **Ivanhoe Tourist Lodge**, 14 Shirley Rd., Grey Lynn, Tel: 09-8462800. **Lantana Lodge**, 60 St. Georges Bay Rd., Tel: 09-3734546. **Picton Street Backpackers**, 34 Picton St., Freemans Bay, Tel: 09-3780966. **Georgia Backpackers Hostel**, 189 Park Rd., Grafton, Tel: 09-3099560.

Plumley House, 515 Remuera Rd., Tel: 09-5204044 (situated a bit outside of town, but ideal as a departure point for hitch-hikers). **Hekerua House**, 11 Hekerua Rd. Waiheke Island, Tel: 09-3728371 (Waiheke Island can be reached by ferry only; the guesthouse is situated in lovely countryside).

North Shore Caravan Park, 52 Northcote Rd., Takapuna, Tel: 09-4182578 (for campers; 4 km north of Harbour Bridge). **Remuera Motor Lodge**, 16 Minto Road, AKL-Remuera, Tel: 09-5245126 (next camping site and motel at Greenlane exit).

Restaurants

Clarry's Restaurant, 99 Parnell Rd., Tel: 09-3095902 (fresh fish).

Cin Cin on Quay, Ferry Building, Quay St., Tel: 09-3076966 (Trendy restaurant for people in the public eye; Italian cuisine).

Harbourside Restaurant, 1th Floor, Ferry Building, Quay St., Tel: 09-3070556 (popular meeting-place at the harbor, spectacular views; open daily from 11:30 a.m.).

Jurgen's Restaurant, 12 Wyndham St., Tel: 09-3096651 (historical flair, New Zealand cuisine, very expensive).

Kerouac's Café, 33 Vulcan Lane, Downtown, Tel: 09-3770091 ("In"-place with pleasant atmosphere; Italian cuisine and sidewalk café).

Mexican Café, Upstairs, 67 Victoria St., West Auckland, Tel: 09-732311 (your local Mexican around the corner).

Miller's Coffee Shop, Mills Lane (off Queen St.), Tel: 09-3020716 (with own coffee-roasting establishment).

Orchards Restaurant, 159 Lincoln Rd., Henderson, Tel: 09-8387006 (vegetarian food).

Papillion, 170 Jervois Rd., Ponsonby, Tel: 09-3765867 (New Zealand cuisine served in a beautiful garden).

Sails Restaurant, The Anchorage, Westhaven Drive, Tel: 09-3789890 (at the harbor, with splendid skyline panorama).

Wheelers and Avisons, 43 Ponsonby Rd., Tel: 09-3763185.

For Night-Owls: **Lorne St**, 26 Lorne St., Tel: 09-3099770 (open daily 12 noon–6 a.m.).

Open Late Café, corner Ponsonby/ Richmond Rd., Tel: 09-3764466 (open daily: 7 p.m.–3:30 a.m.). **24 Hour Café**, 9 Customs St. East, Tel: 09-309 5641 (open 24 hours daily, New Zealand cuisine).

Museums

Aotea Centre, Queen St. (changing exhibitions in the foyer).

Auckland City Art Gallery, Kitchener St., Tel: 09-3077704 (open daily from 10 a.m.–4:30 p.m.; changing exhibitions, mainly New Zealand artists).

Auckland Museum, Auckland Domain, Grafton Rd., Tel: 09-3067067, open daily from 10 a.m.–5 p.m., admission free).

Motat, Great North Rd., Western Springs, Tel: 09-8467020 (Mon–Fri 9 a.m.–5 p.m.; Sat, Sun 10 a.m.–5 p.m.; admission 10 NZ$. Exhibition documenting the history of technology to the present day.

Rugby International Museum, Unit 10, 39 Porana Rd., Takapuna, Tel: 09-4440914 (an absolute must for sports-fans – all about rugby, a typical New Zealand sport.

Tips and Trips

Beaches: The best swimming is near the city at Judges Bay, Okahu Bay, Mission Bay, Kohimarama and St. Heliers Bay. Don't forget to watch out for the change of tide at all these beaches. In the north, good beaches are situated between Cheltenham and Long Bay, and along the Whangaparaoa Peninsula. The west coast is a surfer's paradise: Best wind and surf conditions are prevailing at Piha, Karekare, Bethells, Whatipu and Muriwai.

Bungee Jumping: The almost legendary New Zealand test of courage is called *Bungee Jumping* – the hair-raising jump from a high point (usually a crane), with one's body securely fastened to elastic bands, the *bungee*. Those raring to jump can get down to brass tacks in Auckland: Freemans Bay, Halsey St., Downtown, Tel: 09-3030030 arrange jumps off the top of a crane; those in search of the authentic experience might prefer to put their courage to the test in Queenstown, the birth-place of *Bungee Jumping*.

Devonport: The ferry from Auckland to Devonport runs every half and full hour. On weekdays, the last ferry leaves Devonport at 11 p.m., on weekends at 10 p.m.

Explorer Bus: This bus service connects the most important tourist attractions: Victoria Park Market, Bungy Jumping, Mission Bay Beach, Underwater World, Auckland Museum and Parnell Village. Buses run every hour from 10 a.m. to 4 p.m, the fare is ca. 15 NZ$, and one can get on or off the bus at any of the stops.

Helicopter Roundtrips: Experience Auckland from the air or go heli-fishing in the Hauraki Gulf with Helicopter Line, Mechanics Bay, Solent St., Tel: 09-3774406.

Horseracing: Next to watching horseracing, betting is one of the major passions of the "Kiwis". One of the best places to indulge in both is Aucklands most important racetrack.

Alexandra Park Raceway, Greelane Rd, Tel: 09-6305660 (Times and dates of the races are published in the daily papers). The most important race to take place here is the *Auckland Cup*, at the beginning of December.

Howick Colonial Village: 20 houses and villas from the early Auckland years, surrounded by lovely gardens and flowers: Lloyd Elsmore Park, Bells Rd., Pakuranga, Tel: 09-5769506, open daily 10 a.m.–4 p.m.

Jazz: Live jazz is performed in the **Cotton Club**, 222 Ponsonby Rd., Ponsonby, Tel: 09-3787888 (Wed–Sat from 8 p.m.) and in the **Killarney St. Bar and Brasserie**, 1 Killarney St., Takapuna, Tel: 09-4899409 (Sun 1–4 p.m. and 7:30–10:30 p.m.). **Fullers** offers jazz on a ship. The **Kestrel Jazz Ferry** gets going on Friday and Saturday nights. Info: 09-3774074.

Kelly Tarlton's Underwater World: 23 Tamaki Drive, Mission Bay, Tel: 09-5281994. A chance to view sharks and giant turtles at close quarters, daily from 9 a.m.–9 p.m.

Markets: Victoria Park Market: 50 stalls selling international wares, opposite Victoria Park, Victoria St. West, Tel: 09-3096911, daily from 9 a.m.–7 p.m.; live music on some weekends).

Maori Culture: The Maori-Group Pounamu gives a concert daily at 11:15 a.m. and 1:30 p.m. Excellent guided tours of the Maori collection in the Auckland Museum take place 45 minutes prior to the concerts. Information and reservation: Tel: 09-8387876 or 3090443.

Mountain-Bike Tours: The agency Ross Adventures arranges excursions on 18-gear bikes to Motutapu Island in the Hauraki Gulf. Information: Tel: 09-3774074.

Pavilion of New Zealand: This pavilion, created to represent New Zealand at the world exposition (EXPO) in Brisbane, Australia, has been reassembled in Montgomerie Road, near the airport (20 minutes from downtown). Here visitors can experience a fascinating caleidoscope of various bits and pieces of typical New Zealand , with visual attractions from past and present. Information: Tel: 09-2560111.

Rental Cars: Cars and caravans can be rented from the **Maui Agency**. The **Leisure Port Agency** (same owners) runs two service- and car-return centers in Auckland and Christchurch. This means that visitors renting a car in Auckland (on North Island), can return it to the agency in Christchurch (on South Island).

Information from: *Maui*, Leisure Port, Richard Pearse Drive, Mangere (near the airport), Tel: 09-2753529.

In the Auckland region, the following firms offer good terms and rates:

ACE Tourist Rentals, 39 The Strand, Parnell, Tel: 09-3092258.

Dollar Save Car Hire, Tel: 09-3660646.

Hardy Cars, used cars and caravans, Tel: 03-5481681, Fax: 03-5481581.

Views: The Observation Deck on top of the BNZ Tower (125 Queen St., city center) gives spectacular views across the city, the harbor and the Hauraki Gulf (admission 2NZ$; Mon–Thur 9 a.m.–5 p.m.; Fri until 8:30 p.m.; Sat 10 a.m.–1:30 p.m.).

Zoo: The **Auckland Zoo**, Motions Rd., Western Springs, Tel: 09-3783819, is open daily from 9:30 a.m.–5:30 p.m. and can be reached by bus from Customs Street.

Festivals / Special Events

Since the founding of the city in 1840, the *Auckland Regatta* takes place at the Waitemata Harbour every year on January 29.

The *Auckland Port Festival* is celebrated on the first weekend in March at the Princess Basin. In addition to various culture and sports events, the *Dragon Boat Races* and the *Mardi Gras*-Parade are the highlights of the festival.

Round the Bays: On the last Sunday in March ca. 1000 joggers start on a 9.2 km run around the harbor bay. (Start: 9 a.m.; finish: St. Heliers Bay; starting fee: 10 NZ$).

Airlines

Air New Zealand, Quay St., Auckland 1, Tel: 09-3797515. Ticket reservations: Tel: 09-3573000. Arrival information: Tel: 09-3573030. Departure information: Tel: 09-3672323.

British Airways, Information and reservations: Tel: 09-3568690.

Lufthansa, Lufthansa House, Level 10, 36 Kitchener St., Tel: 09-3031529.

Qantas: Tel: 09-3578900.

Singapore Airlines, Tel: 09-3032129.

United Airlines: Reservations: Tel: 09-3793800. Information: Tel: 09-2750789.

Consulates

Australia: Union House, 32-38 Quay Street, Tel: 09-3032429.

Great Britain: Fay Richwhite Building, corner Queen and Wyndham Street, Tel: 09-3032973.

Japan: 6th Floor, National Mutual Centre, 41 Shortland Street, Tel: 09-3034106.

USA: Corner Shortland and O'Connell Street, Tel: 09-3032724.

Western Samoa: Samoa House, 283 Karangahape Road, Newtown, Tel: 09-3031012.

Tourist Information

AUCKLAND: Auckland Visitor Centre, Aotea Square, 299 Queen Street, Tel: 09-3666888 (open Mondays–Fridays 8:30 a.m.–5:30 p.m.; Sundays and public holidays 9 a.m.–4 p.m. Also in the Pavilion on QE II Square.

Auckland Airport International Terminal, Tel: 09-2756467 or 2767467 (24-hour-service).

AA-Centre, 99 Albert Street, Tel: 09-3774660 (Mondays–Fridays 8:30 a.m.–5 p.m.; information and maps; free service for members of corresponding national automobile associations. The **AA** also maintains additional branches in several New Zealand cities).

Auckland Regional Council, Tel: 09-8177134 (Information on regional events, country walks, beaches and forests).

MANUKAU : Manukau Tourist Information Centre, George Bolt Memorial Drive, P.O. Box 53064, Tel: 09-2755321 (on the road from the airport into town; good, relaxed service; daily 8:30 a.m.–8:30 p.m.).

TAKAPUNA: North Shore Visitors Centre, 94 Hurstmere Road, Tel: 09-4868670.

GREAT BARRIER ISLAND: Information Centre, Safari Tours, Stonewall Store, Pah Beach, Tryphena, Tel: 025-923678.

The **Department of Conservation (DOC)** has opened a number of offices in Auckland and its environs:

AUCKLAND: corner Karangahape Road. and Liverpool Street, Newton, Private Bag 8, Tel: 09-3079279.

KAWAU ISLAND: Tel: 09-4228882.

LITTLE BARRIER ISLAND and **MOTOURA ISLAND**: Radio contact from Auckland **DOC**.

RANGITOTO ISLAND: Tel: 09-3727348.

TIRITIRI/MATANGI ISLAND: Tel: 09-4794490.

MOTUIHE ISLAND: Tel: 09-5345419.

GREAT BARRIER ISLAND: Port Fitzroy, Tel: 09-4290044.

WARKWORTH: 1 Baxter St., Tel: 09-4259081.

ACROSS THE NORTHLAND

BAY OF ISLANDS
WAITANGI
CAPE REINGA

The term Highway 1 may be reminiscent of important national roads in other countries, but there's nothing legendary about the the first few kilometers of New Zealand's number one. Leaving Auckland over the Harbour Bridge, with a last glance at Westhaven Harbour and the skyline, there is still a stretch to go on smooth road before reaching the verdant countryside around Albany. Your eyes can take their time getting used to the composition in shades of green. The landscape changes all the time between farmland and bushland. It's not worth stopping before the hotsprings of **Waiwera**, open to visitors daily from 9:30 a.m. to 10 p.m. The ferry trip to **Kawau Island** from Sandspit is also interesting. The ferry operates several times throughout the day, including around 10:30 a.m. There is also a ferry running from Auckland to Kawau Island. If you wish to visit **Mokohinau Island**, take the turn-off to Leigh.

Once in **Brynderwyn Hills**, after about 120 kilometers, you will be rewarded with a wonderful view of vast plains and soft rolling hills that stretch to the horizon. **Bream Bay** extends along

Preceding pages: Beach near Cape Reinga. Left: Driving up north leads into the history of the Maori.

the eastern coast for miles. The impressive **Bream Head Cliffs** tower in the background just beyond the bay.

Whangarei, which is home to approximately 42,000 inhabitants, lies at the far end of the bay. It is the largest town in the Northland. Although well-known in New Zealand for its oil-refineries, it is of no historical interest. A visit to the **Clapham Clock Museum** can be combined with a scenic drive to the **Parahaki War Memorial**, which is situated on the summit of the 242 m hill of the same name.

The drive along the Ngunguru Road heading towards **Tutukaka** is worthwhile, even if you don't fish. Tutukaka is a popular destination for those planning a deep-sea fishing trip. The catch in these waters includes swordfish, snapper or even a shark.

Those seeking tranquility and with time to spare are advised to head east at Whakapara, along the rough **Russell Road**. This is a beautiful stretch of country to drive through, and if you later miss the kauri forests on the west coast, you can see some of these enormous trees at the **Ngaiotonga Scenic Reserve**.

Visitors with less time to spare can continue along Highway 1 until **Kawakawa.** This is where one may leave the highway, after visiting Kawakawa.

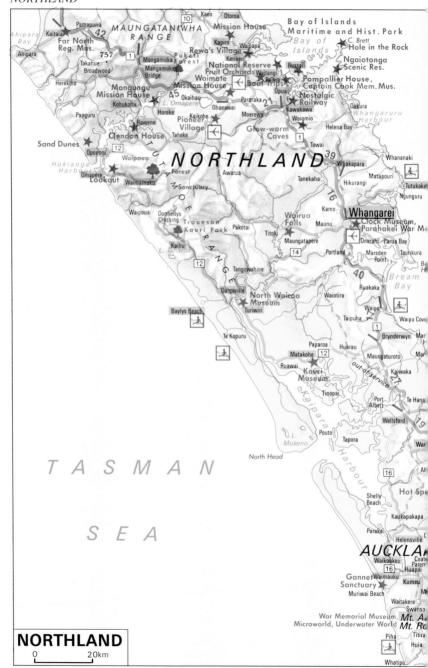

NORTHLAND

MAUNGATANIWHA RANGE

Kaeo   Otoroa   Mission House

Bay of Islands
Maritime and Hist. Park

Bay of Islands

C. Brett   Hole in the Rock

Ahipara Bay   Kaitaia   Pamapuria   42

Far North Reg. Mus.   Ahipara   Herekino   757   Takahue   Broadwood

Kapiro   Rewa's Village   Waipapa   Kerikeri

Puketi Forest   National Reserve   Fruit Orchards   Waitangi   Paihia

Ngaiotonga Scenic Res.

Mangamuka   Mangamuka Bridge   45   Okaihau   L. Omapere

Pompallier House, Captain Cook Mem. Mus.

Mangungu Mission House   Kohukohu   Panguru   Rawene

Waimate Mission House   Boat Trips   Opua

Nostalgic Railway

Horeke   Kaikohe   Pioneer Village   Taheke   Ohaeawai   Pararaka   21   Moerewa   Kawakawa   Waiomio   Oakura

Whangaruru Harbour

Sand Dunes   Opononi   12   Waipoua   Clendon House

Glow-worm Caves   1   Towai   Helena Bay

Hokianga Harbour   Omapere   Waimamaku   Lookout   Forest Sanctuary

N O R T H L A N D   39   Whakapara   Whananaki

Awarua   Tanekaha   Hikurangi   Matapouri   Tutukaka   Ngunguru

Waipoua   Donnellys Crossing   Trounson Kauri Park   Pakotai

Wairua Falls   Kamo   16   Maunu   Whangarei   Clock Museum, Parahaki War M

Kaihu   L. Taharoa   Titoki   Maungatapere   Portland   Onerahi   Parua Bay   Taurikura

Bream H

14   Marsden Point   40

12   Tangowahine   Ruakaka   *Bream Bay*

Dargaville   North Wairoa Museum   Turiwiri   Waiotira   Waipu   Waipu Cove

Baylys Beach   Taipuha   1   Bryderwyn   Mar

Te Kopuru   Paparoa   Huarau   Maungaturoto   Mar   Matakohe   12   Kaiwaka   Ruawai   Kauri Museum   *out-of-service*   27

Tinopai   Port Albert   Te Hana   Wellsford   19

Pouto   Tapora   *L. Mokeno*   War   North Head

T A S M A N   *Kaipara Harbour*   16   Al   Hot Sp   Shelly Beach   Kaukapakapa   Paraka   Helensville   AUCKLA

S E A   Waikoukou   Coate   Parem   Gannet Sanctuary   Waimauku   16   Huapai   Kumeu   M   Muriwai Beach   Waitakere   Swanso   Mt. A   War Memorial Museum,   Mt. Ro   Microworld, Underwater World   Piha   Titira   Huia   Whatipu

Signs indicating railway crossings are something of a rarity in New Zealand, and only significant during summer months. This is when the **nostalgic train** lets off steam three times a day in the middle of town. The railway lines cut right across the town's main thoroughfare for the first kilometers. **Opua** is the train's final destination. Departure times are at 9:15 a.m., 12 noon and 3 p.m., and the return journey takes about two hours altogether.

Opua is accessible by car as well. If you wish to go to the **Bay of Islands**, a popular tourist resort, drive on to Paihia. However, Russell is a quieter and more pleasant place to start the journey. A ferry connecting Opua and **Okiato** operates daily between 6:40 a.m. and 8:50 p.m. at about ten-minute intervals. Before boarding the ferry, don't forget to have a meal at the **Ferryman's Restaurant** on the pier. It is considered one of the best restaurants in the north by many connoisseurs. The food is so good that some guests have often missed the last ferry because of it!

There is an alternative route from Kawakawa to Russell. This road passes through very scenic countryside, and goes along the **Waikare Inlet** for part of the way. But it does add about 45 kilometers to the journey.

Idyll at the Sweet, Blue Penguin

Times have changed in these parts. In the good old days there were deplorable conditions in Kororareka, which means "sweet, blue penguin," as **Russell** used to be called. Life in Russell, or the "hellhole of the Pacific," as the town came to be known, was only bearable under the influence of alcohol.

Today, Russell is a quiet and idyllic country town. It only comes to life during the high season between December and the end of April or during *Labour Day Weekend* (the third weekend in October)

51

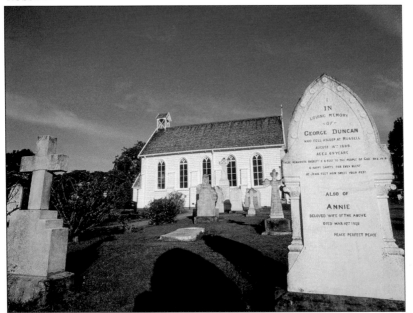

at the finish of the *Auckland to Russell Coastal Classic Regatta*. A rock band plays nightly in the bar of the **Duke of Marlborough Hotel**, and the beer flows freely from the tap. The bar is not located in the hotel of the same name.

Once the celebrations are over, the town becomes peaceful again. After all, the days of the whalers are long gone. They came to Kororareka at the beginning of the 19th century to stock up on provisions, and the town soon developed into the largest European settlement in the entire country. A short time later, New Zealand's first capital city was founded in nearby **Okiato**. It is hardly any wonder, as the Treaty of Waitangi had been signed on the side of the Bay of Islands. Okiato didn't remain the capital for very long, however. After nine months, Captain William Hobson, decided to make Auckland the capital of New Zealand. The "old" capital was

abandoned and the notorious town of Kororareka was re-named Russell.

In any discussion involving the Bay of Islands' past, the name of which was provided by Captain Cook in 1769, it is essential to mention a Maori called Hone Heke Pokai. He chopped down the flagpole flying the Union Jack on top of Flagstaff Hill four times in protest of the exploitation of the Maori people by the British. Hone Heke Pokai also attacked the town of Russell in 1845. Not only did this trigger war between the Maori and Pakeha, the town of Russell also went into a state of decline, losing any political significance it may have had. The contemporary visitor may consider this a bit of good luck. The community of Russell, with its 1000 inhabitants, has remained quite untouched by the hustle and bustle of city life, making it the ideal place to start discovering some of the 157 islands of the Bay of Islands group.

The elegant and well-known **Duke of Marlborough Hotel** is situated next to the pier. This was the first hotel in New

Above: Christ Church was built in 1836 and is among the oldest churches in the country.

Zealand to be given a license for alcohol. Although it has burned down four times since it was established, the hotel still has a lot of its original British charm inherited from the turn of the century.

The *pohutukawa* tree-lined beach promenade leads the visitor into New Zealand's past. A *pa* stronghold is situated only a few steps away from the hotel. The *pa* was turned into a gin mill when the whalers came to this region. It has become a souvenir shop in the meantime. Things change with the times in Russell.

The Gables, New Zealand's oldest restaurant, is located here as well. Built in 1847, it has a charming atmosphere and a splendid view of the Bay of Islands. It is just the place for a romantic dinner by candlelight. The **Captain Cook Memorial Museum** is set a bit back from the promenade. Among the objects exhibited in the museum is a miniature of Captain Cook's ship, the *Endeavour*, on which he reached New Zealand in 1769.

The **Pompallier House**, which bears witness to the attempts of the missionaries to bring light to this "hole of darkness", lies at the end of the promenade. There you will also find **Christ Church**, New Zealand's oldest church, with its shining white walls. The adjacent cemetery became the final resting place for some seafarers. The oldest grave dates back to 1836, and the most important grave bears the name of the Maori Tamati Waka Nene.

BAY OF ISLANDS

The **Bay of Islands Maritime and Historic Park**, which runs a visitor center in Russell, concentrates more on present-day events than history. Conservation officer Shaugham Anderson has a useful tip for adventurous vacationers: "If you are fit, and don't mind exerting yourself, the trail leading to Cape Brett is very remote and beautiful!". The eight-hour hike runs through hilly countryside,

touching the coast only briefly. Accommodation (12 beds) is available in the old lighthouse at Cape Brett.

The underwater trail in one of the **Motuarohia Island** lagoons is quite unique, and should be included in any tour of the Bay of Islands. Equipped with snorkel and flippers, visitors can have close-up views of the island's underwater world, which boasts numerous species of fish and plants – a real adventure.

For those seeking something a little less strenuous, the magnificent sandy beaches on **Urupukapuka Island** are the ideal place to relax. This is the largest island of the group. Details concerning camping sites and transportation can be obtained from the park ranger at the Visitor Centre. Tourists are also informed about the park's biggest problem: Oppossums, brought to New Zealand from Australia, have become a real menace not only here but also elsewhere in the island country. They eat the roots of the *pohutukawa* trees, which, because of their striking red blossoms, have become something of a national symbol. These trees blossom in Northland in the Bay of Plenty and in Coromandel during the long summer months. *Project Crimson* has been launched to save the pohutukawa trees, which the New Zealanders simply call the "Christmas Tree", from becoming extinct.

Paihia, on the other side of bay, is a different place altogether. Several souvenir shops, tourist information, travel agents and take-away restaurants line the streets. A popular trip among the many offered, and certainly a worthwhile one, is by catamaran through the Bay of Islands as far as **Piercy Island** and the **Hole in the Rock**. This trip is arranged for you by Fuller Northland.

WAITANGI

It was only because of **Waitangi** that Paihia became famous. On February 6,

1840, Captain William Hobson, as a representative of the British Crown, signed a treaty with a large number of Maori chieftains representing the first inhabitants of Aotearora, "the land of the long white clouds." Two important principles were embodied in the treaty. The Maori agreed to serve the British sovereign, and demanded in exchange the right to own their land, forests, fishing grounds and other properties. Maori and Europeans were to develop the country together.

When the first European settlers came to New Zealand, they coexisted with the Maori, but friction had developed over the years, so that a treaty became vital in order to reestablish a state of peace.

Trade in supplies and provisions for ships had been replaced by traffic in weapons. Prior to the signing of the treaty, political unrest over land rights had become widespread. It was hoped that the *Treaty of Waitangi* would establish law

and order. The treaty is now well over 150 years old, yet the conflict between the Maori and white New Zealanders has not been completely resolved.

Waitangi was proclaimed a National Reserve. Visitors are welcome to stroll around the reserve, visiting sites of historical interest. The best approach is along the **Nias Track**. Before setting out, it is advisable to watch the extremely interesting and informative 30-minute slideshow at the visitors' centre. Starting there, the track leads to the 35-meter long **Maori war canoe**. It is considered the world's largest canoe, and can accommodate 80 oarsmen. Nowadays *Ngatokima-tawharua* is only used on very special occasions. Then the paddles are attached to the ceiling of the canoe house in neat rows, waiting for the opportunity to stir up memories of the Maori past.

Beyond the canoe house, the trail continues to the **Treaty House**, an outstanding example of English Georgian architectural style. **Whare Runanga**, located nearby, is an example of Maori art. Op-

Above: Traditional art is displayed before the Maori meeting house in Waitangi.

ened in 1940, the assembly hall was built for all Maori.

A well-kept lawn covers the hills of the treaty grounds. From here, visitors have a splendid view of Hobson's Beach and the Bay of Islands.

If you enjoy a touch of nostalgia, take a trip through the Bay of Islands on the *R. Tucker Thompson* schooner. The vessel is anchored just before the bridge in the direction of Paihia. The old ships exhibited in the nearby **Shipwreck Museum** are no longer seaworthy. Almost everything that went aground in the past centuries off the coast of the Bay of Islands is exhibited inside the three-master *Tui*. The restaurant on board is under German management. The collection was put together by Kelly Tarlton, the same man who set up the above mentioned Underwater World.

History is also the focal point of any visit to **Kerikeri**, 26 kilometers down the road. With its 1400 inhabitants, this tourist resort doesn't seem terribly exciting at first glance. A few kilometers to the north of the town center there is an idyllic harbor, with two buildings of historic interest. The **Kerikeri Mission House**, built in 1821, and sometimes called Kemp House after the family that lived in it for over 140 years, is the oldest building in New Zealand. It is surrounded by trim gardens. The building by the name of **Old Stone Store** was built a few years later. The façade of the house has changed as little as the interior even though it was completely restored in 1997. A small souvenir shop is scheduled to open on the ground floor and a museum on the first floor.

There is a magnificent view of the surrounding countryside, and specifically of **St James Church**, built in 1878. A Maori stronghold has been created at the nearby **Rewa's Village**. The **Stone Store Restaurant** veranda is a pleasant place to enjoy a refreshing cup of tea and a piece of quiche.

Kerikeri is hidden behind a lush green bamboo curtain, which protects the numerous kiwi and citrus fruit plantations from wind and weather. These fruits are harvested between April and May each year.

A creative and varied arts scene has established itself throughout the entire region of the Bay of Islands over the past years. The well-known, if somewhat eccentric, Austrian painter Friedensreich Hundertwasser is probably its most famous representative. He has been living in the Bay region since 1973 more or less on a regular basis. Hundertwasser became famous in New Zealand, predominantly among younger people involved in environmental issues, because of his concept for a new New Zealand flag. However, the sophisticated green spiraling fern was not able to replace New Zealand's traditional flag modeled on the Union Jack.

One Million Dollar View Road and Rainbow Warrior

A secondary road leads from Kerikeri back to Highway I, which you should take northbound. About 13 kilometers beyond **Kapiro**, there is the next turn-off leading to the coast. The Matauri Bay Road is tarred only as far as **Otoroa**, where it then turns into a gravel road. Apart from the local school bus which winds its way slowly across the hills, there is hardly any traffic for the next 16 kilometers. **Matauri Bay** consists of a collection of houses, behind which the road makes its way downhill towards the sea. This particular part of the street is called *One Million Dollar View Road* by the locals.

Until quite recently, the white sandy beach was the bay's major attraction. But this changed on July 15, 1990, when the **Rainbow Warrior Memorial** was dedicated on a nearby hill. The propeller of the Greenpeace ship *Rainbow Warrior*

adorns the monument. The ship set sail on numerous occasions, protesting the atomic-bomb tests carried out in Pacific waters by the French, until the French Secret Service bombed the ship while it was anchored in Auckland Harbour, killing a Greenpeace photographer. For a long time after this incident, diplomatic relations between France and New Zealand were very icy. To the delight of many divers, the *Rainbow Warrior* was "buried" a few sea miles off the coast of **Motukawaiti Island**. With its varied examples of flora and fauna, the wreck has become an attraction among divers.

Wainui and **Tauranga** are two more beautiful bays in the Matauri region. The tarred road starts again at Te Ngaere Bay and passes by Whangaroa before meeting up with Highway 10. Weather permitting, you should plan at least one full day for this part of your trip.

Above: Cape Reinga is considered the springboard for Maori souls into the other world. Right: The Cape Reinga lighthouse.

The fresh sea air stimulates an appetite, and what better place to stop for refreshments than **Mangonui** at Doubtless Bay. You can eat at any time of day at the local fish and chips shop situated at the northern end of the town, and run by Neil Moffat. The shop is built on stilts which stand in the water, but figuratively speaking, Neil certainly didn't build his shop on sand. Many *Kiwi* mouths start to water at the very mention of Neil's fish and chips shop. In fact, many Northlanders say the best fish and chips in the entire region are to be had here. Only Neil contradicts them: "The best in the world!"

The road continues along **Doubtless Bay** for a few kilometers. Sometime between A.D. 925 and 950, the Maori patriarch Kupe first set foot on New Zealand soil after his long journey from *hawaiki*, the land of his forefathers. It was Captain Cook who actually gave the bay its name. While sailing these waters on December 9, 1769, he contemplated as to whether the bay was an island or a peninsula. After giving the matter much thought, Cook finally came to the conclusion that it was actually a bay, and he was right. Having reached this decision, Cook continued on his journey, and a Frenchman, Jean François Marie de Surville, became the first European to set foot on this soil. However, he didn't make a very good impression with the locals. After a confrontation with Maori leaders, he destroyed their entire village. When Marion du Fresne landed in New Zealand three years later, the Maori took revenge. Marion du Fresne had to pay with his life for what had been inflicted upon them three years earlier. Before his death, the Frenchman made a valuable discovery, which was to bring a great deal of money as well as fame to the Northland region. After felling a kauri tree (*Agathis australis*), he recognized the extremely hard quality of its wood. Although the Maori had been using kauri wood for their long canoes, they did not cut down the giant trees for commercial purposes.

The kauri industry began to flourish around 1840, under the influence of European settlers. It reached its zenith in 1906. In that year alone, 440,000 cubic meters were processed. Although the kauri trees require centuries to grow to their maximum height, it only took the wood-cutters a couple of years before the last kauri tree was felled. As a result, the kauri industry came to a standstill.

Those planning a boat trip in Doubtless Bay are advised to try their luck in **Taipa.** This is where the majority of locals keep their yachts. Heading for the coast, the road makes its way westwards for the next 20 kilometers, meeting Highway 1 at **Awanui.**

CAPE REINGA

At this point travelers have to decide what to do: From now on a "one-way" road covers the remaining 109 kilometers to **Cape Reinga.** Caution: The road that leads to Te Hapua is a gravel road that

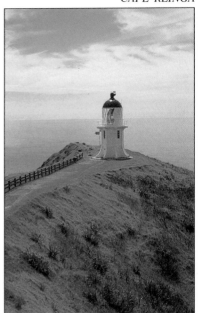

becomes very difficult to drive on in wet weather. If you don't wish to drive the entire distance yourself, **Waipapakauri Beach** is the ideal place to start an organized tour of New Zealand's most northerly region.

It is situated approximately nine kilometers from the turn-off to Waipapakauri. Not only is the little town located right on the coast, tours on their way to Cape Reinga stop here every morning in order to pick up additional passengers before continuing the journey along **Ninety Mile Beach.** Although the beach is actually only 60 miles long, this doesn't alter the fact that the coastal scenery here is very beautiful.

Access to the road is primarily dependent on the tide. It is only possible to drive along Ninety Mile Beach to Te Paki Stream Road during low tide. Notice of tide times is given in the tourist newspaper entitled *Look North.*

When traveling along this stretch of road, it is essential to take great care. The tide has been known to rise up to 3.8 m

CAPE REINGA
0   20km

within six hours. If you have rented a car, be sure to read through your contract very carefully before setting out along Ninety Mile Beach. The majority of rental companies don't allow their cars to be driven along this stretch of road. Vehicles have been known to get stuck in the sand on a number of occasions – and that puts an abrupt end to what would have been a wonderful trip.

Once a year, the Ninety Mile Beach serves as the largest fishing ground anywhere in New Zealand: At the end of February, the *Surfcasting Snapper Fishing Contest* is organized by Tony Brljevich. More than 1000 participants from all over the world come to New Zealand each year in order to take part in this competition. And each of them entertains the hope of catching a seven-kilo snapper and winning the prize money, amounting to 75,000 NZ$. Many of the visitors ar-

riving at Ninety Mile Beach this time of year may also be tempted to come because of the wild beach parties that take place in the normally sleepy town of Waipapakauri.

According to Maori mythology, souls leave Aotearoa at an 800-year-old *pohutukawa* tree on Cape Reinga, and begin their journey from there home to *hawaiki*, the country of the Maoris' ancestors.

Looking northwards from the **Cape Reinga lighthouse**, you can see the point where the Pacific Ocean and the Tasman Sea meet, or you can look eastwards along the coast to the **Surville Cliffs**, New Zealand's most northerly point. The return journey to Waipapakauri Beach leads through the interior of the **Aupouri Peninsula**. Stop at **Houhora Heads** on the way back for a visit to the **Wagener Museum**, which has numerous exhibits of Maori arts and crafts. **Mount Camel** lies on the other side of the bay. With its elevation of 245 m, the term "mount" sounds rather ludicrous. Camel is an ap-

Right: Long, wide beaches and excellent fishing are both typical of the Northland.

propriate designation, however. When Captain Cook first sighted the hill, its shape reminded him of a kneeling camel.

The western part of Ninety Mile Beach and Cape Reinga makes New Zealand's North Point popular among tourists. New Zealanders prefer the more peaceful atmosphere of the east coast, especially the region near **Rarawa Beach**, which stretches along the Great Exhibition Bay starting at Ngataki, north of Houhora. The enormous sand dunes at **Tauroa Point,** to the northwest of Ahipara, are equally popular with both tourists and New Zealanders. This destination is ideal for four-wheel-drive vehicles and rock-pool fishing.

Those who have had their fill of outdoor activities, and want a taste of city life should make their way to **Kaitaia**. New Zealand's most northerly town still shows a strong Balkan influence. A large number of immigrants from southeastern Europe came to this region during the last century and earned their living as gum diggers. They usually found the dark yellow blocks of resin by digging in the vicinity of the trees, or obtained it directly by cutting into the bark.

They have long since had to give up their jobs in this field, but now regard New Zealand as their new home. The **Yugoslavian Cultural Club** on Commerce Street, Kaitaia's main street, is still in business.

Kauri Trees in Waipoua Forest

Highway 1 heads south from Kaitaia via the Maungataniwha Range. There are some hiking trails through the **Raetea Forest** that ultimately lead to kauri trees. There isn't much of interest along this route other than the **Waimate Mission House**, New Zealand's second oldest building, and the **Church of St John the Baptist**, built in 1871. It's best to branch off towards the west at **Mangamuka Bridge**, following the road that runs along the Mangamuka River. This route is characteristic of the idyllic Northland countryside, where time appears to have

59

come to a standstill. The small wooden piers situated along the banks of the river are falling apart. Grass grows over wrecked cars. Most of the fisherman have long since left town. Four kilometers farther along, there is a ferry-crossing to **Rawene** from Hokianga Harbour.

Before continuing your journey on Highway 12 in the direction of Opononi and Opamere, visit the historic Clendon House in Rawene. There is a splendid view of the sand dunes on the other side of the bay from here, as well as from the lookout, situated about half way along the route to Waiotemarama.

Farther south, the town of **Waimamaku** is the gateway to the famous kauri forest region, known as **Waipoua Kauri Forest**. This region has been a nature preserve for years and is therefore a legally-protected conservation area. Even

Above: The kauri tree of Tane Mahuta, with its record-breaking dimensions. Right: The giant trees met their end at the beginning of the 20th century.

so, the 2000 year-old trees, though no longer threatened ty the axe, have been affected by pollution. Their years appear to be numbered. Those wishing to see them should hurry before it's too late. Keep in mind, however, that mass tourism always has its negative sides. Until now, visitors have been permitted to walk around the forest at their leisure.

Since the roots of the kauri trees grow very close to the surface, they are often trampled on and subsequently destroyed by visitors to the forest, often causing the big trees irreparable damage. It is hoped that wooden walkways and more stringent regulations within the forest grounds will help to preserve the trees.

The approach to **Tane Mahuta** is mostly by way of gravel road leading to the 387-m Wairau summit. There is a large parking lot situated on the road, about a 5-minute walk away from the forest. The **God of the Forest**, approximately 1200 years old, with its 55 meters and circumference of 13.7 meters, is the largest kauri tree in New Zealand. Not quite as large, but just as spectacular are the trees known as the **Father of the Forest** and the **Four Sisters**, located a few minutes' drive to the south on the turn-off leading to **Te Matua Ngahere**. It takes about 15 minutes on foot to reach the Father of the Forest and only three minutes to get to the Four Sisters from the parking lot. After so many spectacular sights, the landscape seems rather monotonous for the next few kilometers. There are a number of turn-offs leading to the **Trounson Kauri Park** before entering **Kaihu**. A large number of hiking trails have been laid out in this park.

Beaches at Dargaville and Wine on the Outskirts of Auckland

Those wishing to see the beach again should turn off at **Dargaville**, and head towards the lovely **Baylys Beach**. Dargaville, a town on the banks of the Wairoa

River with 5000 inhabitants, is not a very exciting place. Highway 12 takes a sharp turn to the right just beyond Dargaville, and crosses the Wairoa river heading towards Turiwiri. It reaches the town of **Matakohe** after another 45 kilometers. The **Otamatea Kauri and Pioneer Museum** is located here, founded by Merv Sterling. The 75 year-old man lives for "his" museum, which houses many exhibits charcteristic of life in Northland. Kauri trees and their gum are a predominant feature. The museum is certainly worth visiting and a good place to start or end a tour of Northland.

There is access to Highway 1 again at **Brynderwyn**. The closer one gets to Auckland, the more traffic one finds on the road. Suddenly you cherish the peace and expansiveness which permeates the Northland region. Although it seemed like a tranquil city at the start of your New Zealand tour, Auckland now appears to have the same hectic pace characteristic of any large city in the world. It doesn't take long to get used to the

solitude and tranquility of the rural regions, so that even the smaller towns seem hectic in comparison.

If you are not quite ready for Auckland's busy streets, it is advisable to drive to the right at Wellsford on Highway 6, in the direction of **Helensville**. This, via **Waimauku**, is the best approach to the **Auckland Wine Trail**, which winds around the slopes of the Waitakere Ranges on its way to Huapai and Kumeu. The transition from the quiet countryside of Northland to Auckland's busy city life may be made easier with a glass of wine at (for example) **Coopers Creek Winery**, situated directly on Highway 16, three kilometers outside Kumeu. If you are tempted to partake in more than one glass, it is advisable to spend the night in Kumeu or Waikoukou. There are very stringent laws in New Zealand against driving under the influence.

Whatever your decision, the drive to New Zealand's secret capital of Auckland takes only about 30 minutes from here.

NORTHLAND

Accommodation

DARGAVILLE: *LUXURY:* **Kauri House Lodge**, Bowen St., Tel: 09-4398082. *MODERATE:* **Motel Hobsons' Choice**, 212 Victoria St., Tel: 09-4398551. **Northern Wairoa**, Tel: 09-4398925. *BUDGET:* **Greenhouse Hostel**, 13 Portland St., Dargaville, Tel: 09-4396342.

KAITAIA: *MODERATE:* **Kauri Lodge Motel**, 15 South Rd., Tel: 09-4081190. **Loredo Motel**, 25 North Rd., Tel: 09-4083200. **Reef Lodge**, Rangiputa Beach, Tel: 09-4087100.

BUDGET: **90 Mile Beach**, The Park, P.O. Box 71, Tel: 09-4067298 (cabins and camping; 18 km from Kaitaia at the Waipapakauri Ramp; on 90 Mile Beach). **Main Street Hostel**, Pukenui, 235 Commerce St., Tel: 09-4081275.

KERIKERI: *LUXURY:* **Riverview Park Lodge**, 28 Landing Rd., Tel: 09-4078741. **Bay of Islands Country Lodge**, R.D. 3 (at the Puketona Junction), Tel: 09-4077801.

MODERATE: **Central Motel**, Main Rd., Tel: 09-4078921. **Homestead Motel**, Tel: 09-4077063. **Orchard Motel**, Kerikeri Rd. and Hall Rd., P.O. Box 132, Tel: 09-4078869.

BUDGET: **Aranga Holiday Park**, opposite the BP Service Station, Tel: 09-4079326 (cabins and camping). **Hone Heke Lodge**, Hone Heke Rd., Tel: 09-4078170.

MANGONUI: *MODERATE:* **Acacia Best Western Motel**, Mill Bay Rd., Tel: 09-4060417. **Hotel Mangonui**, Beach Rd., Tel: 09-4060003. *BUDGET:* **Old Oak Inn**, Mangonui, Tel: 09-4060665. **Coppers Beach Motel**, Coppers Beach, Highway 10, Tel: 09-4060271.

OPONONI: *MODERATE:* **Oponui Resort Motel/Hotel**, Waterfront Main Rd., Tel: 09-4058858. *BUDGET:* **Te Rangimarie - House of Harmony**, Opononi, Tel: 09-4058778.

PAIHIA: *LUXURY:* **Abel Tasman Lodge**, Marsden Rd., Tel: 09-4027521. **Autolodge**, Marsden Rd., P.O. Box 28, Tel: 09-4027416. **Waitangi Resort Hotel**, Tel: 09-4028200. **Beachcomber**, 1 Seaview Rd., Tel: 09-4027434.

MODERATE: **A1 (Ayvon Motel)**, Davis Crescent, Tel: 09-4027684. **Dolphin Motel**, 69 Williams Rd., Tel: 09-4028170. **Paihia Sands Motel**, Marsden Rd., P.O. Box 2, Tel: 09-4027707. **Seaspray Motel**, 138 Marsden Rd., Tel: 09-4027935. **The Bayswater Inn**, Marsden Rd., Tel: 09-4027444.

BUDGET: **Smiths Holiday Camp**, Opua-Paihia Rd., Tel: 09-4027678. **Lodge 11 Backpackers Hostel**, Kings Rd., Tel: 09-4027487.

RUSSELL: *LUXURY:* **Te Maiki Villas**, Tapeka Rd., Tel: 09-4037046. *MODERATE:* **Duke of Marlborough Hotel**, The Strand, Tel: 09-4037829. **Flagstaff Homestead**, Wellington Street, Tel: 09-4037862. **Motel Russell**, Matauwhi Bay Road, Tel: 09-4037854. **Russell Holiday Park**, Long Beach Rd., Tel: 09-4037826. *BUDGET:* **Arcadia Lodge**, Tel: 09-4037756.

WHANGAREI: *MODERATE:* **Ascot Motel**, 7-9 Matipo Place, Tel: 09-4381559. **Grand Hotel**, corner Bank and Rose St., Tel: 09-4384279. **Kamo Motel**, 352 Kamo Rd., Tel: 09-4351049.

BUDGET: **Hatea House Hostel**, 67 Hatea Drive, Tel: 09-4382173. **Tropicana Holiday Park and Motel**, Heads Rd., Tel: 09-4380687. **Youth Hostel**, 52 Punga Grove Ave, Tel : 09-4388954.

Restaurants

DARGAVILLE: **Lighthouse Restaurant**, Harding Park, Tel: 09-4397133 (lovely interior, wall-panelling with *kauri-* and *rimu-*wood.

KAITAIA: **Beachcomber Restaurant**, 222 Commerce St. Plaza, Tel: 09-4082010 (seafood and lamb specialities).

OPUA: **Ferryman's Restaurant and Bar**, Opua Store Building, Tel: 09-4027515 (this historic building is situated in the harbor next to the car ferry dock; one of the best Northland restaurants; seafood and lamb specialities).

PAIHIA: **Bistro 40**, 40 Marsden Rd., Tel: 09-4027444 (historic building with impressive view). **La Scala**, Selwyn Rd., Tel: 09-4027031 (fish; speciality of the house: Seafood Extravaganza for 25-40 NZ$). **Tides Restaurant**, Williams Rd., Tel: 09-4027557.

WHANGAREI: **The Myth of Vine Street**, 58 Vine St., Tel: 09-4387849.

Museums

DARGAVILLE: **The Otamatea Kauri and Pioneer Museum**, Matakohe (30 minutes south of town at Highway 12; everything connected with *kauri-*wood and *kauri-*gum; open daily 9 a.m.–5 p.m.; Tel: 09-4317417).

Northern Wairoa Museum, Harding Park, Dargaville (exhibition documenting Maori culture and pioneer age; open daily 9 a.m.–4 p.m.).

KAITAIA: **Far North Regional Museum**, Commerce St., (history of Northlands; open Mondays–Fridays 10 a.m.–5 p.m., Sundays and public holidays 1 a.m.–5 p.m.). **Sullivan's Nocturnal Park**, Fairburn near Kaitaia (daily 9:30 a.m.-dusk; guided tours to see kiwis and fireflies).

KERIKERI: **Rewa's Village**, opposite the Old Stone Store (Maori fortification; impressive view over the bay).

RUSSELL: Captain Cook Memorial Museum, York St. (daily 10 a.m.–4 p.m., Sundays 2–4 p.m.).

WAITANGI: Waitangi National Reserve, Tel: 09-4027437, 3 kilometers north of Paihia (Maori art, history and nature at New Zealand's "cradle" – the famous *Treaty of Waitangi* was signed here). Get into the spirit of the place at the Visitors Centre, which puts on a good slide show, then proceed on the Nias track to the Maori war canoe at Hobson's Beach, the Treaty House and the Maori congregation house *Whare Runaga*. The Waitangi National Reserve, spawling across 1250 acres, is classified as a historical monument; open daily from 9 a.m.–5 p.m.

WHANGAREI: Clapham's Clocks Museum, Town Basin, Water St. (ca. 1000 exhibits; open Mon–Fri 10 a.m.–4 p.m., Sundays and public holidays 10:15 a.m.–3 p.m.). **Northland Regional Museum and Kiwi House**, Highway 14, ca. 4 km toward Dargaville, Tel: 09-4389630 (Victorian flair in and around the Clarke Homestead of 1885; Tuesdays–Sundays 10 a.m.–3:30 p.m.).

Warkworth and District Museum, Parry Kauri Park, turnoff from Highway 1 into McKinney Rd. (local history; open in summer 9:30 a.m.–4 p.m.; in winter 10 a.m.–3:30 p.m.).

Tips and Trips

BAY OF ISLANDS: The favorite local sport is deep-sea fishing: for information, contact Skipjack, P.O. Box 216, Russell, Tel: 09-4031082 or Game Fishing Charters, Maritime Building, Pahia, Tel: 09-4027311. The old wooden schooner *R. Tucker Thompson* sails the Bay of Islands between November and April. Start daily at 9:30 a.m. in Opua and at 10 a.m. in Russell. Info: Tel: 09-4027421. In Summertime the ferry between Paihia and Russell runs daily every hour from 7 a.m. to 9 p.m, on friday from 7 a.m. to 10 p.m.

CAPE REINGA: Fullers Northland (Paihia, Russell, Kaitaia and Mangonui) arrange day trips to Cape Reinga (including a visit to the Wagener Museum and a drive along Ninety Mile Beach). The only Maori tourist operation, Cuzzy Leisure Tours, offers similar trips from Kaitaia (24 Allen Bell Drive; Tel: 09-4081853).

HISTORIC HOUSES: Don't miss the following historic houses situated in the Northlands: Waimate Mission House (built in 1832; Waimate North; daily 10 a.m.–4:30 p.m.), Kemp House (Kerikeri; daily 10 a.m.–4:30 p.m.), Clendon House (The Esplanade, Rawene; 10 a.m.–4 p.m.), Mangungu Mission House (Hokianga Harbour, near Horeke; weekends and holidays 12 noon–4 p.m.) and Pompallier House (The Strand, Russell; 10 a.m.–4:30 p.m.).

HOKIANGA HARBOUR: The ferry between Kohukohu and Rawene – an important connection between the two towns for travelers in the direction of Hwy 12 – operates daily from 7:45 a.m. to 6 p.m.; crossing time is 10 minutes; the fare is 10 NZ$ for cars and 10 NZ$ for passengers.

KAWAU ISLAND: The ferry to Kawau departs from Auckland three times a week, (departs 10 a.m., returns 4 p.m., 45 NZ$) or daily from Sandspit near Warkworth (70 km north of Auckland).

KAWAKAWA: During the summer months a nostalgic steam locomotive operates on the track to Opua (departure three times daily: 9:15 a.m., 12 noon and 3 p.m.; the journey takes two hours).

PAIHIA: A "must" is the boat trip across the Bay of Islands, including a visit to Moturua Island, Otehei Bay, Cape Brett and the "Hole in the Rock": Fullers, P.O. Box 145, Paihia, Tel: 09-4027421.

Festivals / Special Events

NINETY MILE BEACH: The *Surfcasting Snapper Fishing Contest* takes place at the end of February near Waipapakauri Beach. 750 NZ$ prize money.

WAITANGI: On February 6, the anniversary of the *Treaty of Waitangi* is celebrated with a buoyant festival in the historic area of the National Reserve. The *Waitangi Festival of Maori Arts and Crafts* takes place a few days prior to the anniversary.

Tourist Information

BAY OF ISLANDS: **Information Centre**, Maritime Reserve, Paihia, Tel: 09-4027345 (daily 9 a.m.–5 p.m.). **DOC, Bay of Islands Maritime and Historic Park**, Park H.Q. and Visitor Centre, Pitt St., Russell, Tel: 09-4037685 or Kerikeri Station, Landing Rd., Tel: 09-4078474 Kerikeri.

DARGAVILLE: Information and AA Office, Normandy St., Tel:09-4398360 (Mon–Fri 8:30 a.m.–5 p.m.).

HOKIANGA: **Visitor Information Centre**, Omapere Beach, Tel: 09-4058869 (Mon–Fri 9 a.m.– 5 p.m.).

KAITAIA: **Public Relations Information Office**, Jaycee Park, South Rd., Tel: 09-4080879 (Mon–Fri 9 a.m.–5 p.m.).

WAIPOUA FOREST SANCTUARY: **Visitor Centre**, Dargaville-Rawene Hwy (50 km north of Dargaville), Tel: 09-4390605. Trounson Kauri Park, Dargaville-Rawene Hwy, Tel: 09-4390615.

WAITANGI: DOC, National Trust, Tau Henare Drive, Tel: 09-4027437.

WHANGAREI: **Visitor Information Centre,** Tarewa Park (daily 9 a.m.–5 p.m.); **AA**, 7 James Street, Tel: 049-4387079. **DOC**, 48 Kaka Street, Tel: 089-4380299.

ON COROMANDEL PENINSULA

COLVILLE
COOKS BEACH
HOT WATER BEACH

When heading south out of Auckland, you will notice that there isn't a harbor bridge to carry traffic outside city limits. Instead, all traffic moves along a wide, well-covered, multi-lane highway. Those planning to spend a few weeks traveling around New Zealand should enjoy the unique feeling of driving on this modern type of road. You, and various parts of your body, will soon have get used to traveling on single-track bumpy gravel roads and one-way bridges instead.

The highway dwindles and then comes to an end in the **Bombay Hills** district, about 43 kilometers outside Auckland. While the majority of tourists feel that the region marks the start of any New Zealand tour, many Aucklander feel that New Zealand doesn't exist beyond the Bombay Hills. Anything farther south is regarded as extremely provincial.

The name Bombay is derived from the Indian fruit and vegetable merchants who originally settled in this region. The large fruit and vegetable farms are still run by Indians who immigrated some time ago. The fruit and vegetables sold at the various stalls are reasonably priced. It's a

Preceding pages: The spectacular rock formations of the Cathedral Cave on Coromandel. Left: In Colville time and gas pumps appear to have stood still.

good idea to buy some healthy food for lunch at Coromandel.

To the south, Highway 1 to the south continues on to **Hamilton**, located in the fertile plains of the Waikato region, over Huntly and Ngaruawahia. This route is generally used by those who do not have time to spare.

Coromandel: Gold is Forever

One of New Zealand's most scenic spots comes after a turn off just outside Pokeno in an easterly direction. The town of **Thames**, gateway to Coromandel, is approximately 115 km from Auckland. This peninsula has remained unspoiled by tourism, and is lesser known than other regions. Coromandel has dense forests which cover the hillsides, stretching to the north of the peninsula. The landscape changes constantly. Virgin beaches and remote hiking trails give way to islands á la Robinson Crusoe and to quiet villages. This is the perfect place to unwind in peace. People in the smaller villages tend to have a "counter-culture" lifestyle. Many of them have turned their back on city life for good and don't seem to miss the bright lights of Auckland. The west coast tends to be less commercialized than the east coast, according to popular opinion.

SOUTH OF AUCKLAND

0   20   40km

ER I.

CURY
    ISLANDS
        RED MERCURY I.
AT
CURY ISLAND

OHINAU I.

ercury
y
hedral Cove
ei
Hot Water Beach
akite C O R O M A N D E L
                THE ALDERMEN IS.
    SHOE I.
Pauanui
Kauri
c Res.   SLIPPER I.
    P E N I N S U L A

Y

Whangamata

25

Gold Mines
Waihi   Waihi Beach
o
        Athenree

P   A   C   I   F   I   C

O   C   E   A   N

MAYOR
ISLAND

MATAKANA
ISLAND

Bird Colony
    WHITE I.

Katikati   *Tauranga*
Kama   Omokoroa Beach   Mount
varu   Harbour   Maunganui
amaku   Bethlehem   MOTITI I.
A   Te Puna   Matapihi
a   **Tauranga**   Papamoa Beach
Okauia   Historical   Maketu
        Village
nata   Pyes Pa   Te Puke "Kiwifruit Country"
    Forest   Oropi   Pukehina
Te Poi   Paengaroa
    Park   Pongakawa   2   Matata

B a y

o f

P l e n t y

MOTUHORA I.

roire   33   BAY OF PLENTY
        Lake   Okere   Thornton
53   Rotorua   Falls   L. Rotoiti   L. Rotoehu   Edgecumbe   30   Whakatane
ruru   5   Agrodrome   Mourea   L.   Awakeri   Ohope
        Ngongotaha   Rotoma   Te Teko   Taneatua   Opotiki
Rainbow & Fairy Springs   Lake Rotoma   30   Kawerau   Kutarere
    Bath House, Mus.   Rotokawa
ichfield   **Rotorua**   L. Okataina   Ruatok North   Waimana   2
    Thermal Area   Owhata   Te Wairoa
    Maori Cult. Centre   Buried Village   Waiohau
Tokoroa   Forest Park   Lake
        Horohoro   Tarawera   • Mt. Tarawera 1111
Kinleith   Thermal Area   L. Rotomahana   Oponae
    30   Waimangu   Rotomahana
    Ngakuru   Kerewhakaaiitu
Maraetai   Waikite   Waiotapu Thermal
    Atiamuri   Valley   Waiotapu   Wonderland

1

63
2
27
42
2
26
32
34
14
46

69

Thames became both rich and famous during the gold rush period. The first cries of "Gold!" were heard in 1852. In the ensuing years, as many as 18,000 people flocked to Thames in the hope of finding the precious mineral. But the gold rush days are over, and the population has dwindled to a mere 7000. Memories of Thames' gold rush days are kept alive in the **Mineralogical Museum** or during a "murder week-end" in the Brian Boru Hotel, built in 1868.

A narrow road makes its way north along the shores of the **Firth of Thames**, where Captain Cook landed on November 21, 1769. This route is especially scenic from the middle of December until the end of January. The ancient *pohutukawa* trees are then in full bloom, adding splashes of red to the landscape. There are plenty of opportunities for stops all along the road. Those wishing to take a refreshing swim will enjoy the splendid beaches and coves, which line the route all the way to Coromandel. In **Tapu**, you can discover traces of gold-digger history.

The town of **Coromandel** – consisting of 1000 souls, a handful of stores, handicraft shops and potteries parked along the only main street – is a recomendable stop. The Driving Creek Pottery produces bricks and terracotta wares besides pottery. Barry Brickell supplies himself in wood for the kiln and clay from his own land using a narrow-gauge train he built himself. The track is now 3 kilometers long and includes four bridges, a doubledecker bridge, two tunnels, three zigzag switches and two spiral climbs leading to a lookout platform at the end of a jungle ride. (Kennedys Bay Road, Tel: 07-8668703, daily departures 10 a.m. and 2 p.m., in summer additionally at noon and 4 p.m.)

Right: Barry Brickell's own narrow-gauge railway takes visitors around the jungle-like forest near Coromandel.

COLVILLE

The "counter-culture" town is entirely self-governing through the Cooperative Society Ltd. The **Colville General Store** is the town's main supplier. Make sure you fill up your tank here since this is the last gas station before heading north up the peninsula.

The store offers primarily organically-grown fruit and vegetables, muesli and dried fruits, as well as homemade wine and jam. But even in this remote region, reality encroaches upon the visitor. The people of Colville are struggling to save Coromandel from destruction. What once occupied a small number of adventurers, is, should the New Zealand government have its way, soon to be transformed into the business of international mining companies.

The plan is to mine the remaining gold in large quantities by way of modern technology, which would destroy as much as 70 percent of the surrounding countryside through open-pit mining, the most ecologically devastating form of mining. Until now, it has been possible to have these plans stalled, due to continuing citizen protest and court cases against the government's decision.

Deserted Beaches at a Sacred Mountain

The continuing journey becomes a very dusty matter. From here on there are gravel roads all the way to **Colville Bay**. At the end of Colville Bay, there is a turnoff leading to **Cape Colville**. This road runs along **Mount Moehau**, regarded as sacred by the Maoris. According to Maori legends, Tamatekapua, captain of the *Arawa* canoe, is buried near here. If you want to trace Tamatekapua's footsteps, you can tackle the climb to the top from Te Hope Stream (Port Jackson Road) or from Stony Bay, on the east coast. Both take approximately four

hours. **Port Jackson** and **Colville Farm Park** are situated in an extensive bay (with a nice camping ground). Many New Zealanders regard this as Coromandel's finest beach. However, the excursion to the bay is a 26 kilometer single-track road. Make sure you obey the street signs marked *No Exit*! The road ends at **Fletcher Bay**.

There is nothing of great interest on the journey from Port Jackson to Fletcher, unless you want to tackle the three-hour hike to Stony Bay, where you have to wait for a farmer to give you a lift back towards Waikawau Bay. There is no public transportation here.

To approach the bay and the Farm Park by car, head towards Colville on the way back.

Stony Bay's high waves and excellent wind conditions make it primarily popular among surfers. For those preferring something more peaceful and less exposed to wind, **Little Beach** at Kennedy Bay is an alternative. There is a group of summer houses here. The best views of the entire coastal region can be had from the nearby **Lucas Lookout**.

From this point on, the road turns uphill into the mountains. Abandoned mines situated at the foot of **Mount Tokatea** (480 m) bear witness to the gold rush days. Even back then, the gold diggers who looked up from their work in the mountains could enjoy a rare sight: From the pass, it is possible to see the west coast and east coast at the same time.

From here, the road makes its way back downhill towards Coromandel. On the way, however, it is worth paying a visit to artist Barry Brickell's one-kilometer long miniature railway running through the green wooded area. Barry escorts groups of tourists on the 30-minute trip through the forest at 5:05 p.m. every day. At the end of the trip, visitors can have a look at some examples of Barry's pottery exhibited both in the house and around the yard. Barry also runs an "International Academy of Art," reminiscent of the hippy era. The whole place has a

certain charming chaotic flair about it, and isn't far from Coromandel.

On any trip through New Zealand you will often meet people like Barry Brickell. This type of New Zealander makes an impression on the tourist in the way that they don't live off the land, but live with the land. They have managed to realize their dreams by developing an individual lifestyle.

After a trip to the "wilderness," there's is probably no better place to have the typical British 5 o'clock tea than on the terrace of the **Firlawn House** in Coromandel. Built in 1881, it had its heyday during the Victorian era. At that time, large numbers of Aucklander arrived by steam ship across the Hauraki Gulf. During the gold rush and kauri boom, they certainly knew how to let their hair down at the notorious Coromandel parties. But things have changed. Even during the

Above: The typically luxuriant vegetation of Coromandel. Right: Beachlife on Hot Water Beach.

summer months, Coromandel's population never exceeds 4000 – and the pace here is always slow.

COOKS BEACH

The road out of Coromandel takes you over to the east coast, either on Highway 25, or on the narrower road through the mountains, both of which are not tarred. **Whitianga** doesn't have much to offer, unless you are a sport fisherman. Organized shark, kingfish and marlin fishing trips to the waters of the South Pacific start from here.

There are three major attractions on the other side of Mercury Bay: **Cooks Beach, Hahei** and **Hot Water Beach.** Those living in Whitianga cross with the ferry from Ferry Landing Wharf, built in 1840, the oldest brick pier in Australasia. The ferry operates between 7:30 a.m. and 6:30 p.m. daily as required. Since the three places are only accessible by car, it is more convenient to drive directly to the region via Coroglen and Whenuakite.

The **Shakespeare Cliff Scenic Reserve** lies to the northwest of Cooks Beach. A memorial of stone recalls Captain Cook's visit here between November 5 and 15, 1769. This special spot offers a splendid view across Mercury Bay, and an ideal opportunity to wander along the beaches at Lonely Bay and Cooks Bay. They are situated on the right side. Locals prefer the friendly family atmosphere at the beach of the **Purangi Estuary**.

HOT WATER BEACH

Were Captain Cook to see the beach that bears his name today, he would certainly not want to anchor here. Cooks Beach is nothing more than a collection of summer houses. For this reason, it's best to drive on to the small town of **Hahei**, where a splendid, protected sandy beach and one of the best hotels for miles around is located. If you decide to spend the night at the **Hay-Lyn Park Lodge Hotel**, you can go on two trips the next morning, both of which have to be taken

while the tide is out. One of the tours is a 40-minute hiking tour to **Cathedral Cave**, a magnificent beach, concealed by towering cliffs formed by waves, wind and weather. It's so beautiful here that visitors have been known to make a day-trip out of a short visit. The other tour to the equally beautiful **Hot Water Beach** has to be postponed until the following day. Nature has more surprises in store for you here, some accessible with a shovel. The waters from underground thermal springs flow just below the sandy surface. If you dig a hole into the sand during low tide, you can enjoy a relaxing bath. But be careful – sometimes the water is boiling.

Before going on the journey back south, you should stop at the **Purangi Winery**. It lies about 500 meters beyond the fork to Hahei Beach on Cook Beach Road, on the way to the ferry landing. Bill, Mike, Bob, Anneka and Debby produce ten different types of wine in their winery, with fruit grown in their own organic orchards, of course. The food

Above: Bill, operator of the Purangi Winery, has several fruit wines on tap.

served at the winery is also very good: Sea-food cocktail with fresh homemade bread, followed by a lemon gin, is recomended by Bill.

The mining opponents' slogan is "Coromandel – too precious to mine." After relaxing on the scenic peninsula's silver beaches, taking a dip in its waters and enjoying a glass of wine on the shady Purangi Winery veranda, anyone will find it easy to identify with this slogan.

Our journey continues southward on Highway 25. The **Twin Kauri Scenic Reserve** is just outside the town of **Tairua**. A special sight here is the twin kauri trees, which are about 100 years old. The walk around the reserve takes 20 minutes. These trees are the last of Coromandel's vast kauri forests, which disappeared into the insatiable jaws of Tairua's sawmills.

Pauanui lies on the opposite side of the harbor, and is only accessible from Hikuai. Apart from its beautiful beach and the luxurious **Puka Park Lodge**, Pauanui also has another attraction in Doug Johansen, the slightly unusual tour operator. He likes to think of himself as *Kiwi Dundee*, and operates a large number of tours that are a mixture of nature study and adventurous survival training.

When it's time to leave Coromandel, pick up Highway 2 once more at the town of **Waihi**, which became famous and infamous because of its gold mines. You will reach **Tauranga**, situated on the Bay of Plenty, after a 62-kilometer drive along the extensive Tauranga harbor.

The **Bay of Plenty** was also given its name by Captain Cook – because of the warm and generous welcome given by the Maori when he first landed here. However, he wasn't given this kind of welcome when he landed near present **Gisborne** some time earlier, on October 9, 1769. The Maori showed him no generosity, and Cook responded by naming it the Bay of Poverty. Even explorers can be spiteful for posterity.

COROMANDEL
AND ENVIRONS

Accommodation

COLVILLE: **Farm Parks** (these are operated by the Department of Conservation; camping sites are equipped with toilets and fresh water, some with grill areas) in Fantail Bay, Port Jackson, Fletcher Bay, Stony Bay and Waikawau Bay.
COOKS BEACH: *BUDGET:* **Cooks Beach Motor Camp**, R.D.1, Tel: 07-8665469.
COROMANDEL: *MODERATE:* **Firlawn House**, Kapanga Rd., Tel: 07-8668947 (historic building). **Coromandel Colonial Cottages Motel**, Rings Rd., Tel: 07-8668857.
HAHEI: *MODERATE:* **Hay-Lyn Park Lodge**, Hahei Beach, Christine Terrace, Tel: 07-8663888 (among the best in Coromandel).
PAUANUI: *LUXURY:* **Puka Park Lodge**, Private Bag, Pauanui Beach, Tel: 07-8648088.
TAURANGA: *BUDGET:* **Bell Travellers Lodge**, 39 Bell St., Tel: 074-5786344.
THAMES: *LUXURY:* **Coastal Motor Lodge**, 608 Tararu Rd., Tel: 07-8686843.
MODERATE: **Brian Boru Hotel**, 200 Richmond St., Tel: 07-8686523. **Hotel Imperial**, 476 Pollen St., Tel: 07-8686200. **Crescent Motel**, Corner Jellicoe Crescent and Fenton St., Tel: 07-8686506.
BUDGET: **Tui Lodge**, State Highway 25, Whangapoua Road, Tel: 07-8668237. **Sunkist Lodge**, 506 Brown St., Tel: 07-8688808. **Dickson Holiday Park**, Victoria St., Tel: 07-8687308.
WHITIANGA: *MODERATE:* **Mana-nui Motorlodge**, 20 Albert St., Tel: 07-8665599. **Oceanside Motel**, 32 Buffalo Beach, Tel: 07-8665766.
BUDGET: **Coromandel Backpackers Lodge**, 46 Buffalo Beach Rd., Tel: 07-8665380. **Buffalo Beach Resorts**, Eyre St., Tel: 07-8665854. **Harbourside Holiday Park**, 135 Albert St., Tel: 07-8665746.

Restaurants

COROMANDEL: Firlawn House, Kapanga Rd., Tel: 07-8668947 (Five-o'clock-tea is served on the verandah, or you can have dinner in historic rooms).
THAMES: La Casa Restaurant, State Highway 25, Main Rd., Te Puru, Tel: 07-8682326. (Barbecue and spicy Mexican food). **Old Thames Licensed Restaurant**, 704 Pollen St., Tel: 07-8687207. Delicious seafood.
PAUANUI: Keith's Licensed Restaurant, Pauanui Boulevard, Tel: 07-8648825 (elegant and expensive).

WAIHI: Grandpa Thorn's Restaurant, 4 Waitete Rd., Tel: 07-8638708 (elegant, in the upper price category).

Museums

THAMES: Museum of Mineralogy, corner Cochrane and Brown St. (in summer daily 11 a.m.–4 p.m.; collection of minerals).
COROMANDEL: School of Mines Museum, Rings Road, (daily 10 a.m.–noon and 1–4 p.m.). **Stamper Battery**, Buffalo Rd., (here rocks are ground to extract gold-dust, Wed-Sun 10 a.m.–4 p.m.).

Tips and Trips

Kiwi Dundee: Doug Johansen's famous trecks and hikes – a mix of survival-training and nature studies – start from Pauanui. Info: 07-8658809.
Murder Weekend: Those who've always admired Agatha Christie and her creations Miss Marple and Hercule Poirot, might want to try a nostalgic murder hunt in the Brian Boru Hotel (in summer). Info: Barbara Doyle, Brian Boru Hotel, 200 Richmond St., Thames, Tel: 07-8686523.
Rafting: Wildwater trips: Aotearoa Adventures, Coroglen, R.D. Whitianga, Tel: 07-8663808. **Canoeing tours:** Pauanui Canoe Safaris, 59 El Dorado Landing, Pauanui, Tel: 07-8648160.

Tourist Information

COROMANDEL: Coromandel Information Centre, Kapanga Rd., Tel: 07-8668598 (daily 9 a.m.–4 in summer; daily 10 a.m.–3 p.m. in winter). **DOC**, Kapanga Rd., Tel: 07-8666869.
MATAMATA: Information Matamata, 45 Broadway, Tel: 07-8887260.
MORRINSVILLE: Morrinsville and District Public Relations Association, Thames St., Tel: 07-8895575.
PAEROA: Paeroa and District Public Relations Office, Belmont Rd., Tel: 07-8628636.
TAURANGA: Information and Visitor Centre, The Strand, Tel: 07-5788103.
TE AROHA: Public Relations Office, 102 Whitaker St., Tel: 07-8848052.
THAMES: Information Office, 405 Queen St., Tel: 07-8687284.
WAIHI: Information Centre, Waihi Arts Centre and Museum, Kenny St., Tel: 07-8638368.
WHANGAMATA: Public Relations Office, Port Road, Tel: 07-8658340.
WHITIANGA: Information Centre, 66 Albert St., Tel: 07-8665555.

THE HEART OF
NEW ZEALAND

HAMILTON
WHANGANUI NATIONAL PARK
NEW PLYMOUTH
EGMONT NATIONAL PARK
ROTORUA
LAKE TAUPO
TONGARIRO NATIONAL PARK

HAMILTON

Leaving Auckland on Highway 1 with its three lanes heading south, it's a 130-kilometer drive to the town of Hamilton. Even if the last 50-km stretch follows the banks of New Zealand's largest river, the **Waikato**, there's no sight truly worth stopping for along the entire route. The river disappears behind a sea of houses once you reach **Hamilton.**

Ten years ago, you wouldn't have lost sight of the river at all at this point. But times have changed a great deal. The fertile soil of the Waikato region, the damp and mild climate and the hard-working dairy farmers and cattle breeders have made Hamilton a very affluent town. Modern business centers and bank buildings flank Anglesea and Victoria Streets, the city's two main thoroughfares. Most tourists just pass through the university town of Hamilton, which has about 100,000 inhabitants. Although there are pleasant walks along the banks of the Waikato River, around Lake Rotoroa, or through the gardens of the city, most visitors would agree that the best thing about

Preceding pages: A bird's eye view of Mount Ngauruhoe with Mount Ruapehu in the background. Left: In Rotorua the Maori cook their food underground.

Hamilton is its highways leading south. This is where the active heart of North Island beats, and the tourist is faced with a difficult choice: To travel on Highway 3 towards New Plymouth (231 km), with a turn-off to the impressive **Waitomo Caves** and the possibility of visiting the **Tongariro National Park**, or to stay on Highway 1 and turn onto Highway 5 just beyond Tirau, heading towards Rotorua (108 kilometers), and continuing on this route until Lake Taupo, 188 kilometers down the road. You can reach Tongariro Park on this route as well (283 kilometers). If you are short of time and cannot decide which route to take, the second one is the most interesting.

Hamilton – New Plymouth

In Hamilton West, several highways branch off in different directions. If you want to go to New Plymouth, follow the signs to Highway 3. This route travels through the fertile Waikato farmlands, towards Otorohanga (interesting Kiwi House). The bridge over the Puniu River is just beyond Te Awamutu, at which point **King Country** begins. The landscape can thank King Tawhiao for its name. This Maori monarch died in 1894. In 1860, he took over the regency of a kingdom, which various Maori tribes had

79

HAMILTON

WAIKATO

Raglan
Harbour

Raglan   Te Uku   23   New Tamahi

Waikato Mus.
Rukuhia

Ngahinapouri

Bridal
Veil Falls

959 Pirongia

Pirongia   Te Awamutu

Oparau

Forest Park   Pokuru   Toka

*Kawhia
Harbour*

Kawhia   31   Tihiroa   Wa

Albatross Point

Taharoa

31

Otorohanga

Waitomo
Caves   3   Kiwi Ho
Bird Pa

Hangatiki

T A S M A N

Marokopa

Waitomo Caves,
Museum

Te Kuiti

S E A

Tirua Point

24   Eight Mile
Junction   Waipa

Piopio   4

3   Ben

Mangapehi

52   Aria   58

Awakino
Mokau

27   Mangatupoto   Onga

Matiere

26

Tongaporutu   Waitaanga   Okahuk

North

Ahititi   40   Ofura

Pukearuhe

43   Taumarunui

Taranaki   Bight

Uruti   K

Owha

Taranaki Museum,   Waitara   Motunui
Historic Buildings   Bell Block   50

New Plymouth   Urenui

Tikorangi   Tahora
Lepperton

Oakura   3a   Kohuratahi   *Whanganui*

3   Egmont
Village   Inglewood   Retaruke

20   Kaimata   Whangamomona   Na

Pukeiti
Rhododendron   Okato Trust
45   North
Warea   Egmont   Tariki   *TARANAKI*   *Nat.*

Taranaki   Lookout   Midhirst   Huiroa   **Bridge To Nowhere**

C.   2517   43   *Park*
Egmont   Rahotu   Mt. Taranaki   Toko   Puniwhakau   Hor

National   Dawson   Stratford   Pioneer Village   *MATEMATEAONGA RA.*   746   0
Oaonui   Park   Falls   Ngaere

Kaponga   Eltham   Moeroa   Raetihi

Opunake   Auroa   Kapuni   3   Pipiriki
Museum

Pihama   Ngamatapouri   Makakaho   Jerusalem

Manaia   45   Normanby   4
Tawhiti Museum
Hawera   Mokoia

Korinti   Kakatah

ROTORUA–LAKE TAUPO–TONGARIRO

Paparangi   Atene

0   20   40   60km

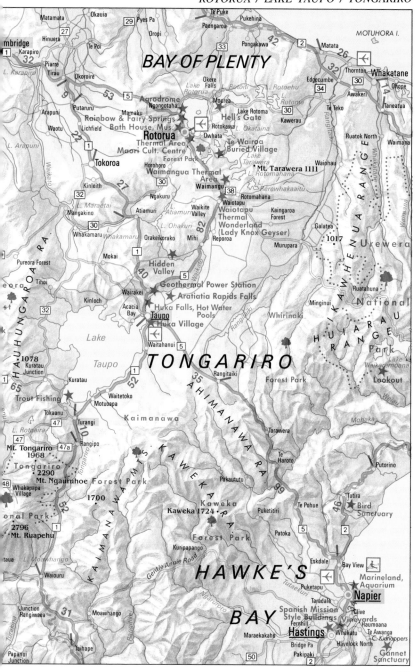

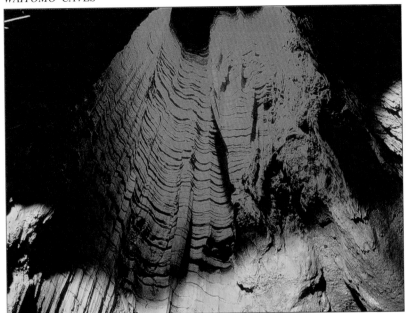

established in order to protect themselves from the growing influence of white settlers. Taking his followers with him, Tawhiao fled to the south in the aftermath of the Battle of Orakau in 1864. They established their new "kingdom" in the surroundings of the present-day Te Kuiti. The local **Maori Assembly Hall** is worth visiting. There were hardly any Pakeha in this region until 1885.

The majority of tourists take the turn-off to the right at Hangatiki, and follow the signs to the **Waitomo Caves**, approximately eight kilometers further. Without a doubt, these caves are the region's main attraction.

The **Glowworm Grotto**, which is visited by floating along on an underwater river, made the caves famous. The glowworms' lights suddenly went out in 1979. A team of experts discovered that the high level of carbondioxide, caused

Above: Color play in the Waitomo Caves.
Right: The gentle landscape with herds of sheep is typical in King Country.

by the large number of visitors breathing in the caves, was responsible for the problem. Subsequently, the Department of Conservation ordered the caves to be temporarlily closed. After the caves were reopened, only a small number of visitors were permitted to enter the caves for brief periods at a time. Now the glowworms are glowing again. It's practical to combine the excursion with a visit to the **Waitomo Museum of Caves**. Waitomo has a lot more to offer than "just" glowworms. But most visitors are in such a hurry that they seem to forget this.

Lost World and the adventure of being lowered down the rock face have become other major attractions over the past years. Those looking for excitement can be lowered 100 m down into the depths of the **Mangaopu Cave** on a rope. Once you get down into the cave, there is a five-hour organized expedition through the underworld. If this isn't adventurous enough, there is another alternative called black-water rafting in the **Ruakuri Cave**. Here you are equipped with a rubber ring

around your waist and a protective helmet with a flashlight attached to it, so that you can make your way through the waters of the cave.

No wonder some people are only too glad to get back onto Highway 3, to once again feel the solid ground under their feet and the warmth of the sun on their skin. If you take the turn-off just beyond Te Kuiti at Eight Mile Junction, heading south on Highway 4, you will already be on route to the Tongariro National Park. Still another sporting adventure awaits you at **Taumarunui**. This time it's a canoe trip on the Wanganui River.

WHANGANUI NATIONAL PARK

The **Whanganui National Park** covers one of the largest areas of relatively untouched bushland anywhere on North Island. The **Wanganui River**, which flows through the park, springs from the snows of the Tongariro National Park in the heart of the country. It winds its way 300 kilometers through hills and forests until it reaches the west coast and the Tasman Sea. This broad river, subject of many legends, first served the Maori and then the European settlers as an important waterway to the heart of North Island.

The Wanganui has become a very popular place to recover from modern life. Hundreds of day-trippers rent canoes or take organized boat rides from Taumarunui along the middle stretch of river, which meanders through pristine bushland and ancient *pa* sites. There are various stops during the trip which allow you to visit places like **Pipiriki**, a major port of call during the steamboat days. Such trips are more enjoyable during the summer months, as it can get quite damp and cold in the winter. Not only is Wanganui an El Dorado for trout fishers, an abundance of brown trout and rainbow trout can also be found in many rivers throughout the country.

There are few "well-beaten" trails in this relatively new park. But the park's two main trails through the lush podo-

carpus forests are well-worth discovering. The **Matemateonga Track**, taking you over ancient Maori trails from Whanganui as far as the province of East Taranaki, is suitable for hikes lasting two or four days. At the beginning of these clearly-marked trails with their good huts – and at your final destination – you have to provide for your own transportation. If you wish to start out from the Wanganui River, you will have to be taken there or picked up by a jet boat. Detailed information can be obtained from the Park Administration Office in Wanganui or Taumaranui.

The second hiking trip of three or four days duration takes you along the **Mangapurua-Kaiwhakaauka Track**, which connects the two tributaries of the Wanganui River. The best time for hiking is during late summer and autumn when the bushland is usually dry and the weather

Above: Mount Taranaki gazes over New Plymouth and environs. Right: A kiwi, the national animal and pride of the nation.

conditions predictable. It is another 43 km from Taumarunui to **National Park**, gateway to the Tongariro National Park.

If you remain on Highway 3 at the Eight Mile Junction, you will reach the coast at **Awakino**. From this point, the drive takes you along the Tasman Sea, towards the west. Another stop is just before **Urenui** (Sir Peter Bucks' famous monument is now in sight), and afterwards you should look straight ahead until **Mount Taranaki** suddenly appears on the horizon. The city couldn't wish for a more beautiful landmark, especially when the volcano is covered with snow during the winter months. The old name of Mount Egmont has been replaced by the Maori name of Taranaki.

NEW PLYMOUTH

New Plymouth, with its 45,000 inhabitants, is no exception to the rule that most of New Zealand's cities have surroundings which are more attractive than the acutal cities themselves. Although

New Plymouth is full of energy in the true sense – it has numerous gas and oil deposits – it has little which is of interest. Among its more intriguing buildings are **St Mary's Church** on Vivian Street, the oldest stone church in the country; **Hurworth Cottage** on Carrington Road, a wooden farm house built in 1855; **Richmond Cottage** on the corner of Ariki and Brougham Streets, which housed the first settlers in the area, as well as **The Gables** on Brooklands Park Drive, a "hospital" built in 1848. All of them give insight into the history of the first Taranaki settlers. Lovingly restored, they are open to the public.

Now it's time to put on your backpack, good strong hiking shoes, and start out for Mount Taranaki, formerly known as Mount Egmont. The National Park has still retained its old name.

EGMONT NATIONAL PARK

Mount Taranaki, standing at 2517 m, extends above the North Island's west coast like the huge reminder of an earlier volcanic era. Its cone forms the center of the circular national park.

Hikers should not underestimate the hiking trails on Mount Taranaki. It's subject to rapid changes in weather conditions, due to its proximity to the coast. You are advised to take along waterproof clothing for longer hikes.

The excellent trail leading around Mount Taranaki has become something of a tradition among keen hikers. It can be done in two phases. The complete tour takes three to four days, often passing through very rugged terrain with splendid views of the volcanic plains and the green countryside.

It's also possible to undertake a hike through the flat bushland on one of the trails from the Puakai and Kaitake Ranges on the mountain's northwest flank leading to the sea. The **Pukeiti Rhododendron Trust** is situated be-

tween these two mountain ranges. It is most beautiful when its eponymous rhododendrons are in full bloom.

The park is acessible from **North Egmont**, about 30 km from New Plymouth. For those approaching from the south, there are comfortable places for overnight stays in **Dawson Falls** on the eastern slopes of Fantham Peak. There's a convenient approach to the park a bit further on the eastern slopes, near the small town of **Stratford**. From here you can reach the little ski-slope at the end of the road leading uphill. Far away from the tourist resorts, this park is usually deserted, so it's possible to enjoy the rugged and dramatic scenery of this region at its best.

But even if you are traveling by car, Mount Taranaki can best be enjoyed during a day trip. In New Plymouth you should purchase everything you require for a good picnic, so that you are ready to start your trip around Taranaki. If you first stop at Stratford, you can take the above-mentioned turn-off to the national

urious garden. The best time to visit is in November when the flowers are in bloom. This is also when New Plymouth celebrates its *Rhododendron Festival*, at which more than 60 gardeners open their gates to the public.

Ferns as high as trees line the next 29 km of the route all the way from Pukeiti to New Plymouth, accompanying the weary traveler at the end of a most recommendable day trip.

ROTORUA

Those heading south via the town of Rotorua will also pass the Waikato Hospital. You should stay on Highway 1 at the large intersection (the right-hand turnoff heads towards New Plymouth) and drive towards Cambridge. The roads divide after 52 km, at **Tirau**: Highway 1 goes straight to Taupo and Highway 5 to Rotorua. You should be clear as to which route you are going to take. Rotorua is an absolute "must", despite the large number of tourists here.

There is only one town in New Zealand that you can recognize even with closed eyes, and that's **Rotorua**. The unmistakeable smell of sulphur gives it away. Even as you are approaching the town, vapor rises into the air from the public mud pools in Kuirau Park. Signs warn against entering the fenced-off areas. Numerous mud pools bubble all over the town.

But things aren't quite as active as they may seem when you first arrive in Rotorua. The geothermic activity has dropped drastically since the end of the 1960s. The reason for this was an increasing number of hotels offering their guests hot thermal water. It was only after the Department of Conservation imposed restrictions on the private use of thermal water that the previous level of geothermic activity returned to the geysers and mud pools. Rotorua, "the small lake," is still the biggest tourist resort.

park. Or you may want to visit the nearby **Pioneer Village**, after which you can follow the Wiremu Road to the volcano. From now on there are numerous possibilites to turn off onto one of the roads marked "no exit" to the right and drive to the foot of the mountain. Hiking tracks often lead all the way up to the summit of the mountain. However, the weather can change very suddenly here. The farmers follow the rule of thumb, that the southwest wind brings rain, while the north wind brings sunshine and warmth.

The vast, flat Taranaki farmland has a large number of ideal picnic spots. The Pukeiti Rhododendron Trust is the perfect place to stop for afternoon tea. But to get there involves decifering the way through a labyrinth of roads, and everyone is certain to lose his way at least once before finally arriving at the coveted destination. Tea is served in the Trust's lux-

Above: An artist at work in the Maori Arts and Crafts Institute. Right: Champagne Pool at Waiotapa is a favorite photographic motif.

Maori and Mud Pools

If you plan to follow the trails of the Maori when you visit Rotorua, you will notice that, like everybody else, the Maori have also commerzialised almost everything they have to offer. Unfortunately, many of their traditions have been lost in the process. Those seeking unspoiled Maori tradition should continue on to the east coast, for example.

If you decide to stay overnight in Rotorua, it's best to head for **Fenton Street**. Make absolutely sure your motel or hotel room has a private spa pool – this is a must in Rotorua. Not only do you find numerous hotels and motels on the southern edge of the town – it is also the center of the tourist attractions.

Your first destination should be the **Whakarewarewa Thermal Reserve**. The main entrance is at the **New Zealand Maori Arts and Crafts Institute**. There is an interesting exhibition of Maori arts and crafts on display in the adjoining museum. You can also watch apprentice Maori craftsmen at work. This is also where you start your (highly-recommended) guided tour of the thermal region. The other entrance of the reserve is at Fenton and Froude Streets. It's much quieter there, and you first pass through the Maori village of **Whaka**. Allow yourself ample time, and take care to adhere to the rules and regulations displayed on signs throughout the village. Remember, 50 Whaka Maori actually live here. They are not a tourist attraction. Visitors are requested not to enter the public baths, for example, even if they are not used during the day by the Maori villagers. Avoid the hot pools as well, they are used by Maori women to cook their Christmas turkey. The nutritional advantage here is that the thermal water draws the salt out of the food, making it healthier.

The **Assembly Hall**, known as *marae* in the Maori language, is worth visiting. You shouldn't miss the Maori burial ground either, since it is the only one of its kind anywhere in New Zealand. The

the *Te Amokura* dance group at the **Ro-towhio pa**. It takes place at around 12:15 p.m. every day.

This performance is considered one of the most interesting of its kind anywhere in New Zealand. After the concert, you can visit the small museum on the right side. There is a hand-made Maori cloak (*korowai*) on exhibit at the museum made of some 20,000 feathers and only for display purposes. The characteristic grass skirts, however, are made daily and in keeping with tradition, cut with shells. The **Whaka International School of Weaving** gives two-week intensive courses for anyone interested in mastering the art of Maori weaving.

There are more examples of Maori traditions in the **Ohinemutu** settlement on the banks of Lake Rotorua to the north of the city center. A visit to the settlement gives insight into Maori village life. **St Faith's Anglican Church**, built in 1910, marks the heart of the village and is surrounded by a lovely old cemetery. Photography is forbidden inside.

Sheep, Trout and a Hot Bath

If you want to continue on the path of Maori tradition in the evening, you should enjoy one of the many Maori concerts in conjunction with a traditional *hangi*. But take care not to get lost in the density of the cultures. Very often, tradition turns into a popular tourist show at these concerts. The THC Hotel is probably the best-known place for them. In 1990, the management was able to boast that the number of visitors had now reached one million. The food served at the *hangi*, an integral part of any concert, is prepared in underground ovens with steam from the hotsprings.

Rotorua not only has Maori culture. The so-called farmshows are also characteristic of the town. The best of these takes place in the **Agrodome of Ngongo-taha**, 10 kilometers to the north of Roto-

dead must be buried at least two meters underground, according to New Zealand law. This is not the case in Whaka, however. The hot soil makes it impossible, so the dead are laid to rest above ground.

Whichever way you decide to approach the thermal region, the **Pohutu Geyser** is always the main attraction. It's the largest of New Zealand's geysers, shooting its waters 20 m up into the air from 10 to 25 times a day. The number of water eruptions is dependent on wind conditions. A northerly or easterly wind cools the geyser's hot waters, forcing disappointed photographers to wait a while longer for the next water jet.

The paths leading to the other geysers and mud pools are cleary marked. You should allow approximately two hours for your visit to Whakarewarewa. The highlight of a visit is the concert given by

Above: The Pohutu Geyser in Whaka-rewarewa, evidence of volcanic activity. Right: A game of lawn bowling across from Bath House.

rua. The highlight of the show is when one sheep from each of the 19 different New Zealand breeds takes its place on the stage. A good variety of entertainment is provided at the show, with many interesting examples of New Zealand farm life.

You can stop at the **Rainbow and Ferry Springs** on the way back. Opposite is the "Farm Show," where sheep dogs demonstrate the art of sheep mustering. Also on display: sheering of a sheep, feeding of a lamb using a milk bottle and milking of a cow.

After a busy day of sightseeing in Rotorua, most visitors feel a little weary. It's therefore advisable to spend the evening relaxing in the vicinity of the **Bath House**, also known as **Tudor Towers**. It is the second largest tourist center in Rotorua, after Whaka. Here you can stroll through the beautiful rose gardens in the **Government Gardens**, or watch the golfers playing on the adjoining golf course amid the clouds of steam and mud pools. You may want to visit the **Rotorua Museum** in Bath House. It is open daily until

4 p.m. Bowlers, dressed in the cream color of the British sport's tradition, play in front of the museum's Tudor façade. The **Orchid House** is situated opposite the museum, and from here it's only a stone's throw to the **Polynesian Pools**, where you can take a break in one of the 26 thermal baths to the sounds of Maori music provided by the local Maori radio station.

In this relaxed atmosphere you can think about your plans for the next days – there is much to do in Rotorua. Whaka is only one of four large thermal regions. **Waiotapu**, 30 km farther south towards Taupo, is also well worth the visit. The best time to be there is at 10:15 a.m. when the **Lady Knox Geyser** is made to erupt using soap. Or you may prefer to visit the **Waimangu Thermal Valley**, 20 km farther south and also on the road to Taupo (turn left). It is convenient to combine a visit to Waimangu Thermal Valley with a boat trip across Lake Rotomahana and Lake Tarawera to the sunken village of **Te Wairoa**. Rotorua's Pompeii came

about after Mount Tarawera erupted on June 10, 1886. 153 inhabitants were killed during the eruption. Some of the houses have been excavated and can be toured today.

If you want to visit **Mount Tarawera** yourself, you can reach it via Rotomahana and Brett Road. Private cars are not permitted on the last section of the road leading to the summit. Visitors who wish to go the whole nine yards are requested to book space with an organized tour in a four-wheel-drive jeep for the latter part of the journey.

Organized tours can be booked from Rotorua, including a visit to Waimangu and Te Wairoa – a worthwhile day-trip.

There is an additional active thermal region known as **Hell's Gate**, to the northeast of Rotorua. It is situated along Highway 30, 16 km beyond Whakatane.

Above: Nature and technology live in peaceful and productive cooperation at the Wairakei Geothermal Power Stations.

Rotorua – Taupo

Rotorua bids an electrifying farewell to its visitors. Highway 5 heading towards Taupo (82 kilometers) not only leads to the above-mentioned thermal regions in Waimangu and Waiotapu, it also passes the **Wairakei Geothermal Power Stations**. This is where the underground steam, also visible above ground, is used to generate electricity. The result is a capacity of 200,000 kilowatt hours. Outdone only by Larderello in Italy, Wairakei is the second-largest power plant of this kind in the world. The power station is open to the public from 9 a.m. to 12 noon, and from 1 to 4.30 p.m. daily.

The nearby **Aratiatia Rapids Waterfalls** suffer greatly because of the power station. Their name is only appropriate at 10, noon and 2 p.m.a.m. and 2:30 to 4 p.m. each day, when it's time for the so-called water march. This is the only time when the fall's water supply is not laid dry.

If you want to visit a true waterfall, the

Huka Falls to the south offer a good opportunity to do so. The best approach is from the turn-off to the left beyond Wairakei, where you continue along the course of the river on Huka Road. *Huka* means foam, and the waterfalls certainly live up their name.

LAKE TAUPO

Highway 5 joins Highway 1 a short time later, which leads to **Taupo**. Before you arrive in Taupo, you may want to stop for a short visit to the **Huka Village**, a cross between a pioneer village and a museum. This typical small New Zealand town doesn't have anything special to offer except for its charming location. The view from the promenade embraces the 40-km-long and 30-km-wide **Lake Taupo**, with the snow-covered peaks of the Tongariro National Park mountain range towering behind its southern section. Beautiful Lake Taupo is the "active" center of North Island. The lake fills a huge volcanic crater which last shook the entire region about 1800 years ago. If you want to discover the lake, you can book one of the many boat tours.

De Bretts Aviation conducts flying tours to the volcanoes of Tangariro National Park in biplanes. They leave from Taupo airport. The best time to see the mountains is in the morning.

Before passing the sign indicating that you are leaving the town of Taupo, Highway 5 branches off to the left, heading towards Napier at **Hawke Bay** (144 km). You are about to cross the impressive **Ahimanawa Mountain Range** with its beautiful valleys and rocky slopes. This part of the country is very sparsely inhabited.

Trout and Fanatics

The majority of tourists remain on Highway 1 and drive the 51 km to **Turangi**. There are numerous scenic picnic spots situated all along this route which follows the shore of the lake. **Turangi**, with its 6000 inhabitants, is considered one of the world's best fishing grounds. There is an abundance of trout in the nearby rivers as well as in Lake Taupo. No wonder the inhabitants of Taupo call themselves fish fanatics. What else could they be with such excellent fishing opportunities?

It's very easy to acquire a fishing license. It only costs about NZ$ 10 a day. The license is valid for approximately 40 lakes, rivers and reservoirs. In order to avoid "over-fishing," the government has imposed a bag limit. This means that anglers are not permitted to catch more than three trout a day. In addition, fishing is only permitted at certain times of the year in the four different fishing regions. Detailed information may be obtained from the National Turangi Trout Centre or at the Department of Conservation.

Even if you have little interest in trout fishing, Turangi is the ideal starting point for a trip to Tongariro National Park.

Whether you are planning a trip lasting one or several days, it's best to take Highway 47 from Turangi (Te Ponanga Saddle Road with splendid views of Lake Rotoaira) to the National Park before turning left towards Chateau Tongariro.

Not only do most of the hiking trails start out from **Whakapapa Village**, this also is where the excellent Information Centre run by the Department of Conservation is located. There are also a large number of opportunities for overnight stays, from very basic camping sites to luxury chalets.

TONGARIRO NATIONAL PARK

The most appropriate heading to describe the 75,000 hectare park, located at the very heart of the North Island, is "volcanoes." Indeed, quite a number of important ones are found here. Not only is **Tongariro** New Zealand's oldest and

most popular National Park, having attained world heritage status in the meantime, but it also provides fine examples of characteristic volcanic landscapes.

The snow-covered **Mount Ruapehu**, 2796 m high and boasting a warm crater lake, is the highest and largest mountain on the entire North Island. This giant old volcano offers excellent skiing conditions during the winter in the north (Whakapapa) and in the southeast (Turoa).

Well-marked tracks and cosy mountain huts make Mount Ruapehu and the neighboring slopes very popular with hikers during the summer months. In addition to shorter walks lasting a few hours, you can also go on hikes for up to three or four days. These can take you all the way around the volcano, for example. When hiking in mountainous regions, through bush forests or open grassy

Above: Country houses on the slopes of the Tongariro National Park. Right: "Louie the Fish" with his catch and daughter on Lake Taupo.

plains, it is essential to bear in mind that weather conditions can change rapidly – a great hazard in such surroundings.

The Department of Conservation organizes an extensive summer program (from December to January), including guided hikes and lectures. If you are here during the summer, you shouldn't miss taking part in them.

Mount Ngauruhoe, 2290 m, and still active after all these years, lies to the north of Mount Ruapehu. It last erupted in 1974. Athletic hikers risk the climb up to Mount Ngauruhoe's summit in summer. However, the ascent has to be carefully planned. Those attempting it in winter should be well-equipped with the essential equipment and knowledge.

A fascinating range of craters and colorful volcanic lakes stretches from Mount Ngauruhoe to Tongariro (1968 m). The track leading through this unique volcanic landscape to the hotsprings situated at the **Ketetahi Lodge** with splendid views across Lake Taupo and the countryside to the north is impressive.

As the Tongariro National Park is fairly close to densely-populated areas, there are generally a large number of visitors in the park at any given time. It is therefore advisable to take a tent with you if you are planning to stay a few days.

If you are traveling by car and pressed for time, you should go on the **Whaka-poapanui Walk**. It takes approximately two hours and follows the river bearing the same name. The walk takes you to the magnificent **Taranaki Falls** in about two and a half hours. Both walks start from the information center. Then it's time for a well-deserved lunch – perhaps the trout you caught at Turangi.

After lunch, drive through the National Park Village before continuing the journey on Highway 4, this time heading towards Ohahune. Like most places in the vicinity of Tongariro, **Ohakune** is fairly quiet during the summer months. However, this is not so in winter, when many towns in this region are teeming with skiers heading for Mount Ruapehu. In the evening, there is international après-ski

in the bars and clubs. If you come here during the summer, it's very hard to imagine just how busy it can get in the winter months.

After a short stop, it's therefore best to continue on to **Waiouru** on Highway 1. You should allow yourself plenty of time for frequent stops to take in the magnificent panoramas of the volcanic mountain world on the left side.

Should you want to return to Turangi, take the Desert Road heading north. The best time is at sunset. In the crimson twilight, the entire countryside is transformed into one of the most beautiful regions on the entire North Island. The high tussock grass dances gently in the wind, and the snow-covered peaks of **Mount Ngauruhoe** and Mount Tongariro glisten in the background. If you are very lucky, you may see a spiral of white smoke hanging over the volcano.

Those traveling south should keep of this scenic countryside in mind during the next 115 km. From here to **Bulls**, the landscape is rather monotonous.

HAMILTON AND ENVIRONS
Accommodation
HAMILTON: *LUXURY:* **Eastwood Manor,** 209 Grey St., Tel: 07-8569029. *MODERATE:* **Abbotsford Court Motel**, 18 Abbotsford St., Tel: 07-8390661. **Commercial Hotel**, 287 Victoria Street, Tel: 07-8391226. **Tamahere Motel**, Tamahere, State Highway 1, Tel: 07-8567722. *BUDGET:* **The Silver Birches**, 182 Tramway Rd., Tel: 07-8556260. **New Empire Private Hotel**, corner Empire and High St., Tel: 07-8475467.
CAMBRIDGE: *MODERATE:* **Cambrian Lodge**, 63 Hamilton Rd., Tel: 07-8277766.
WAITOMO CAVES: *LUXURY:* **THC Waitomo**, Tel: 07-8788227. *BUDGET:* **Juno Budget Accomodation**, Tel: 07-8787649.
Restaurants
HAMILTON: **Gainsborough House Restaurant**, 61 Ulster St., Tel: 07-8394172 (New Zealand cuisine; expensive). **Julian's Restaurant**, 259 Grey St., Tel: 07-8566434 (expensive).
Museums
HAMILTON: **Waikato Museum of Art and History**; Maori art (Tainui) and New Zealand history (1 Grantham St.; daily 10 a.m.–4:30 p.m.). **WAITOMO: Museum of Caves**, Tel: 07-8787640 (open daily).
Tips and Trips
OTOROHANGA: **Kiwi House** and **Native Bird Park**, open daily (Alex Telfer Drive, Tel: 07-8737391). **WAITOMO CAVES**: Tours daily 9 a.m.–4 p.m. (additional tours in summer 4:30 and 5:30 p.m.). Tours of the nearby **Aranui Cave** (stalactite cavern) 10, 11 a.m., 1, 2 and 3 p.m. Info on Lost World and Abseiling in the Cave Museum: Tel: 07-8787640.
Special Events
Every year in March the giant *Maori Regatta* takes place in Ngaruawahia near Hamilton.
Tourist Information
CAMBRIDGE: **Waipa District Public Relations**, Cambridge Library, Victoria St., Tel: 07-8276429. **HAMILTON: Visitor Centre**, Municipal Building, Anglesea St., Tel: 07-8393580. **AA**, Victoria/Brice Street, Tel: 07-8391397. **DOC**, Level 1, BDO House, 18 London St., Tel: 07-8383363. **HUNTLY: Waikato District Council**, Huntly Service Centre, Main St., Tel: 07-8287551. **NGARUAWAHIA: Waikato District Council**, 114 Great South Rd., Tel: 07-8248633. **OTOROHANGA: Visitor Information Centre,** 80 Maniopoto St., Tel: 07-8738951. **RAGLAN: Waikato District Council**, Bow St., Tel: 07-8258129. **WAITOMO: Museum of Caves Information Centre**, Main St., Tel: 07-8787640.

NEW PLYMOUTH AND ENVIRONS
Accommodation
NEW PLYMOUTH: *LUXURY:* **Northgate Motor Lodge,** 18 Northgate Rd., Tel: 06-7585324. **Taranaki Country Lodge**, Cnr Devon/Henwood Rd., Bell Block, Tel: 06-7580379. *MODERATE:* **Heritage Lodge**, 115 Coronation Ave, Tel: 06-758216. **Surfers Motel**, 25 Beach St., Tel: 06-7588530. **Tiffanys Motel**, 301 Devon St. West, Tel: 06-7589151. *BUDGET:* **Hostel 69**, 69 Mill Rd., Tel: 06-7587153. **Princes Tourist Court Family Holiday Park**, 29 Princes St., Fitzroy, Tel: 06-7582566. **Youth Hostel**, 12 Clawton St., Tel: 06-7585720. *B & B:* **Carrington Guesthouse**, 32 Carrington St., New Plymouth, Tel: 06-7582375.
DAWSON FALLS: *LUXURY:* **Dawson Falls Tourist Lodge/Konini Lodge**, Manaia Rd., South Mt. Egmont Nat. Park, Kaponga, Tel: 06-7655457.
Museums
NEW PLYMOUTH: **Taranaki Museum**, Ariki St., (collection of Maori art and New Zealand history; Tue–Fri 10:30 a.m.–5 p.m., Sun and public holidays 1–5 p.m.)
Tourist Information
NEW PLYMOUTH: **Information Centre**, Corner Liardet and Leach Sts., Tel: 06-7586086 (Mon–Fri 8:30 a.m.–5 p.m.). **DOC**, Atkinson Bldg., Devon St. West, Tel: 06-7580433. **AA**, 49-55 Powderham St., Tel: 06-7575646. **NORTH EGMONT: DOC, Visitors Centre**, Egmont Rd., Egmont Village, Tel: 06-7568710 (daily 9 a.m.-5 p.m.). **STRATFORD: District Information Centre,** Broadway, Tel: 06-7656708. **DOC**, RD 21, Pembroke Rd., Tel: 06-7655144.

ROTORUA AND ITS ENVIRONS
Accommodation
ROTORUA: *LUXURY:* **Hyatt Kingsgate**, Eruera St., Tel: 07-3471234. **Okawa Bay Lake Resort**, Tel: 07-3624599 (17 km from Rotorua at Lake Rotoiti). **Sheraton**, corner Fenton/Sala St., Tel: 07-3487139. **Solitaire Lodge**, Lake Tarawera, Tel: 07-3628208. **Princes Gate**, 1 Arawa St., Tel: 07-3481179. **Puhi Nui Motor Lodge**, 16 Sala St., Tel: 07-3484182. **THC Rotorua**, corner Tryon/Fronde St., Tel: 07-3481189. *MODERATE:* **Arawa Motor Lodge**, corner Arawa/Ranolf St., Tel: 07-3479469. **Eaton Hall Guesthouse**, 39 Hinemaru St., Tel: 07-3470366. **Grand Establishment**, Hinemoa St., Tel: 07-3482089. **Kerrys Motel**, 43 Malfroy Rd., Tel: 07-3484807. Kuirau Motor Lodge, corner Hinemara/Ranolf St., Tel: 07-3486189. *BUDGET:* **Holden's Bay Holiday Park,** 21 Robinson Ave, P.O. Box 9, Tel: 07-3459925. **Ivanhoe Lodge**, 54 Haupapa St., Tel: 07-

3486985. **Kiwipaka**, 60 Tarewa Rd., Tel: 07-3470931. **Lakeside Motor Camp**, 54 Whittaker Rd., Tel: 07-3481693. **Rotorua Thermal Holiday Park,** Old Taupo Rd., Tel: 07-3463140.

Restaurants

A traditional feature of Rotorua's culinary landscape is the *hangi*, an earth-pit in which the food is cooked slowly using thermal energy. Almost every large hotel offers *hangi*, usually accompanied by a Maori culture-show (ca. 45–55 NZ$).

Aorangi Peak Restaurant, Mountain Rd., Mt. Ngongotaha, Tel: 07-3470046 (lovely view, expensive). **Lakeside Bar and Grill**, Memorial Drive, lakeshore, Tel: 07-3483700 (closed Mondays).

Museums

ROTORUA: The Bath House Art and History Museum (Government Gardens; open to the public Mon–Fri 10 a.m.–4:30 p.m., Sat and Sun 1–4:30 p.m., on public holidays 10 a.m.–4:30 p.m.

Tips and Trips

Rotorua: Vulcano flights with White Island Airlines, P. O. Box 7118, Tengae, Tel: 07-3459832.

Hangi: The *Hangi*-Show at the Tumunui Farm is not so well known and hence less touristy than similar spectacles elsewhere. Information and reservation: Tamaki Tours, Tel: 07-3462623.

Mount Tarawera: Tarawera Mountain Sightseeing Tours (Tel: 073-85179) arrange trips to the volcanic area with 4-wheel-drive vehicles.

Ngongotaha: New Zealand's farm life is on show three times a day (9:15 a.m., 11:00 a.m., 2:30 p.m.) at the Agrodome, Riverside Park, Tel. 07-357-4350.

Rainbow Springs and Farm: Trout and wildlife at close quarters (Main Auckland Highway, Fairy Springs Road, 5 km from Rotorua. Tel: 07-3479301).

Rotorua: Polynesian Pools are the best public thermal baths (Hinemoa St.; daily 9 a.m.–10 p.m.). The Orchids Gardens with Microworld (Hinemaru St.; daily 8:30 a.m.–5:30 p.m.) are situated close by. **Whakarewarewa Thermal Reserve**: Entrance fee 12 NZ$ (including guided tour, but exclusive of concert; daily 8:30 a.m.–5:30 p.m.).

Tourist Information

ROTORUA: Tourism Rotorua, 67 Fenton St., Tel: 07-3485179 (daily 8:30 a.m.–5 p.m.). **DOC** (Bay of Plenty), 48-50 Amohau St., Tel: 07-3479179. **DOC** (Rotorua), 14 Scott St., Tel: 07-3461155. **AA**, Amohau St., Tel: 07-3483069.

LAKE TAUPO AND ENVIRONS
Accommodation

TAUPO: *MODERATE:* **Chelmswood Manor**, corner Lake Terrace and Tremain Avenue, Tel: 07-3782715. **Mountain View Motel**, 12-14 Fletcher St., Tel: 07-3789366. *BUDGET:* **Acacia Holiday Park**, 868 Acacia Bay Road, Tel: 07-3785159. **De Bretts Thermal Leisure Park**, Taupo/Napier Highway, P.O. Box 513, Tel: 07-3788559. **Lake Taupo Holiday Park**, corner Upper Spa Road and Centennial Drive, Tel: 07-3786860. **Rainbow Lodge**, 99 Titiraupenga St., Tel: 07-3785754.

TURANGI: *LUXURY:* **Tongariro Lodge**, Tel: 07-3869746 (for anglers). *MODERATE:* **Settlers Motel**, State Highway 1, Tel: 07-3867745.

BUDGET: **Tongariro Holiday Park**, Ohnanga Rd., P.O. Box 174, Tel: 07-3867492.

Restaurants

TAUPO: Café Renoir, Walnut Village, 77 Spa Rd., Tel: 07-3780777 (art and cuisine in a cosy atmosphere). **Graham Room**, State Highway 1, Wairakei, Tel: 07-3748021.

Tips and Trips

TAUPO: Discover Lake Taupo and the Maori carvings near the lakeshore with the romantic old steamboat *Ernest Kemp* (Info: Kurrahe Cruises, Tel: 07-3783444). The two-master *The Barbary* is also quite an experience. It begins its cruise in Taupo.

TURANGI: Louie the Fish offers the best fishing trips on Lake Taupo. Information and reservation: Lite-Tackle Tours, P.O. Box 192, Tel: 07-3867953.

Tourist Information

TAUPO: Information Taupo, 13 Tongariro St., Tel: 07-3789000 (daily 8:30 a.m.–5 p.m.). **DOC,** Centennial Drive, Tel: 07-3783885.

TURANGI: **Information Centre**, Ngawaka Place, Tel: 07-3868999. **DOC**, The National Trout Centre, Tel: 07-3868607.

TONGARIRO NATIONAL PARK AND ITS ENVIRONS
Accommodation

LUXURY: **THC Chateau**, Mt. Ruapehu, Tel: 07-8923809.

MODERATE: **Alpine Motel**, Ohakune, 7 Miro St., Tel: 06-3858758. **The Hobbit,** corner Goldfinch and Wye St., Ohakune, Tel: 06-3858248.

BUDGET: **Whakapapa Motor Camp,** Mt. Ruapehu, Tel: 07-8923897. **Ski Haus**, National Park, Carroll St., Tel: 07-8922854. **Howards Lodge**, Carroll St., National Park, Tel: 07-8922827. **Youth Hostel**, Ohakune, Clyde St., Tel: 06-3858724.

Restaurants

WHAKAPAPA: THC Chateau, Ruapehu Room, Tel: 07-8923809 (expensive).

Tourist Information

WHAKAPAPA / MT. RUAPEHU: DOC, Tongariro National Park Centre, Tel: 07-8923729. **OHAKUNE: Ruapehu Visitors Centre**, 54 Clyde St., Tel: 06-3858427. **DOC,** Ohakune Mountain Rd., Tel: 06-3858578.

EAST CAPE

BAY OF PLENTY

GISBORNE

UREWERA NATIONAL PARK

Where the Days Begin

The vast and sparsely-inhabited region of the East Cape Peninsula is cut off from the remaining part of the island by the rugged Raukumara mountain range. Not only is there a great abundance of Maori tradition and culture in this part of the country, but Europeans can also feel a sense of their own history: Captain James Cook first set foot on New Zealand's soil here in the year 1769. One aspect makes this region unique in the entire world: It is here that the rays of the morning sun first touch the earth. This phenomenon is brought about by this district's, and the town of Gisborne's, extreme easterly position (longitude of 178 degrees east), in conjunction with the international dateline and the earth's curvature at Gisborne's latitude (38.40 degrees south). East Cape, with its tranquil landscape of sea and hills, and the leisurely lifestyle of its inhabitants won't entice those tourists seeking the excitement and nightlife a large city has to offer. But those who prefer to relax in peace can certainly do so in this region.

Preceding pages: Landscape around the East Cape Lighthouse. Left: The Maori have a strong historical and cultural tradition on the East Cape.

You can discover East Cape by car on the paved Highway 35, which winds its way around 334 km of scenic coastal countryside, from the town of Opotiki on the north point of the peninsula to Gisborne.

Mount Hikurangi, 1753 m high, is situated on the coast to the north of Gisborne and famous literally round the world because the rising sun's rays first fall on this region. Interestingly enough, that the Ngati Porou tribe considered it sacred. The Maori word for the Gisborne district is *Tairawhiti*, meaning "the coast, where the sun shines on the water."

Gisborne is already making plans to celebrate the new century at the end of the present decade. The summit of Mount Hikurangi will be the first place in the world to be touched by the sun's rays in the 21st century. An annual *First Light Festival* has been organized in order to increase the suspense leading up to the final event. It seems more than appropriate that the sun first shines on a place that has more than 22,000 hours of sunshine each year, making it one the sunniest place anywhere in New Zealand.

The **Gisborne Region**, which embraces the largest part of the East Cape Peninsula, stretches to the north beyond Lottin Point (130 km to the south of Opotiki), to the south as far as the Wharerata

99

Range and from the coast as far as the Raukumara Range. 46,000 people live on the 8300 sq. km constituting this region. 17,000 of them are Maori. Compared with other regions in New Zealand, this is a relatively high percentage, contributing to the fascinating diversity in cultural life and history here.

One of the jewels of East Cape is the 115,103 hectare **Raukumara Range,** one of the few regions on the North Island with vast areas of remote and pristine countryside, rugged terrain and almost virgin forests.

Hikurangi, the highest non-volcanic peak on North Island, is the most prominent topographical landmark on the entire peninsula. Together with the Honokawa, Aorangi, Wharekia and Taitai mountains, it forms a spectacular mountain range. The Hikurangi plays an important role in many Maori legends and songs. Its name originates in the times before the Maori settled in New Zealand.

Remains of the now-extinct huge *moa* birds were found at the foot of the mountain. There is also a splendid view of Hikurangi mountain from the coastal road between Opotiki and Gisborne. The **Gisborne Canoe and Tramping Club** owns a lodge on private land on the mountain's northern slopes. It's recommended to leave your name at the information office before starting out.

BAY OF PLENTY

The majority of travelers begin their East Cape tour in **Tauranga** at the Bay of Plenty, about 153 km north of Opotiki. The Maori word *tauranga* means "anchor place for canoes," an appropriate name for a town whose wealth is derived from one of New Zealand's most fantastic harbors.

The route to Opotiki leads to the town of **Whakatane** and runs along the coast for most of the way. This is the region where kiwis grow in great abundance. It

is well worth visiting one of the numerous kiwi plantations in **Te Puke**, known by the locals as "the kiwi capital of the world".

On approaching the town of Whakatane, you can see the volcanic island situated about 48 km from the coast, **White Island**. Clouds of steam and sulphur rise from its crater. Sulphur was mined here at one time. There is also a large colony of birds on White Island. As many as 10,000 pairs of gannets have been known to nest here during brooding time. The island is easily accessible to the curious tourist either by helicopter, charter boat tour or by seaplane from Whakatane.

Opotiki, the starting point for this enchanting trip along the East Coast, has its own fascinating history. It derives its name from the spring known as *o-potiki-mai-tawhiti* above Waiotahi Beach, a name which goes back to the time when the Maori left their original homeland of *hawaiki*. In pre-European times there was a large Maori center here, and even today approximately half of the 8600 inhabitants have Maori origins.

One of the most brutal events in New Zealand's history took place in Opotiki. During a bloody rebellion, the Maori murdered the German missionary Carl Volkner in his Church of St Stephen. The leader of the rebellion, Kereopa, drank the missionary's blood from a chalice, and earned himself the name of *Kaiwhatu*, which means "eye-eater" because he swallowed the pious man's eyes in the church. We shudder to think why the church of St Stephen still stands in Opotiki, and that the missionary is buried here.

Opotiki lies some 350 km from Gisborne, following the coastal road all the way. The villages along the way offer a variety of accomodations – from hotels to camping grounds.

Some of the best examples of Maori carving, as well as *pa* sites and strong-

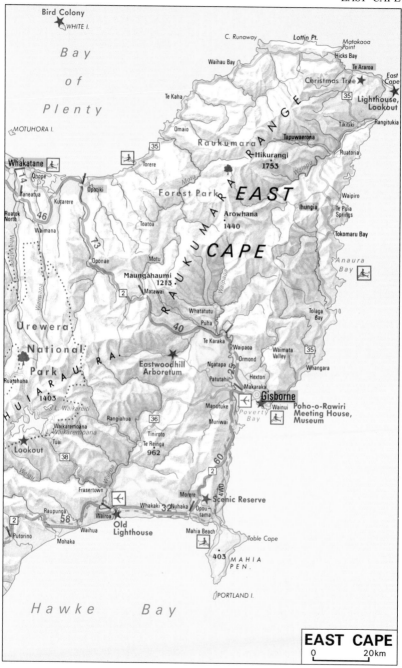

Bird Colony
WHITE I.

Bay

of

Plenty

MOTUHORA I.

Whakatane
Ohope
14
Taneatua
Kutarere
Opotiki
Ruatok North
46
Waimana
73
Oponae
Urewera
National
Park
Ruatahuna
1403
L. Waikareiti
Waikaremoana
Waikaremoana
Tuai
Lookout
38
Fraser town
Raupunga
2
58
Waihua
Putorino
Mohaka

C. Runaway
Lottin Pt.
Matakaoa Point
Hicks Bay
Waihau Bay
Te Araroa
East Cape
Christmas Tree
35
Lighthouse, Lookout
Te Kaha
Rangitukia
Omaio
Tikitiki
Raukumara
Tapuwaerona
35
Torere
Hikurangi
1753
Ruatoria
Forest Park
EAST
Waipiro
Motu
Arowhana
1440
Ihungia
Te Puia Springs
Toatoa
CAPE
Tokomaru Bay
Motu
Anaura Bay
Maungahaumi
1213
Matawai
RAUKUMARA
2
Whatatutu
Tolaga Bay
Puha
40
Te Karaka
Waipaoa
Waimata Valley
35
Eastwoodhill
Arboretum
Ngatapa
Ormond
Whangara
Patutahi
Hexton
Makaraka
HUIARAU
Gisborne
Poho-o-Rawiri
Meeting House,
Museum
Manutuke
Wainui
Poverty Bay
Rangiahua
36
Muriwai
Tiniroto
Te Reinga
962
60
2
Morere
Scenic Reserve
Whakaki
32
Nuhaka
4WD
Opou-
tama
Wairoa
Old
Lighthouse
Mahia Beach
Table Cape
403
MAHIA
PEN.

Hawke   *Bay*

PORTLAND I.

EAST CAPE
0   20km

101

holds of earlier battles, are found in the assembly halls that flank the street. The coast is lined by the native *pohutukawa* trees, the largest of which can be seen in **Te Araroa** (160 km east of Opotiki).

A small road leads from Te Araroa to the **East Cape Lighthouse**, the most easterly light in the entire world. There are 726 steps leading up to the lighthouse, but the climb is well worth it. You will be rewarded with a splendid view across the East Cape.

Approximately 16 km further along the highway, the Pakikora turn-off leads to the **Tapuwaerona Valley** and the **Rip Homestead** run by the Department of Conservation at the foot of Mount Hikurangi. Be sure to find out about road conditions before setting out on this stretch. **Ihungia Rest Area** is situated 21 km down the highway. There are magnificent views from this point.

Above: White Island in the remote coastal regions serves as a perch. Right: Decorative detail of a waka, a Maori war canoe.

GISBORNE

One of the most splendid golden beaches on this coast is located about 6 km from the highway on **Anaura Bay**, 264 km south of Opotiki. A plaque on the shore commemorates Captain Cook's second landing in New Zealand. The Coast Road ends in the harbor town of **Gisborne**, the hub of this region.

The town is of historical importance for both Europeans and Maori. The hill that dominates the town of Gisborne, **Kaiti Hill**, looms over Kaiti Beach, where Captain Cook and his crew first set foot on New Zealand soil. This hill is known as *titirangi* in Maori. It means "cradle", which is supposed to pay homage to the Maori tribes who have lived here for some 24 generations.

From the lookout point on Kaiti Hill, you can admire Gisborne's panorama, its harbor, and three rivers which flow into the sea. Some of New Zealand's largest food processing factories are situated in Gisborne Valley. In addition, Gisborne is

one of the largest wine-producing regions, and has won many international prizes. Wine merchants refer to this region in the oenological department as the "Chardonnay Center of New Zealand".

New Zealand's largest *marae* (place of assembly), **Poho-o-Rawiri,** lies within the town's boundaries, and has housed numerous royal guests in the past. There are also many churches and other *marae* of historical significance on the flat surrounding pasturelands. A "Safari" minibus service takes visitors to the sights of their choice.

The State Highway 2, to Wairoa and Napier, will bring you to the large 365 hectare **Morere Scenic Reserve**, located some 61 km to the south of Gisborne. It offers some beautiful and healthy nature. Amid jungle and flocks of protected native birds, thermal pools entice visitors to relax in their warm waters.

When you leave the reserve, a turn-off to the left leads to the golden beaches and clear waters of the **Mahia Peninsula**, an ideal spot for fishing, diving and swimm-

ing. *Mahia* means "hazy sounds" – so enjoy the symphony of waves, birds and rustling trees there.

The town of **Wairoa** (with 5200 inhabitants and situated on the banks of the Wairoa River), is approximately 98 km from Gisborne. Its pride is the lighthouse, made of solid kauri wood and built in 1877 on Portland Island. When plans were made to have the lighthouse torn down, inhabitants from Wairoa moved it to their town and placed it on the main road. Wairoa is also the eastern gate to the Urewera National Park where travelers from far and wide go to enjoy the popular Lake Waikaremoana.

UREWERA NATIONAL PARK

The **Urewera National Park** is a paradise for those wishing to experience a real jungle adventure on the North Island. It's easy to imagine what this region must have looked like before the Europeans came. The park, a five-hour drive from Auckland, stretches over a very large

area. It is still fairly isolated even today, and embraces the largest regions of jungle on the North Island. The gravel roads take the visitor back into New Zealand's past. The local inhabitants, the Tuhoe, who fought against any form of European intrusion and domination for a long time, still mostly speak Maori. Looking out across the vast expanse of this region from one of the numerous elevated areas, it's easy to understand why it has remained so isolated.

After Lake Taupo, (see the preceding chapter) **Lake Waikaremoana**, whose depth reaches 300 m, is New Zealand's second largest lake. There is a very popular four-day hike leading around the lake. Numerous lodges have been built on the shores of Lake Waikaremoana. You can either swim, sunbathe or catch trout to your heart's content – as long as it doesn't rain for days on end, which, of course, can happen! If the circular walk

Above: The Maori present is given vivid, modern portrayal on a mural.

proves too long for you, you can always arrange to be picked up by boat from one of the lodges.

The highlight of this tour is most certainly **Panekiri Bluff**, which rises to an elevation of 1289 m. There are magnificent views across the Urewera Forest from here. From the summit of Panekiri Bluff, it beomes obvious that the lake was created by a gigantic landslide about 2000 years ago.

Longer walking tours lead to the **Whakatane River Valley** and further on to the East Coast. There are a few short paths over flat terrain to the charming waterfalls, and even here you are surrounded by almost virgin jungle. A short trip takes you to **Lake Waikareiti** with its crystal clear waters.

Those who prefer not to undertake a three-to-four day tour on their own can book a guided tour which includes meals.

Heading south on Highway 2 from Wairoa, it's another 118 km before you finally reach the town of Napier on Hawke Bay.

EAST CAPE
Accommodation

GISBORNE: *LUXURY:* **Sandown Park Motel**, Childers Rd., Tel: 06-8679299.

MODERATE: **Orange Grove Hotel Motel**, 549 Childers Rd., Tel: 06-8679978. **Whispering Sands Beachfront Motel**, 22 Salisbury Rd., Tel: 06-8671319. *BUDGET:* **Youth Hostel**, 32 Harris St., Tel: 079-8673269. **Waikanae Beach Holiday Park**, Grey St., Tel: 06-8675634.

HICKS BAY: *MODERATE:* **Hicks Bay Motor Lodge**, East Coast Highway, Tel: 06-8644800.

BUDGET: **Backpackers Lodge**, Onepoto, Beach Rd., Tel: 06-8644731.

OHOPE BEACH: *MODERATE:* **West End Motels and Tourist Flats,** 24 West End Rd., Tel: 07-3124665.

BUDGET: **Ohope Beach Backpackers Inn**, 1A Westend, Tel: 07-3125173.

OPOTIKI: *LUXURY:* **Magnolia Court Motel**, corner Bridge and Nelson St., Tel: 07-3155444.

MODERATE: **Ranui Motel,** 36 Bridge St., Tel: 07-3156669. *BUDGET:* **Island View Family Holiday** (Camping), Appleton Rd., Waiotahi Beach, Tel: 07-3157519.

TAURANGA: *LUXURY:* **Boulevard Motel**, 261 Waihi Rd., Tel: 07-5783268. **Willow Park Motor Hotel**, 9 Willow St., Tel: 07-5789119. *MODERATE:* **Fountain Court Motel**, 91 Turret Rd., Tel: 07-5789401. **Greenpark Racecourse Motel**, 1460 Cameron Rd., Tel: 07-5410131.

BUDGET: **Bell Travellers Lodge**, 39 Bell St., Tel: 07-5786344. **Backpacker Budget Tourist Lodge**, 44-46 Botanical Rd., Tel: 07-5782382.

TE ARAROA: *MODERATE:* **Kawa Kawa Hotel**, Tel: 06-8644809.

TE PUIA: *MODERATE:* **Te Puia Springs Hotel**, Main Rd., Tel: 06-8646861.

TOLAGA BAY: *MODERATE:* **Tolaga Inn**, Tel: 06-8626856.

WHAKATANE: *MODERATE:* **Cortez Motor Inn**, 55 Landing Rd., Tel: 07-3084047.

BUDGET: **Awakeri Hot Springs** (Camping), Rotorua/Whakatane Highway, Tel: 07-3049117.

Restaurants

GISBORNE: Chalet Rendezvous, Moana Rd., Wainui Beach, Tel: 06-8679777 (speciality: salmon). **L'Escalier Restaurant**, 339 Childers Rd., Tel: 06-8689990.

Museums

GISBORNE: Museum and Arts Centre, Stout St. History of Maori and European art; part of the museum are the historic Wyllie Cottage and The Star of Canada Maritime Museum. A whaling boat from the Te Kaha region and a painting of Captain Cook's arrival at Kaiti Beach (1769) are on display.

Tips and Trips

Bethlehem: Around the Christmas season this small township west of Tauranga is *the* favorite place for stamp collectors from all over the world.

Eastwoodhill Arboretum: This park, founded in 1951 by William Douglas Cook, contains one of the largest "tree collections" in New Zealand on 160 acres of land – 340 different trees represent more than 3000 species of trees (35 km west of Gisborne at the road to Ngatapa and Rere; Tel: 079-39800).

Whitewater Rafting: During the last years Opotika has developed into a center for *Whitewater Rafting*, with rafting tours on the Waioeka River as special highlights. In the section from Wairata to Oponae a number of rapids add to the excitement (Devil's Canyon).

Please note: Travelers have encountered difficulties with Maori living along the East Coast. Large coastal areas are the traditional lands of Maori tribes. Quite a few beach campers and caravaners have been surprised in the morning by Maori demanding a fee – without prior announcement. Some beach- and coastal areas are fenced off to keep visitors out.

The general Maori attitude towards tourists is rather on the cool side, and violent fights between police and Maori are frequent in the north of the region, where some Maori Rastafarians live in a commune. However, these incidents are not the order of the day, and a trip along the east coast should not be missed.

Tourist Information

GISBORNE: Eastland and Gisborne District Information Centre, 209 Grey St., Tel: 06-8686139 (open weekdays 8:30 a.m.–5 p.m.). **DOC**, 63 Carnarvon St., Tel: 06-8678531. **AA**, corner Palmerston and Disraeli St., Tel: 06-8686139.

MOUNT MAUNGANUI: Tourist Information Office, Salisbury Avenue, Tel: 07-5755099 (open Mondays–Fridays 9 a.m.–4 p.m., Saturdays 10 a.m.–12:30 p.m.).

MORERE: DOC, Morere Springs Scenic Reserve, State Highway 2, Nuhaka, Tel: 06-8378856.

RUATORIA: Information Centre, Main Rd., Tel: 079-48505 (Mon–Fri 9 a.m.–4 p.m.).

TAURANGA: Visitor Information, The Strand, Tel: 06-5788103.

TE PUKE: Information Office, Palmer Court, 72 Jellicoe St., Tel: 07-5739172.

WAIKAREMOANA: DOC, Motor Camp, State Highway 38, Aniwaniwa, Tel: 07-8373826.

WAIROA: Information Bureau, Marine Parade West, Tel: 06-8388500 (open Mondays–Fridays 9 a.m.–5 p.m.).

WHAKATANE: District Information Bureau, Boon St., Tel: 07-3086058 (open Mondays–Fridays 9 a.m.–5 p.m.).

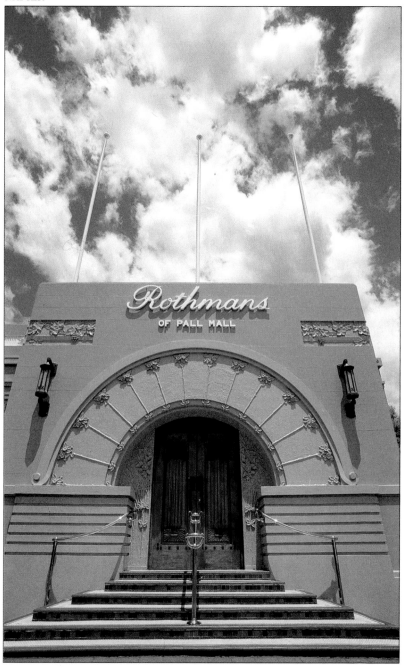

IN THE SOUTH

NAPIER

HASTINGS

WANGANUI

There is a saying that "all roads lead to Rome." In the southern part of North Island all roads lead to Wellington, the capital of New Zealand. Two specific routes, however, can be recommended to the visitor: Either you approach Wellington coming from Napier, and then head towards Hawke Bay traveling through Palmerston North or Masterton (Highway 2); or you are in the Taranaki region (New Plymouth) and travel past Wanganui (Highway 3) along the coast. The routes merge in Levin where you proceed on Highway 1 to Wellington.

NAPIER

On February 3, 1931 at 10:47 a.m., the history of **Napier** seemed to vanish from the earth. An earthquake measuring 7.8 on the Richter scale flattened the city along with the neighboring town of Hastings. 258 people died in this devastating earthquake. However, Napier has long since risen from the ruins to become a flourishing city in the 1990's. For the magazine *North & South*, the entire area around Hawke Bay has progressed into the country's center of optimism. This

Preceding pages: A New Zealand floral specialty, the pohutukawa tree, blooms around Christmas. Left: Art-Deco style in Napier.

recognition is due particularly to the typical weather of this region, where the sun shines more reliably than anywhere else on the island. As a result, fruit and vegetables grow abundantly; more than 20,000 tons of grapes ripen on the vine annually, later to be transformed by 17 well-known wine cellars into the best wines in New Zealand. This abundant natural wealth is the foundation of prosperity in Napier and Hawke Bay.

Visitors can make unique discoveries here. You will look in vain for traces of New Zealands's pioneer days between Marine Parade and Oak Street, but you will find glorious examples of Spanish mission and Art-Deco style of architecture which dominated the reconstruction of the city in the mid-1930's after the earthquake.

The **Criterion Hotel**, the **A & B Building**, **Rothman's Building** (a blue masterpiece at Inner Harbor), as well as numerous buildings between Crave Street and Marine Parade are prime examples lending Napier the title of one of the best-preserved cities of Art-Deco style in the world. The harbor promenade, although less dominated by artistic forms of construction, is certainly worth taking a stroll along. You will see that the ocean plays an important role, even on land. At **Hawke Bay Aquarium** you can

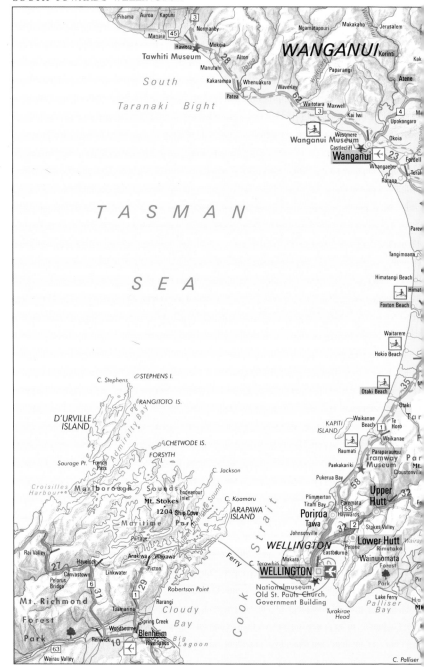

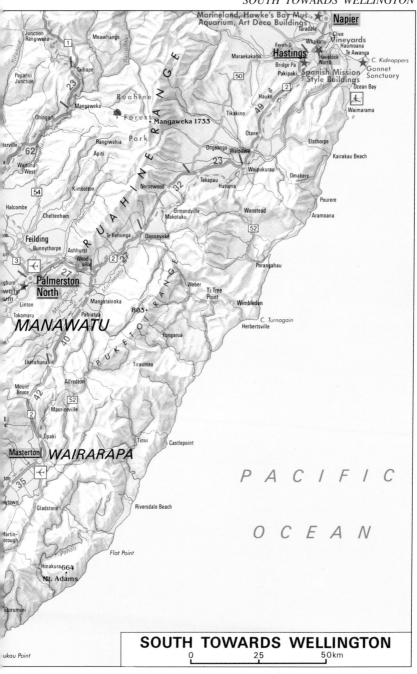

111

observe the plant and animal life of the ocean on three different floors of the building. A dolphin and seal show in **Marineland** is an even livelier attraction. If you who would like some peaceful moments, a climb up **Bluff Hill** (Lighthouse Road) should be part of your itinerary. From the top of Bluff Hill you have a splendid panoramic view over the city, and afterwards you can take a leisurely stroll through Napier's most beautiful residential area. The beaches are not as inviting as elsewhere, since they are covered with a coarse black sand. However, an overnight stay should still be planned into your schedule. The majority of hotels are either located in the vicinity around **Westport** (Meeanee Quay, towards Gisborne, with a windsurfing area across the street) or on the long **Taradale Road** (towards Hastings) which is lined by stately palm trees.

Above: A strange encounter of the third kind somewhere in the region of Wanganui.

HASTINGS

The town of **Hastings** experienced the same fate as Napier, and it is not surprising that this small neighbor is also distinguished with an architectural style typical of the 1930's. You can best get acquainted with the Spanish mission style of the town on the tour marked by signs.

Havelock North, the third town of the group, is smaller and less well-known – without justification. For many *Kiwis,* the community with a population of 9000 on the Tukituki River is a jewel in itself. Its old houses quietly hide behind even older giant trees.If you would like to get a taste of the culinary side of Hawke Bay, then travel past Havelock North towards **Te Mata Peak** (399 m). You will find not only three excellent vineyards here, but also the restaurant **Peak House** – with delicious food, a wonderful view of the bay and, of course, a tasty wine originating from the vineyards next door. A more pleasurable way to end the day in the east is hardly imaginable.

It is important to travel as many kilometers as possible the next day, since most heading south will want to travel the 340 km to Wellington before nightfall. This should be no problem. It is 34 km to Waipawa, and a further 55 km to **Dannevirke**, a Danish stronghold with an over-dimensional figure of a Viking greeting the visitor at the entrance to the town. In 1872, Scandinavians came to the area to cultivate the land around Seventy Mile Bush and help with road construction. Highway 2 runs along these old tracks today, and you may hear more Danish than English in Dannevirke in some of the cafés flying the Danish flag.

In **Woodville** you will have to make a decision. Highway 2 proceeds past Masterton, Upper Hutt and Lower Hutt, through the interior to Wellington. By the way, both Upper Hutt and Lower Hutt are frequently chosen as overnight stops to avoid having to look for a room as soon as you arrive in Wellington.

You will come to **Palmerston North** if you continue further in a westward direction after Woodville. A stop at the popular town square and the **Manawatu Museum** with its collection of Maori and pioneer exhibits is certainly rewarding. You will meet up again with Highway 1 coming from Wanganui at Levin.

New Plymouth – Wellington

Be sure to take a last look at Mount Taranaki before you reach the coast at **Hawera** – and before the New Zealand province surprises you anew. If you were ever crazy about Elvis Presley, but never had the opportunity to do anything about it, you will now get your chance. The **Elvis Presley Memorial Room** in Hawera exhibits a vast collection of records, souvenirs and mementos of him (51 Argyle Street).

Later, when you are traveling through **Patea**, you should take a look at the **Aotea Kanu**, a boat lying on its left side in the center of the city. This boat is 16.5 meters long and made of concrete. It is dedicated to the memory of Turi, who came from *hawaiki* with his family and relatives. The memorial was placed here in 1933 by his descendents. The road then proceeds through hilly farmland, and the coast towards the south lights up time and again as a silver stripe until you reach Wanganui.

WANGANUI

The city of **Wanganui** owes its significance to a river of the same name. The Wanganui River flows into the Tasman Sea and has always been one of the most important means of transportation to the north of the island. It is no wonder that bloody clashes between Maori and Pakeha during the first years of the settlement were so frequent. The quarrels that took place in those days in this farming region are now buried, and the past is only kept alive by the remarkable Maori art collection exhibited in the **Wanganui Regional Museum**, located in Queen's Park.

Wanganui is famous for its gardens and parks. Cook's, Moutoa and Kowhai Park are several worth mentioning. After a visit to the Maori-style **Putiku Church** (Anaua Street), a picnic at **Virginia Lake** is a good introduction to the outdoor adventures around Wanganui. One of the most spectacular experiences in the southern part of North Island is a canoe trip on the Wanganui River. Starting point for the trip is Wanganui itself, where some professional companies offer organized tours, and the appropriate equipment for the trip can be rented. The actual adventure begins after a two-hour bus ride north to **Taumarunui**. The canoe trip takes about three days for athletic participants or five days for those who want a more relaxed pace. It covers over 70 km of river winding through pristine forests, far from civilization. Tents are set up for the night at specified places, some-

times on beautiful terraces overlooking the river. Canoe trips also start at Ohakune in the Tongariro National Park.

The Wanganui River has fervently defended itself against all outside intervention. Steamboats have run aground due to its constantly changing bed. Attempts to develop the region for transportation purposes have failed. The most perfect example of nature's victory over civilization can be found in the **Bridge to Nowhere**, built near the mouth of Mangapura Stream. This unique monument to a failed human attempt to defeat nature stands in the middle of the forest.

Large masses of water have been diverted from the upper reaches of the river for a hydro-power station, but this hasn't detracted anything from Wanganui's charm. The river flows wide and smooth at the beginning, then suddenly spirited and rushing, through the Maori region, which has now been declared the **Whan-**

ganui National Park. This trip is accompanied by the sound of natural music, whose source is the thousands of birds living in the thickets above the steep banks of the river. The canoeing experience ends at **Pipiriki**, where a museum gives an account of Wanganui's history. On the bus ride back to Wanganui (along the beautiful but mostly unpaved River Road), places such as Jerusalem, Athens or Korinth give evidence of the Christian missionaries of earlier days.

In contrast, Highway 3 leading out of Wanganui towards the south offers a bit of relaxation. It meets Highway 1 from Taupo in **Bulls** and in Levin, the road from Napier joins it. From here there is only one destination: Wellington. Stops along the way at the beaches, accessible via side roads in a westerly direction, are worthwhile. **Himatangi, Foxton, Otaki** and **Paraparaumu** are especially inviting at the end of March when New Zealand's crazy beach horse races take place. At any rate, the capital Wellington is only 68 km away at this point.

Above: A fast and comfortable way of getting around, Air New Zealand.

THE SOUTH
Accommodation

DANNEVIRKE: *MODERATE:* **Viking Lodge** (Motel), 182 High St., Tel: 06-3747045.

HASTINGS: *MODERATE:* **Camberley Court Motel**, 801 Omahu Rd., Tel: 06-8768119.

BUDGET: **Hastings Holiday Park** (Camping), Windsor Ave, Tel: 06-8786692.

HAVELOCK NORTH: *MODERATE:* **Cherry Grove Motel**, 91 Napier Rd., Tel: 06-8778122.

BUDGET: **Arataki Holiday Park** (Camping), Arataki Rd., Tel: 06-8777479.

LEVIN: *MODERATE:* **Redwood Lodge Motel,** 368 Oxford St., Horowhenua (Highway 1), Tel: 06-3689319. *BUDGET:* **Levin Park,** Manakau (Highway 1), Tel: 06-3626799.

LOWER HUTT: *BUDGET:* **Hutt Park Holiday Village**, 95 Hutt Park Rd., Tel: 04-5685913.

NAPIER: *LUXURY:* **Snowgoose Lodge Motel,** 376 Kennedy Rd., Tel: 06-8436083.

MODERATE: **Blue Lagune Motel**, 27 Meeanee Quay, Westshore, Tel: 06-8359626. **Marineland Motels**, 20 Meeanee Quay, Westshore Beach, Tel: 06-8352147. **Fountain Court Motel**, 411 Hastings St., Tel: 06-8357387.

BUDGET: **Criterion Backpackers Inn**, 48 Emerson St., Tel: 06-8352059. **Glenview Farm Hostel**, RD 1, Tel: 06-8366232. **Kennedy Park Complex** (Camping), Storkey St., Tel: 06-8439126.

PALMERSTON NORTH: *LUXURY:* **Coachman Motel/Hotel**, 134 Fitzherbert Ave, Tel: 06-3565065 and 06-3577309.

MODERATE: **Always Inn**, 877 Main St. East, Tel: 06-3579978.

PARAPARAUMU: *BUDGET:* **Lindale Motor Park**, Paraparaumu North (Highway 1), Tel: 04-2987933.

UPPER HUTT: *MODERATE:* **Totara Lodge**, Ararino St., Tel: 04-5284152.

BUDGET: **Harcourt Holiday Park** (Camping), 45 Akatarawa Rd., Tel: 04-5267400.

WANGANUI: *MODERATE:* **Oasis Motor Lodge**, 181 Great North Rd., Tel: 06-3454636. **Gateway Motor Lodge**, corner Southern Motorway and Heads Rd., Tel: 06-3458164.

BUDGET: **Alwyn Motor Court**, 65 Karaka St., Castlecliff, Tel: 06-3444500. **Aramoho Holiday Park**, 460 Somme Parade (5 km upriver from Dublin St. Bridge), Tel: 06-3438402.

Restaurants

HASTINGS: Vidal of Hawke Bay, 913 St. Aubyn St. East, Tel: 06-868105 (wine tasting and good food in a garden; closed Sun).

HAVELOCK NORTH: Peak House, Te Mata Peak Rd., Tel: 06-8778663 (daily 12 noon–2 p.m., 6:30 p.m.–midnight; local specialities).

LOWER HUTT: Conservatory Restaurant, Waterloo Rd. and Bloomfield Terrace, Tel: 04-5693279.

NAPIER: Beach Restaurant, War Memorial Building, Marine Parade, Tel: 06-8358180 (seafood). **Wine Growing Estate Esk Valley**, Main Rd. (Highway 2), Bay View, Tel: 070-266411 (wine tasting, restaurant open daily 9:45 a.m.–6 p.m.).

Museums

HAWERA: Tawhiti Museum, Ohangai Rd., Fri-Mon 10 a.m.–4 p.m.; June–August Sundays only). **NAPIER: Hawke's Bay Museum**, 65 Marine Parade, Tel: 06-8357781 (daily 10 a.m.–4:30 p.m., Sat–Sun 1–4:30 p.m.; exhibits from Art Deco to earthquakes). **Aquarium**, Marine Parade (daily 9 a.m.–5 p.m.; 5.15 p.m. fish-feeding time).

Tips and Trips

NAPIER: *Take a Walk*, a guided city-tour with emphasis on the Art-Deco style – arranged by the **Hawke's Bay Art Gallery and Museum** – takes place every Sunday at 2 p.m. **Marineland**, Marine Parade (daily 10 a.m.–4 p.m.; 10:30 a.m., 2 p.m. dolphin and seal shows).

Special Events

Every year (end of March) a horserace is held at Paraparaum Beach (near Kapiti Island); for many Wellingtonians an ideal occasion for a picknick.

Tourist Information

HASTINGS: Visitor Information Center, Russell St., Tel: 06-8780510, (Mon-Fri 8:30 a.m.-5 p.m., Sat 8:30 a.m.-12 noon).

HAWERA: South Taranaki Information Centre, 55 High St., Tel: 06-2788599 (Mon-Fri 9 a.m.-5 p.m., in summer: Sun and public holidays additionally 10 a.m.-3 p.m.).

LOWER HUTT: Visitor Information, 26 Laings Rd., Tel: 04-5706699 (Mon-Fri 9 a.m.-5 p.m., Sat 9:30 a.m.-12:30 p.m.).

MASTERTON: Visitor Information, 5 Dixon St., Tel: 06-3787373 (Mon–Fri 8:30 a.m.–5 p.m., Sun and public holidays 10/11 a.m.–2 p.m.).

NAPIER: Visitor Information, 100 Marine Parade, Tel: 06-8357579 (Mon–Fri 8:30 a.m.–5 p.m., Sat–Sun 9 a.m.–5 p.m.). **DOC**, The Old Courthouse, 59 Marine Parade, Tel: 06-8350415. **AA**, 164 Dickens Street, Tel: 06-8356889.

PALMERSTON NORTH: Information Office, Civic Complex, The Square, Tel: 06-3585003 (Mon–Thur 8:30 a.m.–5 p.m., Fri until 4:30 p.m., Sat 9:30 a.m.–1 p.m.). **AA**, 185 Broadway Ave, Tel: 06-3577039.

WANGANUI: Visitor Information, 101 Guyton St., Tel: 06-3453286 (Mon–Fri 8:30 a.m.–5 p.m., Sun and public holidays 9 a.m.–2 p.m.). **DOC,** 299 Victoria Ave, Conservation House, Tel: 06-3452402. **AA**, 78 Victoria Ave., Tel: 06-3454578.

CAPITAL OF NEW ZEALAND

WELLINGTON

One thing is absolutely sure: Emotions sway between love and hate when it comes to how the *Kiwis* feel about their capital city of **Wellington**. Of course, this assessment also depends upon the personal point of view. Those people who live and work in Wellington are enthusiastic about the city for the most part, and there are many good reasons for this. No other city in New Zealand has such an international flair and atmosphere, both with regard to artistic and culinary tastes. When the sidewalks are rolled up in other cities, so to speak, Wellington comes to life with its numerous bars, pubs, theaters and restaurants. The rents are accordingly high, like in many big cities, but there are lovely residential areas. Despite a population of approximately 330,000, the city offers a variety of outdoor activities close by – on the beaches, at the lakes and in the mountains. The Wellingtonians seem to be content with their lot.

The picture looks a little different, however, for tourists. Visitors making a short stop in the city frequently do not know what to do there and, as a result, quickly take the next ferry to Picton. A lack of downtown atmosphere and touristic highlights seems to be the reason for the hasty departure from the city located in the extreme south of North Island.

Approaching the Windy City

In no way does "love at first sight" apply when approaching Wellington. The two-lane highway leading into the city winds through suburbs and hills, and the last few kilometers are dominated by industrial and harbor complexes. On the horizon you will see looming office and bank buildings.

According to a Maori legend, it was Kupe who first set foot on the shore at Wellington. However, it was the Maori Tara who actually settled this area around the harbor. He had been sent by his father, Whatonga, who lived on Hawke Bay to the north, to explore this southern region. When Tara returned after a one-year journey with a positive report on the area, Whatonga's decision to move was made. He took his tribe to the south where he built fortified settlements on Somes Island and Miramar Peninsula. The Maori still call Wellington *te whanga-nui-a-tara*, meaning "the harbor of Tara."

On January 22, 1840, the first white settlers came to Wellington on the vessel *Aurora*. This ship was underway for the

Preceding pages: Wellington by night. Left: Modern office buildings and shops have taken over the center of the city.

119

New Zealand Company. A few weeks before, Colonel William Wakefield had purchased land from the Maori. With this act, the foundation was laid for the social development and political advancement of the city, named after the Duke of Wellington. It was third choice as capital of New Zealand. Okiato, located in the vicinity of Russell on the Bay of Islands, first graced itself with the title from 1840 to 1841. Auckland had its turn from 1841 to 1865. For most Aucklander, this status hasn't changed even today, although Wellington has been the official capital city since 1865.

The New Zealand Company, an influential commercial trading enterprise, primarily promoted Wellington on its way to prosperity. The company had great hopes (based on Wellington's favorable geographical location in relation to the South Island) that business would flourish, transportation routes would be shorter (also to Australia), and that the travel routes would be safer – since it had always been very difficult to reach the northern part of the island. However, the first years of Wellington's start have a bitter taste to them, as has often been the case in historical success stories.

Fairness and equality were just as foreign to the commercial traders as was the keeping of agreements and treaties. Those who suffered once were again the Maori, who had sold their land – without even knowing it. The brutal clashes over property rights to the south shore of Port Nicholson were only the beginning of a conflict which was to last 30 years. However, the relationship between the Maori and white settlers was troubled for a much longer period of time.

Wellington owes its significance to the economic interests existing right from the start. This still holds true even today: Banks and consulates, international firms and the national host of civil servants have established their headquarters in Wellington.

Although the city is best known as the true capital of New Zealand, it is most infamous for its rather peculiar weather patterns, particularly the constant west winds.

It is no coincidence that one of the most popular radio stations is called *Radio Windy*. For the visitor to Wellington, it is important to dress warm – throughout the year. An umbrella or waterproof jacket should be at hand at all times, even when the sun is shining.

When properly weatherproofed, you can start out on a tour of the city. The best spot to begin is on **Wakefield Street**, where the city information center is located in the **Town Hall**. If you have driven into the city with a vehicle, there is a parking garage right next door at the **Civic Centre**.

The **Michael Fowler Centre**, with one of the best concert and convention halls in New Zealand, also belongs to this building complex. Among others, the National Symphony Orchestra and the National Ballet are at home here. Michael Fowler was once mayor of the city and played an important role in the (controversial) moderization of Wellington.

Between the Harbor and Hills

Wakefield and Willis Streets lead through the business center of the city. After accomplishing the short climb up to Boulcott Street, it is time to enjoy some tranquility. The **Antrim House** on 63 Boulcott Street rests between the high-rise buildings like a serene oasis out of the Edwardian age (built in 1905 as residential quarters). Today it is the office of the New Zealand Historic Places Trust that maintains and preserves numerous historical buildings and monument which are protected.

In Wellington itself, there are three other significant historical buildings. **Katherine Mansfield Birthplace** (25 Tinakori Road, Thorndon) was built in 1888

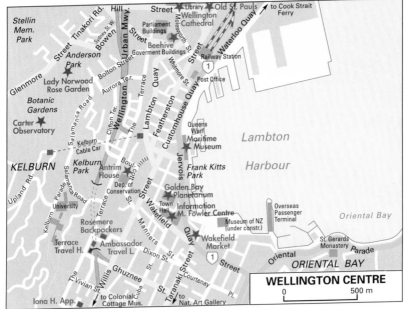

and is today a museum dedicated to the author, who died in 1929. The **Colonial Cottage Museum** was built in 1858 and is located at 68 Nairn Street, Brooklyn. The last and most interesting of these buildings is the **Old St Paul's Cathedral**, which will be mentioned again later.

For those travelers planning to visit national parks another quick stop nearby should not be forgotten. Directly next to the Antrim House are the headquarters of the **Department of Conservation**, usually called DOC for short (59 Boulcott Street), which is responsible for everything having to do with the national parks and national reserves in New Zealand. You can obtain all necessary information, brochures, maps and overnight coupons for the tracks and huts here at the DOC headquarters.

At the north end of Boulcott Street, the **Plimmer Steps** lead down again into the lower part of the city. Generations of seafarers and settlers have stepped down to the harbor by way of these stairs. They

are flanked right and left by small snack-bars and restaurants before reaching **Lambton Quay,** one of the main shopping streets in Wellington.

After about several hundred meters of window-shopping, it is time again for a climb – with the **Kelburn Cable Car.** If you follow the prescribed tour of the city (or if you do not shy away from the easy climb down by foot), you only need to purchase a one-way ticket. Otherwise, it is better to buy the more economical two-trip ticket.

The old days of the cable car are long gone, as is the case with that most famous equivalent in San Francisco. The cable car was put into operation in 1902. In 1972, the aged cars were replaced by sophisticated piece of machinery from Switzerland. Unfortunately, a piece of nostalgic atmosphere has been lost in the process.

In its place, the cable car today travels the 122-m long grade with ease in a total of five minutes. From the end station you not only have a spectacular view across

121

the city and harbor, but also the opportunity to take a peaceful walk through the grounds of the **Botanical Garden** (25 hectares). The cable car's end station was built by Ian Athfield, one of the best-known and innovative architects in New Zealand. His unmistakeable style can be found throughout the city. On the left side is also **Kelburn Village**, with a lot of shops and restaurants, as well as the grounds of the **Victoria University**.

No matter which direction you decide to take, the Kelburn trip should end at the **Lady Norwood Rose Garden.** There are more than 100 varieties of colorful, fragrant roses to be found here, and you can enjoy a lovely lunch at the Tea House located to the left, next to the Begonia House (open until 4 p.m.).

Above: More than a hint of Olde England can be found in this residential area of Wellington. Right: Richard John Seddon stands in front of the New Zealand Parliament, The Beehive.

A "Beehive" as a Center of Power

The tour continues through **Anderson Park** in the direction of Bowen Street. The opposite side of the street below Tinakori Hill (the Northern Walkway leads to the 300 m high lookout with a beautiful view), is the site of one of the oldest parts of the city with a few carefully restored houses from the colonial times (along Sydney Street West).

After crossing under the Wellington Urban Motorway, it suddenly appears in its glory: the center of political power and control in New Zealand. The "Beehive" is located in the center of the **Parliament Buildings** and is the seat of New Zealand government. One look and it is immediately obvious why this place has received the nickname "Beehive." The construction of the conical building was finished in 1981, but signs of wear and tear are already very noticeable.

There has been no parliamentary majority formed to approve a fundamental renovation, due mainly to the fact that no

one knows where the money is to come from and how to convince the voters of the necessity of these highly costly repairs. The older wooden **Government Buildings** dating back to 1876 are situated nearby on Whitmore Street. Their construction also consumed a vast sum of money, even for those days, not to mention the enormous amount of valuable wood used.

Fortunately, times have changed with regard to the use of wood and its conservation. Only the problem of high costs remains the same.

The Beehive appears more impressive from the outside than it does from the inside when you take a tour of the building. The prime minister (who was the Conservative Jim Bolger at the end of 1991) has to be modestly content with just one of the upper floors as compared to his colleagues in other countries. It is interesting to note that a copy of the Treaty of Waitangi is displayed in the conference room of the four Maori representatives. In addition, the portraits of distinguished Maori leaders and various art objects belonging to the first inhabitants of the island can be seen here.

After leaving the "sacred" rooms of the living politicians at the "Beehive", one might take a last look outside at the statue of Richard John Seddon (prime minister from 1893 to 1906).

Aitken Hill begins at the northern corner of the square. On the left side, you will see the **National Library** and the **Alexander Turnbull Library**, both of which not only show varying exhibits of great interest but are also leading archives in their documentation of New Zealand's history.

A few hundred meters further on, you will run into the previously-mentioned **Old St Paul's Cathedral** on Mulgrave Street. It was built in 1866; and if it were up to some of the church officials, this house of worship would have long been reduced to a pile of rubble since it was not prestigious enough for them.

The construction of the **Wellington Cathedral** (on Molesworth Road) did pacify them somewhat. St. Paul's has the opposite visual effect of the Beehive. From the outside, the church looks rather plain. Inside, the impressive New Zealand woodwork with which the church nave is furnished will take your breath away.

Afterwards the tour leads the visitor back to the city center again. Whether you take Featherston Street or the Lambton Quay, you'll find both are lined with glass-faced office buildings, small snackbars and numerous stores and shops. The first houses in the city were built here. They are now long gone – many because they were not earthquake safe, a danger that Wellington (like all of New Zealand) is still faced with to a high degree.

The **Frank Kitts Park** is now the first place offering a bit of greenery. North of the park you will find the **Harbour Board Maritime Museum.** It is located on Jervois Quay and on two separate floors it exhibits everything that has to do with the harbor, the city and the ocean.

Visitors underway on the weekend will surely head in a southerly direction towards **Wakefield Street**, where the shops in the **Wakefield Market** are open from Friday to Sunday. These shops are tucked into a former storage house on the harbor and sell everything you can think of (and even some things you would not). Here again, the international Wellingtonian mixture creates a special atmosphere with an exotic touch.

The **Museum of New Zealand** and the **National Art Gallery** are both housed in the same newly-built building on Cable Street on the grounds of the former harbor. This museum, the only one in the country to be state-supported, can be compared to the Auckland Museum (viz, the Maori section there). Particularly beautiful is the richly decorated meetinghouse from Turanga (Gisborne, as it is called nowadays). Most exhibits and displayed items are related to Maori, Pacific and New Zealand history and culture.

Green Hills and Golden Beaches

Wellington does not have to imply downtown and the hectic pace of the city center. The green surroundings can be ideally explored by *Bus & Walk.* The Wellington City Transportation Office offers 16 trips in and around the city by means of public transportation. These trips take you to such places as the beaches of **Scorching Bay** and **Worser Bay** (near Seatoun), as well as to **Owhiro Bay**, **Island Bay**, and **Lyall Bay**, all of which can be rather blustery since they face the open sea. They are, however, ideal for surfers.

All of the above beaches lie along a route called the **Oriental Parade.** This 39 km-long round-trip tour begins at Port Nicholson Yacht Club. For the first few kilometers, it allows a look at one of the most beautiful residential areas in the city, at the foot of Mount Victoria. Those sunbathers stretched out on the beach at Oriental Bay are not actually touching New Zealand ground. The sand came to this spot as ballast via trade ships from throughout the world.

The Oriental Parade proceeds directly along the water. The end of the tour should take you to a lookout point on **Mount Victoria**. From here you have a magnificent view of the city, the harbor, the hills of Wellington and even of Cook Strait.

Mount Victoria, with an elevation just short of 200 m, is the ideal spot to say good-bye to North Island. And if you see one of the inter-island ferries setting anchor down at Port Nicholson after its 83.6 km trip from Picton, it is time to head down to the harbor. In approximately two hours, the ferry will embark on its journey, leaving Wellington behind; a new adventure in the wilderness of the South Island lies ahead. On the way, in the middle of the bay is tiny **James Island**, where Kupe, the Maori explorer, landed in the 10th century.

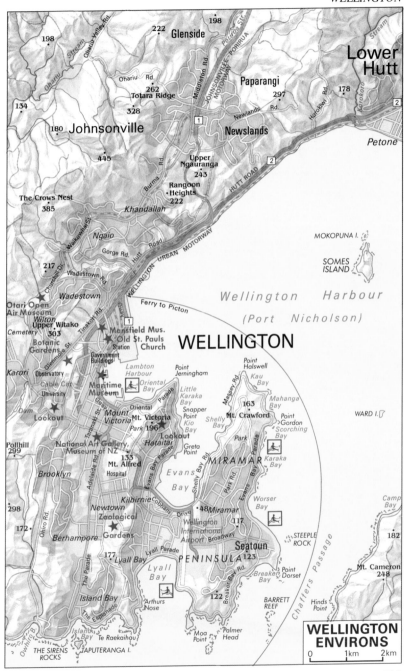

Lower Hutt

Glenside
198
222
198

Ohariu Valley Rd.
Ohariu Stream

Paparangi
297
Rd.
178

Ohariu Rd.
262
Totara Ridge
328

Johnsonville
180
134

Newlands
Newlands Rd.

Petone

445

Upper Ngauranga
243

Burma Rd.

Rangoon Heights
222

The Crows Nest
385

Khandallah

HUTT ROAD

MOKOPUNA I.

Ngaio

SOMES ISLAND

217

Gorge Rd.

Hutt Road

WELLINGTON URBAN MOTORWAY

Wadestown Rd.

Wadestown

Churchill Dr.
Waikowhai St.

Otari Open Air Museum
Wilton
Upper Witako
303
Cemetery
Botanic Gardens

Ferry to Picton

Wellington   Harbour

(Port   Nicholson)

Mansfield Mus.
Old St. Pauls Church
Station

WELLINGTON

Glenmore St.

Lambton Harbour

Point Jerningham

Point Halswell

Karori
Observatory

Government Buildings

Kau Bay

Massey Rd.

Cable Car
University

Maritime Museum

Oriental Bay

Little Karaka Bay

Mahanga Bay

Dam
Lookout

Tinakori Rd.

Mount Victoria
Mt. Victoria 196

Oriental Parade

Snapper Point
Kio Bay

Mt. Crawford
163

Shelly Bay

WARD I.

Pollhill
299

National Art Gallery, Museum of NZ
Mt. Alfred
135

Lookout
Hataitai

Greta Point

Park

Point Gordon
Scorching Bay

Adelaide Rd.

Brooklyn

Hospital

Evans   Bay

MIRAMAR

Park Rd.

Karaka Bay

298

Kilbirnie

Cobham Drive

Camp Bay

Newtown
Zoological Gardens

Evans Bay Parade

Shelly Bay Rd.

Worser Bay

182

172

Ohiro Rd.

48 Miramar
117

Mt. Cameron
248

Berhampore

Wellington International Airport
Broadway

Seatoun
123

STEEPLE ROCK

Chaffers   Passage

The Parade

177 Lyall Bay

Lyall Parade

PENINSULA

Breaker Bay Rd.

Point Dorset

Island Bay

Lyall Bay

Breaker Bay

Hinds Point

BARRETT REEF

The Esplanade

Arthurs Nose

122

Owhiro B.

THE SIRENS ROCKS

Island Bay
Te Raekaihau
TAPUTERANGA I.

Moa Point

Palmer Head

WELLINGTON ENVIRONS

0   1km   2km

WELLINGTON

Arrival

Wellington's airport is situated 8 km from the city center. A bus service connects the airport with the rail terminal (10 NZ$), additional shuttle-buses provide direct services between the airport and the hotels, i.e. Supershuttle (10 NZ$), Tel: 04-3878787. The taxi fare from the airport into town is ca. 15 NZ$. Please note: International departures are levied with an airport tax of 20 NZ$.

Accommodation

LUXURY: **Wellington Parkroyal**, corner Grey and Featherston St., Tel: 04-4722722. **Plaza International Hotel**, 148-176 Wakefield St., Tel: 04-4733900. **Bay Plaza Hotel**, 40-44 Oriental Parade, Oriental Bay, Tel: 04-3857799. **Iona Motel Apartments**, 140 Abel Smith St., Tel: 04-3850404. *MODERATE*: **Trekkers Hotel**, 213 Cuba St. And Dunlop Tce, Tel: 04-3852153. **Ambassador Travel Lodge**, 287 The Terrace, Tel: 04-3845697. **Victoria House Inc**, 282 The Terrace, Tel: 04-3843357. **Hampshire House**, corner 155 Ghuznee and 305 The Terrace, Tel: 04-3843051.
Terrace Travel Hotel (cabins), 291 The Terrace, Tel: 04-3829506. **Tinakori Lodge**, 182 Tinakori Rd., Tel: 04-4733478. **Harbour City Homestays**, P.O. Box 14-345, Tel: 04-3862339 (good accommodation in private homes).
BUDGET: **Maple Lodge**, 52 Ellice St., Mt. Victoria, Tel: 04-3853771. **Rosemere Backpackers**, 6 MacDonald Crescent, Tel: 04-3843041. **Beethoven House Hostel**, 89 Brougham St., Mt. Victoria, Tel: 04-3842226. **Wellington Youth Hostel**, 40 Tinakori Rd., Tel: 04-4736271. **Rowena's Lodge,** 115 Brougham St., Mount Victoria, Tel: 04-3857872.
A large number of accommodations in all categories spread along The Terrace near the city center. Prices in the capital are very high – accommodation at reasonable prices can be found in the "suburbs" of Lower and Upper Hutt or along the West Coast.

Restaurants

Brasserie Flipp, RSA Building, 103 Ghuznee St., Tel: 04-3859493 (pleasant atmosphere, fresh fish is served daily).
Genghis Khan, 25 Majoribanks St., Tel: 04-3843592 (open daily for dinner; a startling experience for the eyes and taste buds: a Mongolian barbecue).
Great Expectations, 60 Ghuznee St., Tel: 04-3849596 (pricey New Zealand cuisine, with live

jazz; open from 5:30 p.m., closed Sun and Mon).
Mexican Cantina, 19 Edward St., Tel: 04-3859711 (a reasonably priced Mexican).
Sakura, 3rd Floor, 181-195 Wakefield St., Tel: 04-3845806 (open Tuesdays – Fridays for lunch and dinner; Japanese cuisine with an exotic touch – culture-buffs dine sitting on *tatami*-mats.
Downtown sports a plethora of good snackbars, salad bars and takeaways, catering to an army of hungry office workers at lunchtime. Wholefood and vitamins are rapidly gaining importance on the list of priorities. Between 12 noon and 2 p.m. eateries are packed to bursting point, and you might have trouble finding a seat.

Museums

National Art Gallery of New Zealand and **Museum**: Cable St., Tel: 04-3859609 (daily 10 a.m.–4:45 p.m.; free admission and guided tours; exhibits of Maori art and culture from New Zealand as well as from the Pacific area).
Wellington Maritime Museum: Wellington Harbour Board Building, Queens Wharf, Tel: 04-4728904 and 4723738 (open Mondays–Fridays 9:30 a.m.–4 p.m.; Sundays and public holidays 1–4:30 p.m.; everything related to the harbor and shipping).
National Cricket Museum: Old Stand, Basin Reserve, Tel: 04-3856602 (October–April daily from 10:30 a.m.–3:30 p.m.; May–September weekdays from 10:30 a.m.–13:30 p.m.; all about the history of cricket, one of the country's most typical sports.
National Library and Alexander Turnbull Library, corner Molesworth and Aitken St., Tel: 04-4743000 (Mondays–Fridays 9 a.m.–5 p.m., Saturdays 9 a.m.–1 p.m.; guided tours Mondays, Wednesdays and Fridays at 2 p.m.).
Wellington Tramway Museum: Queen Elisabeth Park, Paekakariki, Tel: 04-29228361 (open Sundays and public holidays from 11 a.m.–5 p.m.; the historic trams still operate on a track 2 km long).

Tips and Trips

Bus: Those planning to travel all day on the public WCT-buses should invest in a *Daytripper* ticket for 5 NZ$, valid between 9 a.m. and midnight. A *Day Rover* ticket (15 NZ$) allows you to explore the suburbs and surroundigs of Wellington, Tel: 04-8017000.
Cable Car: The cable car runs between Lambton Quay and the Observation Point Kelburn at the Botanic Gardens every 10 minutes: Mon–Fri from 7 a.m.–10 p.m., Sat from 9:30 a.m.–6 p.m. and Sun from 10:30 a.m.–6 p.m. Return fare 2,50 NZ$.

Car Rental: Hardy Cars, used cars and caravans, Tel: 03-5481681, Fax: 03-5481581.

Carter Observatory: Botanic Gardens, Kelburn (open Tuesdays from Mar. to Oct.: 7:30–9:30 p.m.).

City Tours: start daily at 2 p.m. (in summer one additional tour runs at 10 a.m.) from the City Information Centre, Wakefield Street. The fare is 21 NZ$ for adults, 11 NZ$ for children, the tour takes two and a half hours.

Department of Conservation (DOC): Visitor Information Centre, Old Government Building, Tel: 04-4727356. Supplies information and maps of all National Parks, as well as accommodation vouchers for the various huts ; an absolute must for hikers).

Galleries: New Zealand Academy of Fine Arts, Buckle St., Tel: 04-3859267 and 3844911 (exhibitions 10 a.m.–4:30 p.m.); **City Art Gallery**: 65 Victoria St., Tel: 04-732625 (daily 10 a.m.–6 p.m.).

Golden Bay Planetarium: Harris St. (behind the Public Library), Tel: 04-4723053 (shows Sundays and public holidays 1:30, 2:30 und 3:30 p.m.).

Harbor Ferries: The *East by West Ferry* runs a service several times daily from Queen's Wharf to Day's Bay (Information: Tel: 04-4991273).

Markets: Wakefield Market: Corner Jervois Quay and Taranaki St., Tel: 04-4729239 (Fridays 11 a.m.–6 p.m., Saturdays, Sundays and public holidays 10 a.m.–5 p.m.; the largest and most colorful market ion the city). **The Marketplace:** Manthel Motors Building, 186-200 Wakefield St., Tel: 04-3854464 and 3848821 (lower floor daily 9 a.m.–5 p.m.; additional market on the upper floor Saturdays–Sundays 10 a.m.–5 p.m.).

New Zealand Historic Places Trust: Antrim House, 63 Boulcott St., Tel: 04-4724341 (the office gives information on all buildings classified as historical monuments in New Zealand; open during office hours; visiting hours for the house: 12 noon –3 p.m.).

Three further historic buildings in Wellington: **Katherine Mansfield's Birthplace:** 25 Tinakori Rd., Thorndon, Tel: 04-4737268 (Tuesdays–Sundays 10 a.m.–4 p.m.). **Nairn Street Colonial Cottage**: 68 Nairn St., Tel: 04-3849122 (Mondays–Fridays 10 a.m.–4 p.m., weekends 1–4:30 p.m.). **Old St. Paul's Cathedral**: Mulgrave St., Thorndon, Tel: 04-4736722 (Mondays–Saturdays 10 a.m.–4:30 p.m., Sun 1–4:30 p.m.).

Parliament: Free guided tours through "The Beehive" take place daily (Info: Tel: 04-4719503 or 4719999).

Zoo (Wellington Zoological Gardens): Newtown, Tel: 04-3898130 (daily 8:30 a.m.–5 p.m.; best reached by bus No. 11 in the direction of Newton Park; best time for visiting the Kiwi-House is between 10 a.m.–12 noon).

How to get to the South Island

Ferry Departures: Four daily departures are scheduled for the ferries to the South Island: 9:30 a.m. and 2:30, 5:30 and 10:30 p.m. However, if one of the ferries is due for overhauling, there will be only two departures daily and long queues can be expected (mostly mid-March).

Fares (one-way crossing): Adults will pay about 44 NZ$; children ca. 22 NZ$; cars, minibuses and caravans between 150 and 160 NZ$). After arrival, a free bus service connects the ferry dock and the rail terminal.

Alternative: The fast catamaran *Lynx* crosses Cook Strait in just about 2 hours, but the crossing is quite expensive.

Flights: *Skyferry* offers daily flights between Wellington and Picton or Blenheim on the South Island (Information: Tel: 04-3888380).

Festivals / Special Events

The *New Zealand International Festival of the Arts* takes place every two years in March (in years with even numbers), and features ca. 300 cultural events.

Airlines

Air New Zealand, corner Featherston and Grey St., Wellington, Tel: 04-3859911. Reservations: Tel: 04-3859922. Flight information: Tel: 04-3889900. **British Airways**, corner Featherstone and Panama St., Tel: 04-727327. **Lufthansa**, Tel: 09-3031529 (telephone number in Auckland!). **Singapore Airlines**, Norwich Bldg, 3-11 Hunter St., Tel: 04-4739749. **United Airlines**, 26 Brandon St., Tel: 04-4726897.

Embassies

AUSTRALIA: 72-78 Hobson Street, Thorndon, (P.O. Box 4036), Wellington, Tel: 04-4736411.

GREAT BRITAIN: Reserve Bank Building, 2 The Terrace, Wellington, Tel: 04-4726049.

USA: Embassy of the United States, Consular Section, 29 Fitzherbert terrace, Wellington, Tel: 04-4722068.

Tourist Information

Visitor Information, Old Town Hall, Civic Centre, 101 Wakefield St., Tel: 04-8014000 and 4735063 (daily 9 a.m.–5 p.m.). **The Interisland Line Arahura and Aratika Ferry Information Centre**, 3rd floor in Wellington Station, Tel: 04-4982130.

SOUTH ISLAND

MARLBOROUGH SOUNDS
NELSON
ABEL TASMAN NATIONAL
PARK
GOLDEN BAY
HEAPHY TRACK
NELSON LAKES NATIONAL
PARK

A North and South Conflict

Apart from its beautiful scenery, North Island offers the traveler bustling big cities and, above all, New Zealand history. In contrast, nature in its purest form unfolds before your eyes on South Island. Any efforts to experience big-city adventure on South Island will be in vain (although Christchurch residents do not like to admit this).

The traveler in New Zealand can best experience and enjoy the natural surroundings of South Island by visiting any of its eight national parks. You will find sandy beaches in Abel Tasman National Park; the jagged West Coast in Paparoa National Park; the glaciers in Westland National Park; the Milford Sound in Fiordland National Park; and the highest mountain peak in Mount Cook National Park. Another must for many traveling on South Island is Stewart Island. It is not a national park, but is often called New Zealand's "third island".

From the top of South Island in the north to Stewart Island in the south, there are remarkable cities, such as Nelson and

Preceding pages: Sailboats wait patiently on the beach in Kaiteriteri. Left: A dense rain forest embraces the lonely beaches along the Marlborough Sounds.

Dunedin; enchanting natural marvels, such as the Moeraki Boulders and Lake Wakatipu; and history of all kinds. In Akaroa you will be welcomed on arrival in the French language, and in Otago Goldfields Park the memory of the "international" gold rush is still kept alive.

South Island is also the home of "odd" but endearing *Kiwi* personalities: the *Wizard of Christchurch*; the *Coasters* on the west coast; the unruffled farmers in the Catlins; and the hippies residing near Nelson who still have that certain air and flair typical of the 1960s.

Despite the numerous and captivating attractions, it is almost an unwritten rule for many North Island *Kiwis* to take their vacations in Australia rather than to explore their own South Island. The South Islanders try to compensate and counter this slight by calling their island simply the Mainland.

However, the humorous north-south conflict does have a rather earnest aspect to it, which should not be forgotten. For a number of years, North Island was more strongly financially supported than South Island. One could even say that South Island was more or less neglected during this period. A great disparity in the economic development arose between North Island and South Island. The North became industrialized and money flowed.

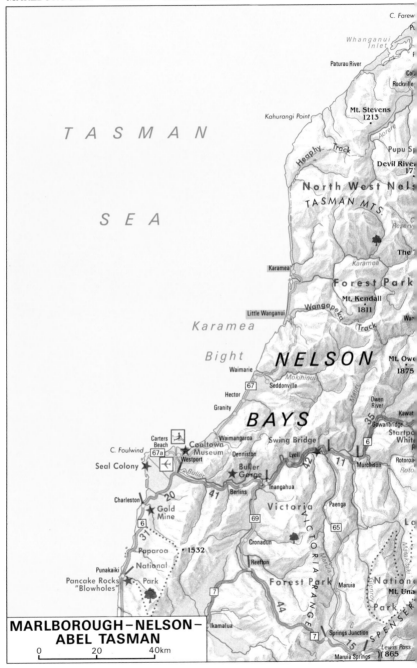

T A S M A N

S E A

Whanganui Inlet

C. Farew
Pu

Paturau River

Col
Rockville

Mt. Stevens
1213

Kahurangi Point

Aorere

Heaphy Track

Pupu Sp

Devil River
17

North West Nels

TASMAN MTS.

Reserv

Karamea

The

Forest Park

Karamea

Karamea

Mt. Kendall
1811

Little Wanganui

Wangapeka

War

Karamea

Track

Bight

N E L S O N

Mt. Owe
1875

Waimarie

Mokihinui

67 Seddonville

Hector

Maruri

Owen
River

Granity

B A Y S

Kawat

Bowanbridge

35

Startp
Whit

Carters Beach

Waimangaroa

Swing Bridge

6

C. Foulwind

67a Coaltown Museum

Denniston

Lyell

42

11

Murchison

Rotoroa

Westport

Buller

Seal Colony

Buller Gorge

Inangahua

Charleston

20

41

Berlins

Victoria

Paenga

La

Gold Mine

6

69

65

31

Cronadun

Maruia

Glenroy

Matak

Paparoa

1532

Punakaiki

National

Reefton

VICTORIA RANGE

Natio
Park

Pancake Rocks
"Blowholes"

Park

Forest Park

Maruia

Mt. Una

7

Ikamalua

44

SPENSER

7 Springs Junction

15

Lewis Pass
865

Maruia Springs

MARLBOROUGH−NELSON−
ABEL TASMAN

0   20   40km

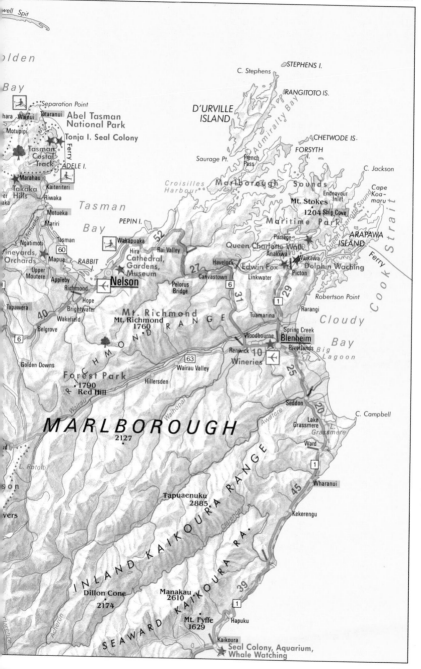

well Spit

olden
Bay

Separation Point
hara · Wainui
Totaranui
Abel Tasman
National Park

Motupipi

Tonja I. Seal Colony

Tasman·
Coastal
Track

ADELE I.

Marahau
Takaka
Hills
ber
Hills
aka

Kaiteriteri

Riwaka

Motueka

Mariri

Ngatimoti

Tasman

neyards,
Orchards

Mapua

RABBIT
I.

Upper
Moutere

Appleby

Richmond

Hope

Tapawera

Brightwater

Wakefield

Belgrove

Golden Downs

Forest Park

1790
Red Hill

Tasman
Bay

PEPIN I.

Wakapuaka

Hira

Cathedral,
Gardens,
Museum

Nelson

Rai Valley

52

Pelorus
Bridge

Canvastown

27

Havelock

6

Linkwater

31

29

1

Picton

Robertson Point

Rarangi

Cloudy

Bay

Big
Lagoon

Mt. Richmond
Mt. Richmond
1760

R A N G E

Tuamarina

Woodbourne

Renwick

10

Blenheim

Spring Creek

Riverlands

63

Wairau Valley

Hillersden

Wineries

25

Seddon

20

Lake
Grassmere

C. Campbell

Grassmere

Ward

C H M O N D

H

MARLBOROUGH

2127

1

Wharanui

45

Tapuaenuku
2885

Kekerengu

I N L A N D   K A I K O U R A   R A N G E

Dillon Cone
2174

Manakau
2610

39

S E A W A R D   K A I K O U R A   R A.

Mt. Fyffe
1629

1

Hapuku

Kaikoura

Seal Colony, Aquarium,
Whale Watching

C. Stephens

STEPHENS I.

RANGITOTO IS.

D'URVILLE
ISLAND

CHETWODE IS.

FORSYTH
I.

Saurage Pt.

French
Pass

C. Jackson

Croisilles
Harbour

Marlborough   Sounds

Cape
Koa-
maru

Mt. Stokes
1204 Ship Cove

Endeavour
Inlet

Maritime   Park

ARAPAWA
ISLAND

Portage

Queen Charlotte Walk

Anakiwa

Waikawa

Dolphin Watching

Edwin Fox

Ferry

Cook Strait

40

6

Wairau

Waihopai

Waiau

Awatere

Clarence

Acheron

Golden
Bay

Admiralty Bay

Ferry

60

Queen Charlotte Sound

The pastoral South Island was demoted, as it were, to the food producer of New Zealand.

Farewell North and Hello South

Most travelers approach South Island via the ferry starting at Wellington – even though the direct flight from Auckland to Christchurch has become a time-saving alternative for many tourists on a tight schedule. The trip with the ferry across Cook Strait between Wellington and Picton is exactly 83.6 km long, takes 3.5 hours, allowing enough time for the visitor to tune in to the other, still unfamiliar part of New Zealand.

Cook Strait owes its name to that renowned, and indeed frequently mentioned captain, who – from his viewpoint on Arapawa Island (off South Island) – looked out across this natural boundary between the two islands. The strait measures 19 km at its narrowest point, yet crossing it can sometimes seem like an eternity. Storms and rough, raging waters are frequent, calm passages are few and far between. Therefore, you should try to enjoy the well protected tranquility in Port Nicholson before the ferry reaches open waters.

It is not only the rolling seas and stormy weather that set many travelers in a contemplative mood when leaving Wellington: The ferry connection often turns out to be a time-consuming bottleneck. This is especially true during the month of March when the ferry *Arahanga* is banned to the shipyard for its yearly general maintenance. Day-long waits are relatively frequent during this period. It is, therefore, essential to make reservations in advance for the ferry trip across the strait. Early reservations are also recommended because the shipping

Right: Every fifteenth New Zealander owns and operates a boat, not surprisingly perhaps considering the beautiful waters.

company, the *Interislander*, and the New Zealand government have not been able to remedy this deplorable state of affairs, even though it has been staring them in the face for these many years. In March of 1991, it even came to pass that outraged tourists, who had been forced to spend three nights in their vehicles in the stand-by line before they could buy their tickets, staged unruly demonstrationa at the ferry dock.

MARLBOROUGH SOUNDS

If you are fortunate enough to begin the ferry ride across the straits in good weather, the crossing will be an extraordinary experience – especially the last few kilometers, where the ferry creeps forward through a broad labyrinth of islands and coves. In 1770, Captain Cook set anchor in these protected waters with his ship, the *Endeavor*. He enjoyed this area so much that he spent more than 100 days anchored at Ship Cove on his visits to New Zealand. At the end of the 18th century, these **Marlborough Sounds** became the point of departure for whaling ships; and fifty years later, the first white settlers followed the path through these bewildering waterways.

Less successful in his navigating abilities, due to lack of orientation, was the captain of the Russian cruise ship *Michail Lermontov*. In 1986, he miscalculated the ideal passageway, and today his former place of work has become a popular diving destination. One of his life boats now serves as seating at a fast-food restaurant in Picton! This demonstrates one more time that the crossing of the **Queen Charlotte Sound** can be a treacherous endeavor even in our age of computers and radars.

Another interesting bit of history comes from **Dieffenbach Point**, which you pass at the end of Tory Channel. This spot was named after an explorer working for the New Zealand Company. Dr.

Ernst Dieffenbach gained some fame through a very simple discovery. He determined the elevation of a mountain by the amount of time it took for his tea-water to boil on it.

In **Picton** you have land under your feet again. This small port city has become an ideal entry point for travelers wishing to explore South Island. If you arrive with the late ferry (approximate arrival time is 10:30 p.m.), or if you land after a stormy crossing and need time to recover, there is a wide range of overnight accommodations available in every price category (also important for the return trip due to long waiting lines). Close to the ferry dock is another ship that has found its final anchorage – the three-master *Edwin Fox*, one of the last belonging to the legendary East India Company.

After your arrival in Picton, there are two possibilities to choose from when starting your tour of South Island. If you travel south towards Christchurch along the east coast (Highway 1), your first stop will be at **Kaikoura**, located 157 km

from Picton. Those who prefer more relaxation should turn west right outside of Picton, towards Nelson and the nearby Abel Tasman National Park.

West from Picton to Nelson and Golden Bay

Travelers who have arrived in Picton in the early evening are recommended to continue on Highway 1 as far as **Blenheim**, and from here via Highway 6 towards Nelson. The drive is longer, but considerably safer in the dark than the winding Queen Charlotte Drive. However, in daylight there is no alternative to the Queen Charlotte Drive, one of the most beautiful scenic roads in New Zealand which is meandering along the rugged coastline.

Should a few top managers in the tourist business have their way, this idyllic countryside will soon be endangered. A Japanese hotel chain has drawn up plans for a gigantic resort here. Up until now, public protests initiated by the citizens of

the area have prevented its construction. As a result of this outcry, the 52,000 hectare area has been declared the **Marlborough Sounds Maritime Park**. The region can best be explored on foot or by boat. The **Queen Charlotte Sound Track** begins at Anakiwa, where the only outdoors school in New Zealand is located. Here participants learn techniques necessary to live and survive in the wilderness. The track has a length of 49 km (approximately 24 hours hiking time, taking four to five days; overnight stays in cabins are possible) and runs along the coast to **Ship Cove**, one of the most historically significant spots in the entire country. Local residents maintain even today that Captain Cook used the trees still standing at the end of the beach at Ship Cove to tie up his ship, the *Endeavor*. Though there may be doubts as to

Above: This trompe l'oeil mural in Nelson creates an unreal vista. Right: An oldtimer braves the sands of time on Trafalgar Street.

the authenticity of this story, the naming of Queen Charlotte Sound is less disputed. On nearby Arapawa Island, Captain Cook hoisted his Union Jack, raised his glass toasting the health of King George III, and christened the sound in the name of his queen.

But those who stand on this historical site today will be perturbed about a more banal problem – namely, the return voyage with the ferry. This should be organized before starting off an exploratory trip through South Island, otherwise the enjoyment of this trip will soon be spoiled. (Information can be obtained at the DOC office in Picton.)

At **Havelock**, Queen Charlotte Drive meets up with Highway 6, heading towards Nelson. Mussel connoisseurs looking for a delicious evening meal should take some time to pay a visit to the port's mussel farm (one of more than 200 farms in the area).

Another picturesque trail through Maritime Park ends across from the small sound. It runs from Elaine Bay along Tennyson Inlet to Penzance Bay. The **Archer, Hard Beech** and **Nydia Tracks** then lead further on to Kaiuma Bay (altogether a 17-hour walk taking two to three days; overnight stays are possible in several huts).

Just beyond Havelock, the highway stretches along a flush landscape past the old gold rush community of **Canvastown** and the Pelorus River. In the summer, at **Pelorus Bridge** the local residents enjoy cooling off in their swimming hole, the best spot far and near. Even for tourists, a swim here is as delightful as a cup of tea at the nearby park.

The **Maungatapu Road** begins at Pelorus Bridge. At the end of Maungatapa Road, several beautiful tracks (some taking several days) start. Among other places, they lead to Nelson and Blenheim. A substantially shorter hike is the nearby Totara Walk, taking approximately 40 minutes.

The road continues on to **Rai Valley** (last chance for a short trip to Marlborough Maritime Park via the Elaine Bay Walk) and then up to the **Rai Whangamoa Forest**. On both sides of the road, the trees spead out in an almost perfect linear formation. It clearly shows that Nelson, still a good 40 km from here, has acquired its wealth not only from fishing, but also from the export of wood (primarily in the form of small chips). A good share of the trees from this region will land some day as a newspaper on a Japanese breakfast table. Behind Wakapuaka, you will have a view of Tasman Bay for the first time.

NELSON

Actually, everything is different in **Nelson**. The people here are generally more relaxed and their lifestyle is easygoing (both traits allegedly stem from Nelson's climate). Not only in the numerous fruit orchards, plantations and vineyards does everything blossom and thrive better than elsewhere, but there are also no limits with regard to the creativity of the local people. The number of potteries, workshops of every size and type, goldsmiths and glassblowers is steadily growing from month to month.

Nestled between the seaport and foothills, Nelson continues to grow up the slopes. Its current population is 35,000. It will celebrate its 150th anniversary in 1992. Yet, never in its history has the city been as popular as today. If posed the question: "Where would you most like to live?" many *Kiwis* give only one and short answer: "Nelson!" – based on its high quality of life.

Nelson is interesting for visitors, too. Although the city offers only few optical highlights, it has a certain flair and atmosphere that can be taken in behind **Christ Church Cathedral** between Trafalgar and Halifax Street, on a stroll along **Tahunanui Beach**, or on an outing to **Rabbit Island**.

Shops and boutiques line Nelson's main streets – the same types found any-

where else in the country. On the other hand, a few cafés stand out from the rest. If you like a rustic scene with a strong aura of flower power from the 1960s, look for a seat between people wearing hand-knit sweaters and sandles under colorful parasols on the street at **Chez Eelco** (296 Trafalgar Street; unfortunately, the culinary quality has recently declined). If reading a newspaper in the traditional coffeehouse atmosphere is more appealing, look for **Pomeroy's**, a nicely decorated café (276 Trafalgar Street).

Refreshed and invigorated from your café visit, you might now start out on foot to the nearby **Queen's Gardens**, or to the **Botanical Reserve,** where New Zealand's geographical center is to be found and the romantic **Maital Valley** begins. Nelson is, by the way, famous for its

Above: Some of the comfortable residences at Tahunanui Beach. Right: Harvesting apples in New Zealand's "fruit orchard" north of Nelson.

parks and gardens. A recommendable tour (especially with a picnic lunch) is the **Queen's Gardens**, **Melrose House**, **Fifeshire House** and **Cathedral Gardens**. The **Founders' Park** is located just a short distance away (87 Atawhai Drive, east of downtown). In this lively pioneer museum, you can retrace Nelson's history, which actually began on November 1, 1841, with the arrival of the first European settlers on the vessel *Arrow*.

The **Boat Marina** in the new yacht harbor gives an indication of the wealth that some Nelson residents have acquired in the meantime. Business is especially good in the nearby freight port. Russian trawlers have been increasingly contributing to the flourishing trade in the past few years by docking here.

The Wakefield Quay and Rocks Road lead along the ocean shore where windsurfers find ideal sailing conditions, sheltered behind **Boulder Bank**, which is a full 16 km long.

At **Hays Corner** it's good-bye to Nelson, but not without taking a short trip to

the **Nelson Provincial Museum** (located in a part of the city called Stoke) and a quick look into the nearby **Isle House** (built in 1886 and surrounded by lovely gardens).

From Nelson it is just a few kilometers to **Richmond**. Here it is best to turn right onto the Richmond by-pass (a stop on the corner at **Craft Habitat**, with its numerous galleries, art studios and salesrooms is worthwhile) and follow Highway 60. For the next stretch of kilometers, fruit orchards will skirt the road. If you have ever wondered how a kiwi grows, you will have ample opportunity to see it. Should the predictions of the farmers in this area prove right, the fruit of the future will be called *nashi* – a juicy fruit hybrid, somewhere between an apple and a pear. Fruit is inexpensively sold directly by the producer everywhere, so stock up on a sufficient supply of vitamins before embarking on further adventures. If time allows and you do not have to rush to catch the morning Abel Tasman ferry at **Kaiteriteri** (departure

time 9 a.m.), then turn off the road to the left behind Appleby towards Redwoods Valley. Even when the roads are marked *highway,* it is slow going. Fortunately so, because expansive vineyards line the way. The best-known wine-growing estate with a tasting tour is the **Seifried Vineyard** in Upper Moutere. Along with Seifried, names such as Neudorf, Rosental, Sarau, or Ranzau call to mind the early German settlers who reached New Zealand in 1843 on the vessel *St. Pauli.* Sarau – once the settlers' main town – has changed its name in the meantime to **Upper Moutere**. Yet, a trace of German atmosphere is still preserved in the shadows of **St Paul's Lutheran Church**.

Close by, nature can be encountered in a completely different way. For example, the family Newport offers an "upside-down zoo," where, in summer, visitors can watch the daily feeding of tame eels; and the horticultural tour given by Colin Pretty guides the visitor through the best fruit orchards and tobacco plantations in the province of Nelson Bays.

ABEL TASMAN NATIONAL PARK

At Motueka you again join up with the main road, and from here it is just 20 km to Kaiteriteri, situated at the southern reaches of **Abel Tasman National Park**. You should be warned in advance that the peaceful days are now apparently a thing of the past. Nature hikes through the park have become extremely popular. Alone in 1990, 24,000 hikers, as well as 50,000 other visitors were registered at the park, and the trend is toward more rather than less. It is only natural that the environment and the pure outdoor experience suffer when faced with such crowds. Especially in the summertime, between Christmas and the end of February, tourism moves in and takes over. There are no vacancies in the hotels and motels; boat trips and the cabins along

Above: Enjoying the fresh air, clear water and clean sands of Bark Bay in the Abel Tasman National Park. Right: The landscape along the Heaphy Track.

the tracks are booked up with certainty. Early reservations are, therefore, essential.

There are two tracks to choose from in this park: One runs along the coastline and the other inland. Both tracks take in **Marahau** in the south and **Wainui Bay** in the north. For the most popular and more crowded **Coastal Track**, you should allow approximately five days (about 20 hours straight hiking; the longest stretch between Awaroa and Whariwharangi Hut takes about five hours). Cabins with up to 28 places to sleep can be found at regular intervals along the trail. Along the **Inland Track** there are considerably fewer cabins (approximately 28 hours of straight hiking; the longest stretch is just less than five hours between Wainui and Clifton via Bird's Cleaning). It holds true for both routes that overnight coupons must be acquired in advance at the DOC office. Even with coupons, there is no guarantee that you will have a spot to stay overnight. The huts are occupied on a "first come, first sleep" basis. It is wise to take a tent along on these routes throughout the year.

Ideal for those who want to hike the coastal track in just one direction, and for visitors who wish to get a feel of the national park on a day-outing, is the ferry boat service offered by Abel Tasman Enterprises (with a bus connection to and from Nelson). The ferry commences its daily service in the summer (end of September to beginning of June) at 9:00 a.m. from **Kaiteriteri** and travels up the coast with various stops during its three-hour cruise to **Totaranui** (arrival time is 12:15 p.m.). The return trip begins here, and on its return trip the ferry will stop at six coves. An ideal day-trip is to take the ferry to **Bark Bay** (arrival time 11 a.m.), hiking from here back to **Torrent Bay** (approximately 2.5 hours), where you can get aboard the ferry *Explorer* at 2:20 p.m. for the return trip.

Depending on your physical condition, these routes can be considerably extended. It is always recommended to take a picnic lunch along because there are no places to buy food – and the beach at Torrent Bay is just one of the perfect rest stops along the way.

The days of peace and quiet at Kaiteriteri are gradually vanishing. In December 1990, the Wilson family, owners of a shipping company which provides transportation to the national park, experienced this change first hand. One evening, thieves broke into one of their boats and completely cleaned it out. The Wilsons could hardly believe their eyes: "Two years ago something like this would have been unthinkable!" Even in Abel Tasman times have changed (unfortunately).

Most visitors start out at Kaiteriteri, although **Marahau** is the actual gateway to Abel Tasman National Park (and the last place for an overnight stay outside of the park). The 10-km long approach to the park begins at the beach at Kaiteriteri, for the most part over gravel roads, but ac-

companied the whole way by beautiful forest and splendid coastal scenery.

Whether at the track's head or end, a rest in the quaint garden of **Park Café** (open daily at 7 a.m.), located at the park's entrance, is a must. Its specialities, "blueberry milkshakes and blueberry crumble cake," prepared personally by its Czechoslovak owner Jirca, are absolutely delicious and must be sampled.

GOLDEN BAY

Most visitors return to Nelson from Abel Tasman National Park. Traveling north from here, you will experience more natural marvels. After passing the **Ngarua Caves** (guided tours daily from 10 a.m. to 4 p.m.), the narrow and time-consuming climb up the **Takaka Mountain** begins. The view from the mountain top is a reward for the strenuous ascent. On the horizon you will see Takaka, the spacious Golden Bay and the emerald Tasman mountains. From Takaka, road access to the northern part of the Abel

Tasman National Park is possible all the way to Totaranui. The **Abel Tasman Memorial** is located on this road.

An ideal spot from which to start trips is the tiny village of **Collingwood** (with a population of 120, 27 km from Takaka). A highway sign right in the middle of town reads "60 Ends." Behind the sign rampant green grows. People in Collingwood need not waste much breath instructing visitors which direction to take!

At first glance, Collingwood gives the impression of being at the end of the world. Even the limited business hours of the town's pub (12 noon to 2 p.m. and 5:30 to 8:30 p.m. – an accurate way of estimating the size of a local population in New Zealand) seems to confirm this suspicion.

Kiwis seldom go astray at Golden Bay. Collingwood has been off the beaten

Above: The sun casts a timid light on the summits of the Nelson Lakes National Park. Right: Giant ferns and rain forest line most of New Zealand's tracks.

track, at least up until now, and this has been good. Here you can go fishing, hiking and rafting in serene surroundings on the **Aorere River**, where a chapter of gold-rush fever lasting just three years was written in 1857.

A climb down to the **Te Anaroa Caves** can be undertaken all alone, or you might want to accompany Jock, the postman, as he distributes his mail for the next five hours each day during the week. (Information can be obtained at the post office, cost NZ$ 25).

Besides the activities mentioned above, you can also take a soothing drink out of the crystal-clear waters of **Pupu Springs** or enjoy the **Wharariki Beach,** one of the most beautiful in the Golden Bay area. **Cape Farewell** is also close by. Collingwood is a wonderful spot for families vacationing with children.

The four-wheel-drive trip to **Farewell Spit** is a must. Along a stretch of 26 km, sand dunes and beaches line the way to the lighthouse at the end of the narrow headland.

HEAPHY TRACK

A trail not far from Collingwood is becoming an alternative to the overcrowded Abel Tasman National Park. Whoever wishes to find solitude for a few days in pristine surroundings will surely be satisfied on the **Heaphy Track**. The 77 km long track, taking four to six days, starts out through an almost untouched primeval landscape. It continues along the rugged west coast, and discloses scenery that is still thoroughly untamed. Altogether, there are ten huts along the way (each with 20 to 40 places to sleep). The longest stretch of track without overnight accommodations lies between **Mackay** and **Lewis Hut**, and is approximately 12 km long.

You may run into difficulties concerning your arrival or departure regardless of the direction you go on Heaphy Track. Although there are telephone booths in **Brown Hut** (Collingwood side) and in **Kohaihai Shelter** (Karamea side), you should definitely make travel arrangements in advance.

Those who wish to return to Nelson on foot can start at Little Wanganui (20 km south of Karamea) on the **Wangapeka Track.** It is about 50 km long and runs through the hilly and thus more difficult terrain of **Northwest Nelson State Forest Park.** 13 huts offer overnight accommodations along the trail. One of them is located near **Little Wanganui Saddle.** This is the highest point along the track, with an elevation of 1087 m, and offers a wonderful panoramic view. Moreover, you can rest up here from the strenuous climb. The track ends in the small town of **Wangapeka**. From Wangapeka, you can reach **Tapawere** on Highway 61 – usually by hitch-hiking.

This return hike is, of course, not everyone's cup of tea. Therefore, Heaphy Track ends for most hikers with a 100 km long drive on Highway 67 from Karamea to Westport.

In 1861, the first homes of the shopkeepers who supplied goods and wares to the gold diggers in nearby Buller Gorge were built in **Westport.** The golden days are long gone. Years later, coal was discovered here and, thereafter, the city was nicknamed Coaltown. Its seaport is no longer of great significance. The unemployment rate among the *Coasters* is quite high. New Zealand's lovely, remote west coast is left without many economic perspectives, although tourism does give a shimmer of hope. This is where once the gold rushers searched for their fortunes; you can now speed through **Buller Gorge** on jet boats (Buller Adventure Center on Hwy 6), or take an underground trip to **Black Water Rafting**. Even those traveling on Highway 6 at a comfortable pace will enjoy the scenery between wooded hillsides and valleys – after all, Buller Gorge is among the most untamed valleys in New Zealand. The area is teeming with reminders of the days of the gold rush; for example, in the town of **Berlins** with its beautiful historical hotel; or in **Lyell**, where a short stroll will take you past the weather-beaten relics of the gold rush and through the old cemetery.

Murchison and its surrounding area again brings to mind how young New Zealand's soil actually is. In 1929, an earthquake shook the area and cost a total of 17 lives. Even today, the region is still revisited by minor tremors. At **Kawatiri**, 35 km from Murchison, the road splits off in two directions. Highway 6 leads further north, and until you can order a cup of fresh coffee in one of the cafés along Nelson's Trafalgar Street, there are almost another 100 km to travel. On the other hand, it's only 25 km to **St. Arnaud**, the entrance to Nelson Lakes National Park (Highway 63 eastbound).

NELSON LAKES NATIONAL PARK

Two large glacier lakes surrounded by mountains and dark green beech trees are the jewels of this enchanting park. It takes about 1.5 hours to drive here from Nelson. The landscape is typical of South Island's highland.

With the exception of summer vacation, **Nelson Lakes National Park** is still pleasantly uncrowded, and the numerous tracks invite the visitor to take day-hikes or adventure tours lasting several days.

The area around **Lake Rotoiti** has been built up the most for tourism. It has good camp sites, a few shops and stores, motels and the park headquarters. The larger and more remote **Lake Rotoroa**, situated a short distance to the west, also offers the same beautiful scenery.

On the **Travers-Sabine Track,** you will experience a magnificent hike taking four to five days. The trail begins at the upper shore of Lake Rotoiti, leads up to **Travers River Valley**, across the mountain saddle and along the Sabine River to Lake Rotoroa. This track, with its woodlands of beech and podocarpus

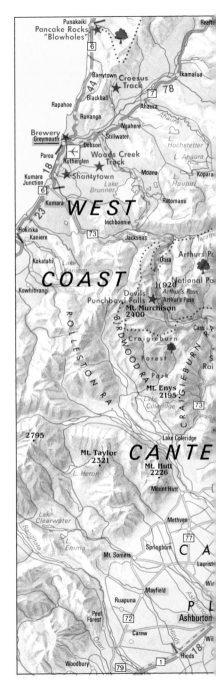

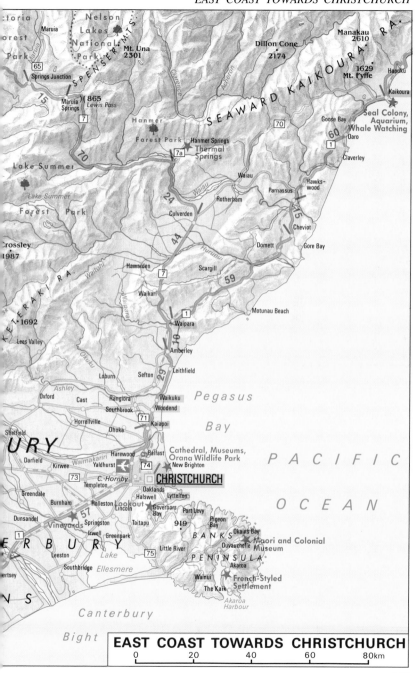

Victoria Forest Park

Maruia

Nelson Lakes National Park

SPENSER MTS.

Mt. Una 2301

Dillon Cone 2174

Manakau 2610

SEAWARD KAIKOURA RA.

Hapuku

1629 Mt. Fyffe

Kaikoura

65

Springs Junction

15

Maruia Springs

865 Lewis Pass

7

Hanmer

Forest Park

Hanmer Springs

7a Thermal Springs

70

Goose Bay

60

Daro

1

Seal Colony, Aquarium, Whale Watching

Claverley

70

Lake Summer

Lake Summer

Forest Park

Clarence

Acheron

Waiau

Waiau

Parnassus

Hawks-wood

Rotherham

Claverley

24

Crossley 1987

KET ERA KIRA RA.

1692

Lees Valley

Culverden

44

Hurunui

Cheviot

Domett

Gore Bay

Walton

Hawarden

7

Scargill

59

Oxford

Cast

Waipara

Waitohi

Waikari

Motunau Beach

1

Waipara

Okuku

Loburn

Sefton

Leithfield

Amberley

29

Pegasus

Ashley

Rangiora

Waikuku

Woodend

Southbrook

Horrellville

Ohoka

71

Kaiapoi

Bay

Sheffield

BURY

Darfield

Kirwee

Waimakariri

Harewood

Yaldhurst

Belfast

73

C. Hornby

74

Cathedral, Museums, Orana Wildlife Park

New Brighton

PACIFIC

Greendale

Burnham

Rolleston

Templeton

CHRISTCHURCH

Oaklands

Halswell

Lyttelton

OCEAN

Dunsandel

57

Springston

Lincoln

Lookout

Governors Bay

Port Levy

Pigeon Bay

Vineyards

Irwell

Greenpark

Taitapu

919

Okains Bay

Maori and Colonial Museum

Leeston

Southbridge

75

Little River

Duvauchelle

Akaroa

CANTERBURY

Lake Ellesmere

BANKS

PENINSULA

French-Styled Settlement

ertsey

Wainui

The Kaik

Akaroa Harbour

Canterbury

NS

Bight

EAST COAST TOWARDS CHRISTCHURCH

0   20   40   60   80km

145

trees, requires some alpine experience, especially around the mountain saddle. From the various valleys you can go on shorter hikes and walks.

The largest river in the northern part of South Island has its source in Nelson Lakes National Park. **Buller River** flows from Lake Rotoiti to the west coast and into the Tasman Sea. The great alpine rift runs straight through the center of the park from west to east. If you would like to try your hand at trout fishing in one of these lakes or adjoining rivers, get out your fishing pole as soon as possible. Information and fishing licenses can be obtained at park headquarters. Do not forget insect repellent. Swarms of sandflies could make your evenings miserable.

If you have already visited Nelson, or if you want to continue further along the east coast to Kaikoura and Christchurch, it is recommended to travel to Blenheim (Highway 63, approximately 100 km) from St. Arnaud and Nelson Lakes National Park.

Heading South from Picton to Christchurch

You will probably arrive with the ferry in **Picton**. Right at the harbor there is a tourist information center where all necessary instructions for further travel south on Highway 1 can be picked up.

It is a 28 km stretch to **Blenheim**, which usually can be covered without any stops. In 1857, the first sheep were introduced to Blenheim, creating the economic basis for the next decades. Today, the entire area is also known for its excellent wine.

Blenheim itself has little to offer. However, the surrounding area covered with extensive vineyards is lovely. One acitivity consists in scouting out the wine-growing estates along the **Marlborough**

Right: A whale dives with the snow-covered peaks of the Kaikoura in the background.

Wine Trail. Merlen Wines, Corbans and Hunter's all lie east of the town's center on Rapaura Road (towards Nelson, Highway 6). Also located in the vicinity are the wineries Cellie Le Brun, Cloudy Bay, Te Whare Ra and Highfield. Despite the tremendous differences in wine taste, all of the estates have one thing in common: They offer visitors vineyard tours and wine-tasting.

An alternative tour to the Marlborough Wine Trail is a visit at **Montana Wines** (directly on Highway 1 on the right-hand side) on the way to Kaikoura. Montana Wines was established in 1973 and has become the largest wine estate in New Zealand in the meantime. It offers tours on the hour from 10 a.m. to 3 p.m. (closed Sundays), as well as wine-tasting and selling.

It makes sense to buy several bottles of wine because in a few hours you might round off a perfect dinner with them. But first, continue on to **Seddon**. On the way you will pass by the colonial **Oak Tree Cottage**, about 1 km from the main road with a small picnic area; and a short distance further on the left side, **Lake Grassmere**. This lake is not especially suited for swimming since salt is extracted on an area of approximately 700 hectares in size. The region's climatic assets are well utilized: The sun and the steady wind contribute to rapid evaporation of the water. What remains is called "white gold." Long ago, the Maori named the lake *Kaparatehau*, meaning "water churned by the wind."

On the right side, you now have an increasingly clear view of the mountains belonging to the two Kaikoura mountain ranges. The snow-covered **Mount Tapuaenuku** towers 2885 m high in the Inland Range. **Mount Manakau's** elevation is 2610 m. It is part of the **Seaward Range**. Huge flocks of sheep graze on the vast areas of this mountainous countryside. After traveling another 60 km, you will again reach the coast at **Wharanui**,

where **St. Oswald's Anglican Church** is a sight to see (founded in 1927). From this point on, the coves and bays are worth a stop. There is also a special attraction which has given the coastline leading up to Kaikoura its name. *Kaikoura* means "the place where crayfish is eaten" in the language of the Maori, and no visitor should ignore the tip. This ocean specialty (a crayfish is similar to a lobster) is offered at numerous stands for the next 50 km along the highway. It goes without saying that freshness and quality are the best anywhere. Here is where we come back to that perfect dinner previously mentioned. The crayfish along with a bottle of fine wine from a Marlborough province winery can be enjoyed together with a visit to **Kaikoura**.

KAIKOURA

For many years, this town, today with a population of about 3000, was apparently away from the beaten track for tourists. Hardly anyone turned off Highway 1

to explore this area on the tiny peninsula with its natural simplicity and beautiful scenery. In the meantime whales have done their part to make Kaikoura more attractive, thus drawing tourists. Nowhere else in the world do huge sperm whales, orcas and dolphins come so close to the coast. The sperm whale feels most at home at a depth of 2000 m and the shoreline at Kaikoura drops off to this depth right beyond the harbor.

Several companies offer whale-watching tours here. However, the days when rubber rafts daringly approached the whales almost within reach are now gone. Today, the Department of Conservation has declared a safety zone of 300 m to protect the sensitive animals. A guarantee that a whale or dolphin is actually sighted on these three-hour tours cannot be given (departures depend on the season and tides). Many visitors have returned from the water rather disappointed. A "swim with the dolphins" expedition allows to to quite literally swim with these ocean mammals.

climb up to the cliffs at **Whalers Bay** for the early return trip (two hours long).

Northwest of Kaikoura, in **Mount Fyffe State Forest**, is another interesting area for hiking and enjoying the wonders of nature. Fyffe Peak, at a height of 1602 m, can be climbed via two routes. Both begin close to the **Hinau Picnic Area**; however, the climb up **Goldmine Creek** and **Fenceline** is recommended. For a round-trip tour (up the mountain at Gold-mine Creek and down via the road), you will need about six hours. For those hikers who wish to stay overnight, Mount Fyffe Hut at Tarn Saddle offers six simple places to sleep.

Despite the influence of tourism, Kaik-oura itself has kept its small town atmos-phere – with a typical shopping street, a shoreline promenade and a sandy beach. There are not many activities to partici-pate in, except on the weekend if you are an avid movie-goer. The local cinema is unique. Its seats, old and almost of his-torical value, have been collected from movie theaters all over New Zealand (open Friday through Sunday).

It is hard to lose track of things in Kaikoura. On the other hand, the town can be enjoyed from viewpoints ac-cessible via the **Scarborough Terrace**. The spectacular, colorful view here is not easy to relinquish!

While traveling south for the next few kilometers, numerous coves will tempt you to stop. The coarse, sandy beaches with high surf are, however, less suitable for swimming. After covering another 134 km, you will arrive at **Waipara**. Besides St. Paul's Church, there is little to see here. More interesting is a short jaunt on Highway 7 to **Hanmer State Forest Park** (68 km).

In no other park in the country are there so many different species of trees. They can best be discovered and admired along the **Conical Hill**, **Mount Isobel** and **Waterfall Tracks**. Not only is the coniferous forest enticing, but also the

Consolation, in this case, can be found on land since Kaikoura has a few other interesting attractions. The **Peninsula Walk** runs along two different routes – the shoreline walk and the cliff walk. The walks can be started at **South Bay** or from the parking lot at **Point Kean**. The shoreline route will take about 2.5 hours. Keep the high and low tides in mind since the starting place at Point Kean is under-water at high tide and not passable. The shoreline walk takes you along the coast, and lively seals and seabird colonies can be observed.

The 1.5 hour cliff walk guides you past fantastic viewpoints rich in contrast, overlooking the ocean with majestic, snow-covered mountains on the opposite side. An ideal combination of the two trails would be to start at Point Kean along the coast and then take the narrow

Above: The ocean has intricately carved the coast near Kaikoura. Right: Friendly faces on the way to Christchurch.

148

Hanmer Springs. Although these thermal waters were discovered by William Jones, they were named after the settler Thomas Hanmer. The springs are known to ease the pain of chronic arthritis and also some skin disorders, but even "healthy" visitors enjoy a dip in the warm, relaxing waters just for the sake of it. Hanmer Springs (with three thermal pools among other attractions) is open for the general public daily between 10 a.m. and 8 p.m. (entrance fee: NZ$ 3). In the wintertime, the nearby **Amuri Ski Field** opens up another outdoor alternative.

Traveling further westward, you come across **Lewis Pass** at an elevation of 865 m and **Springs Junction** on the way to **Reefton** (129 km) in the direction of the west coast near Greymouth. This link across the northern part of the Southern Alps is chosen by very few travelers. Most tourists continue their trip south via Hwy. 1 at Waipara. The vast landscape of the **Canterbury Plains** stretches out ahead. This area is one of the most fertile farming and grazing regions in the country.

Waikuku, **Woodend** and **Kaiapoi** all have something in common – they are located on **Pegasus Bay**. Within a few minutes walk, you can reach long, wide, sandy beaches (caution is called for since the beaches are not all patrolled). These beaches are guaranteed to be deserted except during holiday and vacation periods.

Christchurch, 20 kilometers away and the capital of Canterbury Province, has a population of approximately 300,000; it is not only the economical and political center of South Island, but also the third-largest city in the entire country.

Caution is recommended because the city indeed consists of a confusing system of one-way-streets that makes driving difficult. Arriving in downtown Christchurch from the north, follow Cranford and Sherborne Streets, and then turn right onto Bealey Avenue. Colombo Street begins a few hundred meters up Bealey Avenue to the left. Colombo Street will take you to Cathedral Square, leading to the heart of Christchurch.

149

MARLBOROUGH SOUNDS
NELSON
ABEL TASMAN NATIONAL PARK
THE EAST COAST

Accommodation

BLENHEIM: *LUXURY:* **Ugbrooke Country House**, Ugbrooke, R.D.4, Tel: 03-5757259 (historic flair; turn off Highway 1, turn left in Dashwood; 26 km south of Blenheim).
MODERATE: **Blenheim Motel**, 81 Main St., Tel: 03-5780559.
BUDGET: **Blenheim Motor Camp**, 27 Budge St., Tel: 03-5787419.
COLLINGWOOD: *MODERATE:* **Collingwood Motel**, Haven Rd., Tel: 03-5248224.
BUDGET: **Collingwood Motor Camp**, Tel: 03-5248149. **Pakawau Beach Camp**, Tel: 03-5248327 (12 km to the north).
HANMER SPRINGS: *LUXURY:* **Alpine Spa Lodge**, corner Harrogate and Amuri Dr., Tel: 03-3157311.
MODERATE: **Percival**, Main Rd., Tel: 03-3157062. **The Chalets**, Jacks Pass Rd., Tel: 03-3157097.
HAVELOCK: *MODERATE:* **Garden Motel**, 71 Main Rd., Tel: 03-5742387.
BUDGET: **Rutherford Youth Hostel**, 46 Main Rd., Tel: 03-5742104.
KAIKOURA: *MODERATE:* **Kaikoura Motel**, 11-15 Beach Rd., Tel: 03-3195999. **Panorama Motel**, 266 The Esplanade, Tel: 03-3195053. *BUDGET:* **The White House Backpackers**, 146 The Esplanade, Tel: 03-3195916 (Owner Ashley King knows the area well and gives valuable tips). **Youth Hostel**, 270 The Esplanade, Tel: 03-3195931.
KAITERITERI: *LUXURY:* **Kimi Ora**, Tel: 03-5278027 (bungalows; with vegetarian restaurant).
MODERATE: **Torlesse Coastal Motel**, Rowling Rd., Little Kaiteriteri, Motueka, Tel: 03-5278063. **Farm Cottage Holiday**, Kairuru, 20 minutes from Kaiteriteri, Tel: 03-5288091 (farm-holidays).
BUDGET: **Kaiteriteri Sunbelt**, Martins Farm Road, Tel: 03-5278123. **Kaiteriteri Beach Motor Camp**, Tel: 03-5278010 (central; on the beach, next to the Abel Tasman Ferry).
KARAMEA: *MODERATE:* **Karamea Township Motel**, Wharf St., Tel: 03-7826838. **Little Wanganui Hotel**, Last Resort, Waverly St., Tel: 03-7826617 (18 km to the south of Karamea).
BUDGET: **Karamea Holiday Park**, Tel: 03-7826758.
MOTUEKA: *LUXURY:* **Motueka Garden Motel**, 71 King Edward St., Tel: 03-5289299.
MODERATE: **Abel Tasman Motor Inn**, 45 High St., Tel: 03-5286688. *BUDGET:* **The White**

Elephant Backpacker, 55 Whakarewa St., Tel: 03-5286208.
MURCHISON: *LUXURY:* **Moonlight Lodge**, S.H.65, Maruia Valley, Tel: 03-5239323 (32 km to the south). *MODERATE:* **Mataki Motel**, Hotham St., Tel: 03- 5239088. *BUDGET:* **Riverview Holiday Park**, Box 99, Tel: 03-5239571.
NELSON: *LUXURY:* **Cambria House**, 7 Cambria St., Tel: 03-5484681 (one of the nicest accommodations in Nelson, with only four rooms).
MODERATE: **Anchor Lodge**, 7 Roto St., Tahunanui, Tel: 03-5486007. **Leisure Lodge Motor Inn**, 40 Waimea Rd., Tel: 03-5482089. *BUDGET:* **Backpackers Beach Hostel**, 80 Tahunanui Drive, Tel: 03-5486817. **Tasman Towers**, 10 Weka St., Tel:.03-5487950. **Paradiso**, 42 Weka Street, Tel: 03-5488817 (the ultimate backpacker with swimming pool and sauna,). **Richmond Holiday Park**, 29 Gladstone Rd., Tel: 03-5447323.
PICTON: *LUXURY:* **The Picton Whalers Inn**, Waikawa Rd., Tel: 03-5737002.
MODERATE: **Aldan Lodge Motel**, 86 Wellington St., Tel: 03-5736833. **Broadway Motel,** 113 High St., Tel: 03-5736563. *BUDGET:* **Bavarian Lodge**, 42 Auckland St., Tel/Fax: 03-5736536 (expect fresh-baked bread and cakes, the owners, Gerhard and Hanni, are from Bavaria). **Blue Anchor Holiday Park**, 70-78 Waikawa Rd., Tel: 03-5737212. **Sail-on-Inn Backpackers**, 34 Auckland St., Tel: 03-5736598. **The Lazy Fish**, Tel: 03-5736055 (in the Marlborough Sounds near Dieffenbach, only acesible by boat).
ST. ARNAUD: *LUXURY:* **Alpine Lodge Rotoiti**, Private Bag, Tel: 03-5211868 (accommodation for backpackers also offered at reasonable prices).
BUDGET: **Nelson Lakes National Park Camp,** West Bay, Tel: 03-5211806 (reservations through the park-ranger from 8 a.m.–5 p.m.).
TAKAKA: *MODERATE:* **Golden Bay Motel**, Commercial St., Tel: 03-5259428. *BUDGET:* **Shady Rest**, 141 Commercial St.; **Pohara Beach Camp**, Tel: 03-5259500 (9 km to the east).
WESTPORT: (see information on the west coast).
WOODEND: *MODERATE:* **Wayside Motel**, 79 Main North Rd., Tel: 03-3127616.

Restaurants

KAITERITERI: **Park Café**, Tel: 03-5278158 (open daily from 7 a.m.; at the entrance to the Abel Tasman National Park).
MOTUEKA: Old Cederman House, 4 km north of Motueka on the road to Kaiteriteri, Tel: 03-5289276. Built ca. 1870 in Victorian style; tea and snacks in a lovely garden. **Gothic Gourmet**, 208 High St., Tel: 03-5286699 (New Zealand specialties are served in a renovated church).

NELSON: Brown House, 52 Rutherford St., Tel: 03-5489039 (New Zealand specialities served until 6 p.m., dining with candlelight in a 110-year-old cottage; closed Mondays). **Hitching Post**, 145 Bridge St., Tel: 03-5487374 (salads, pizza, steaks). **Trailways Restaurant**, 66 Trafalgar St., Tel: 03-5487049 (fish and lamb dishes). Numerous cafés and restaurants along Bridge St.

Museums
KAIKOURA: **Aquarium**, The Esplanade (open daily; free admission).
NELSON: Provincal Museum, Isle Park, Stoke, Tel: 03-5479740 (Tuesdays–Fridays 10 a.m.–4 p.m.; Saturdays, Sundays and public holidays 2–5 p.m.; history of the province Nelson Bays; large historic photo-collection).
PICTON: The three-master *Edwin Fox* lying at dock in the harbor can be visited daily from 8:30 a.m., 4 NZ$

Tips and Trips
Abel Tasman National Park: Guided four-day hiking-tours with comfortable accommodation: Abel Tasman National Park Enterprises, Motueka 3, 234 High St., Tel: 03-5287801. Canoeing-trips along the coast, charter boats and guided tours from Abel Tasman Kayaks, Marahau, Tel: 03-5278022.
Car Rental: Hardy Cars, used cars and caravans, Tel: 03-5481681, Fax: 03-5481581.
Collingwood: Participate in delivering the mail on the *Scenic Mail Run:* Info: Jock and Jo Lill, Tel: 03-5248188.
Farewell Spit and Aorere Valley: Information and tours in the Golden Bay area: Collingwood Safari Tours, Tasman St., P.O. Box 15, Collingwood, Tel: 03-5248257 and 5248313.
Heaphy Track Aerotaxi: This private airline operates flights between Karamea – Collingwood – Nelson. Hikers can arrange to be picked up at the end of the track for air transport to their departure points (for 3 passengers 220–292 NZ$ per flight).
Kaikoura: Whale Watch, Kaikoura Railway Station, Tel: 03-3195045 and Nature Watch Charters, 90 The Esplanade, Tel: 03-3195662 are the only licensed agencies offering whale-watching. Various firms offer diving-trips (with dolphins) as well as bird- and seal-watching. Dolphin Encounter, 58 West End, Tel: 03-3196777
Motueka: Trips along the *Wine and Craft Trail* between December 1 and March 31 daily: Pretty's Tours, Tel: 03-5289480.
Nelson: Handicraft products are on sale at Craft Habitat (at the Waimea Pottery; Richmond By-Pass, Tel: 03-5447481; weekdays 9 a.m.–5 p.m.; Sat 10 a.m.–4 p.m. Nightlife in Nelson: The Cactus Club,

120 Bridge St; Shakespeare, 89 Hardy St. or Club Horatios, 23 Halifax St.
Sailing: Those wishing to explore the area around the Abel Tasman National Park by sea can charter a boat from Kaiteriteri Yacht Charters, Dehra Doon Rd., Tel: 03-5286274. Similar offers in Pohara.

Festivals / Special Events
MOTUEKA: The people of Golden Bay hold their riotous *Hop and Beer Festival* in Riwaka (Sports Ground) at the beginning of January.
NELSON: At the beginning of March, all culinary delights of the province Nelson Bays are on display at the *Taste Nelson Festival* in Founders Park. Every Saturday a colorful *Vegetable- and Flea-Market* takes place in the city center.
WESTPORT: The beginning of the fishing-season is celebrated in the middle of October with the *Whitebait Festival.*

Tourist Information
ABEL TASMAN NATIONAL PARK: Visitor Centre, 406 High St., Motueka, Tel: 03-5289117 or in Totaranui, 1 Commercial St., Takaka, Tel: 03-5258026 or in Marahau.
BLENHEIM: Information Centre, Queen St., Tel: 03-5789904 (weekdays 9 a.m.–5 p.m.; add. opening on Saturday mornings in summer).
HANMER SPRINGS: Hanmer Springs Business and District Promotion Association, Conical Hill Road, Tel: 03-3157128 (weekdays from 9 a.m.–5:30 p.m.; Saturdays from 9 a.m.–1 p.m.).
Hanmer Forest Park: Information Centre, Jollies Pass Road, Tel: 03-3157128.
KAIKOURA: Information Centre, The Esplanade (opposite Memorial Gardens), Tel: 03-3195641 (Mondays–Fridays 9 a.m.–5 p.m.).
MARLBOROUGH SOUNDS MARITIME PARK: Department of Conservation (DOC), opposite the train station, Picton, Tel: 03-5737582, or **Momorangi Bay Motor Camp**, Queen Charlotte Sound, Tel: 03-5737865.
MOTUEKA: Visitor Information, 236 High Street, Tel: 03-5286543.
NELSON: Nelson Regional Promotions Office, corner Trafalgar and Halifax Street, Tel: 03-5482302, (daily 9 a.m.–5 p.m.).
NELSON LAKES NATIONAL PARK: Park Headquarters, View Rd., St. Arnaud, Tel: 03-5211806. **PICTON: Marlborough Promotions Information Centre**, Picton Foreshore, Tel: 03-5737513 (weekdays 9 a.m.–4 p.m.; weekends, public holidays 10 a.m.–3 p.m.).
TAKAKA: Golden Bay Information Centre, Commercial St., Tel: 03-5259136 (daily Dec–Apr 9 a.m.–5 p.m.; May–Nov 10 a.m.–4 p.m.).

SOUTH
ISLAND

Nelson
Nelson
Marlborough
Wellington

West
Coast
Canterbury
Christchurch

Timaru

Southland
Dunedin

Invercargill

Stewart I.

MAGICAL CENTER
OF THE SOUTH

CHRISTCHURCH
BANKS PENINSULA

CHRISTCHURCH

If the tricolored French flag were to wave above **Christchurch** today and the residents of the city spoke fluent French, not a single *Kiwi* could rightly complain. After all, for a many years the British were reluctant to settle this region. In the first place, they were frightened off over disputes regarding land rights with the Maori. In contrast, the French quickly took the matter into their own hands. In 1839, the Frenchman Captain Jean Langlois decided to settle courageous and hardy countrymen and countrywomen on the Banks Peninsula. However, he had made his plans without consulting his European neighbors. Suddenly, the reluctant British felt that their Union Jack should fly above this part of New Zealand's South Island and made reference to the newly-signed Treaty of Waitangi to underscore their intentions.

One countryside and two interested parties – a delicate situation had arisen and had to be reckoned with. The Maori, true "owners" of the land, had their rights and demands more or less ignored by

Preceding pages: Christchurchers socialize on the square in front of the cathedral. Left: Towncrier Stephen is a living monument in Christchurch.

both the French and British. In this one respect, the two European nations were very much alike. They therefore put up with each other during the first few years, for better or worse.

The French ended their colonial presence in New Zealand in 1849, and thereby paved the way for British settlement of the region. From that point on, this part of New Zealand became more British than Great Britain itself. A result of this distinctive characteristic is that Christchurch uses the slogan "A Touch of English" to promote its prestige. The cliché expresses it even more clearly – Christchurch is regarded as the most British city outside of Great Britain.

At least the downtown area around the cathedral confirms this reputation. This area of town was transformed into a pedestrian zone a number of years ago, and it is the ideal spot to start an adventurous exploration of Christchurch. Cathedral Square is also the undisputed center of interest in the city.

Shortly after the city's founding on December 16, 1850, **Cathedral Square** already gained significance. In 1879, laws were passed in the place where today stamps are sold across the counter. The government buildings on the west side of the square have relinquished their functions and now serve as the city's post

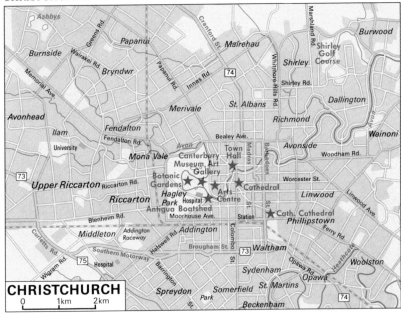

office. Since 1881, the opposite side of the square has also achieved a certain importance. After a construction period of 16 years, the **Christchurch Cathedral** was finally completed. Its bell tower reaches 65.5 m into the heavens. 133 steps lead up to a fantastic panoramic view of the city and, on a clear day, of the snow-covered Southern Alps.

The Wizard

For many foreign visitors, the main attraction of the city can be found in front of the Cathedral. "It" stands on two legs: **The Wizard**. Many local residents have doubts as to the sanity of this self-declared magician. His identity as well as his speeches are extremely controversial. For Christchurch's tourism, The Wizard is worth more than his weight in gold. The city is the only one in the world that can claim its own official magician. The

Right: "The Wizard" proclaims truths in various ous shades in front of the cathedral.

156

Union of New Zealand Art Galleries has declared him a "living work of art." The Wizard, whose name is Ian, and who was born in Australia, tries to more than live up to this honorable distinction. He has founded his own political party, maintains a private army (size and significance has not yet been disclosed), and pays no taxes, as you might expect. There is a very thin line between truth and legend in the person of the Wizard.

Weekdays around 1 p.m., the Wizard will scold, scoff, curse and philosophize about heaven and earth, of which he has his very own point of view. His map shows the world upside-down. There is no guarantee that you will meet up with the entertaining Wizard in his white or black priest robes. If he does not show up, you should start your tour of the city because the Wizard look-a-likes that are romping around the square cannot compare in the least to the original.

The best time to visit the square is definitely midday. In the summer, live music, art activities and snack stands are spread

out across it. However, this place should be avoided at night. An increasing number of assaults on tourists and passers-by has been registered in 1991.

Parks and Gardens, Avon River and Arts Centre

Worcester Street begins behind the statue of John Robert Godley. The statue was molded out of Russian cannonballs captured in Sebastopol and is dedicated to the city founder. A touch of Japan surrounds the store windows of the numerous duty-free shops – because Christchurch is a must for Japanese tourists – and many come here to get married in one of the charmingly romantic churches. The next statue you come across is standing on **Oxford Terrace.** It is dedicated to the Antarctic explorer Robert Falcon Scott. Scott was the second person to reach the South Pole and is a prime illustration of the close relationship that exists between Christchurch and the Polar Sea. A closer look at this affinity

will be discussed later. First priority on the program is a glance at the abundance of nature. As you will readily see, taking a walk through Christchurch demonstrates that it rightly deserves its nickname, the Garden City.

The path along the **Avon River** going upstream leads under old, stately trees. The **Bridge of Remembrance** is dedicated to those who died in World War I. Right behind the bridge, the unexciting business district joins Cashel and High Streets (partially a pedestrian zone). It is more pleasant to follow the Avon River further upstream. It does not matter which side of the river you choose to stroll along (on the left you will find **St Michael's Church**, completed in 1872, and the historical building belonging to the Pegasus Press on 14 Oxford Terrace; on the right you can enjoy the peace and quiet of the promenade). The most important thing is to finally arrive at the **Antigua Boatsheds.** Since 1882, watersports fans started out from here on short, relaxing canoe rides on the Avon River,

157

adding to that typical English feeling. The 26.1 km long river, which the Maori called *otakaro*, meaning "place to play," and which the white settlers called *Shakespeare*, is passable in just one direction only on these trips. The first half of the canoe trip starts out going upstream because the boat renters have learned from their negative experience that many a canoeist with a weak constitution could not make the return trip going upstream (rentals daily from 9:30 a.m. to 4 p.m.).

When returning from a walk or canoe trip, the best place to relax and recuperate is at **Le Café**, located in the Arts Centre. The café is also a popular meeting place for parents who wish to check up on their children's college achievements since Christ's College is located across the way. Between meat pies and fruit cake, they can casually keep an eye on the college activities which are meant to prepare their children for life.

The University of Canterbury was housed in the buildings of the present day **Arts Centre** between 1876 and 1973. Only the laboratory of the research scientist Sir Ernest Rutherford (specialist in the field of atomic fission and Nobel prize winner in chemistry in 1909) gives witness to the days when the buildings served as an institute of higher learning. Today, art, artists and culinary kitchens have moved in. In more than 150 workshops, galleries, studios and restaurants, a dynamic scene has established itself, which especially comes to life on the weekend.

Every Saturday and Sunday between 10 a.m. and 4 p.m., more than 100 stands present a colorful variety of items: leather goods, woodwork, wool sweaters, glass art, jewelry and silver work, silk paintings and design furniture. In addition, there is a vast selection of the multicultural and international cuisine available in the ethnic melting pot that is New Zealand.

At 12 noon another of Christchurch's living "monuments" takes the floor. Stephen Symens, Esquire, has been employed since 1989 as the official **Towncrier**; with his British looks, he does not have to emphasise the fact that his roots are on "the island."

In the evening, there is no question as to what to see and do. If you wish to experience something quite different in Christchurch, then you should stop in at **Dux de Lux** at least once. Dux de Lux is a mixture of vegetarian restaurant, rustic pub with its own home-brewed beer, and contemporary insider club (in the summer there is seating outside in the beer garden).

Across the street from the Arts Centre and on the other side of Rolleston Avenue, you meet up again with reminders of the Antarctic. Behind the neo-Gothic façade of **Canterbury Museum**, one of the best Antarctic exhibits in the world is exhibited (Hall of Antarctic Discovery). This is not at all surprising, since Christchurch is still the departure point for many expeditions to the Polar Sea. The first curator of the museum, in 1870, was Sir Julius von Haast, who made a name for himself as a geologist exploring and surveying South Island. Visitors who travel from Queenstown along the west coast will come across his name again. A 563 m high pass in that region carries his name. Adjacent to the back side of the Canterbury Museum is the **McDougall Art Gallery**, exhibiting a colorful variety of international paintings and sculptures.

After this intense encounter with culture and history, it is time for a walk through the nearby **Botanical Garden** for some relaxation in natural surroundings. Founded in 1863, the botanical garden covers an area of 30 hectares along the Avon River, and is an inviting place for peaceful strolls among aged trees and cultivated flower beds. This garden is just

Right: Late afternoon mood on the steps of Christchurch Cathedral.

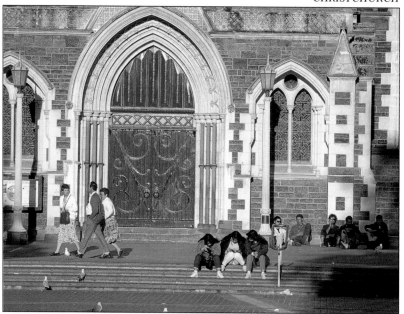

a part of the green belt of the city. An El Dorado for joggers and cyclists is **Hagley Park**, next to the botanical garden to the west. Many important cricket matches, New Zealand's number one sport, have been played out on the green at Hagley Oval. After victories, especially when they are against Australia and England (arch-rivals on the cricket field), half of the country is in turmoil, and even the Prime Minister gets involved by inviting the heroic team to an official reception.

Now it is back to the old part of the city, specifically to **Rolleston Avenue**. If you walk further on towards the north, within a few meters you will reach **Christ's College**, which was mentioned earlier. This all-men's private school is a further example of the English architecture typical in the city. It is worthwhile to take a quick look behind the walls of the college and get a feel of the atmosphere. Afterwards, it is best to turn right onto Armagh Street, passing by the **Cranmer Club** built in 1864 and located on a square with the same name. A bit later,

on the right side of the street, you will run into the **Canterbury Provincial Government** building complex on Durham Street. The buildings are among the most beautiful neo-Gothic constructions in New Zealand (1859 – 1865).

A bridge spans the Avon River and leads to **Victoria Square**, the second most central spot in Christchurch. Here you will find a statue of Queen Victoria, as well as one of James Cook. The municipal authorities of Christchurch are especially proud of their **Town Hall**, located on the other side of the Avon River. Its official opening took place in 1972. Tours of the town hall are offered, but visitors will not miss much if they limit themselves to a photograph of the unique fountain in front of the building.

If a glance at the nearby flower clock reveals that you have already spent too much time dreaming along the river and visiting the Arts Centre, don't worry. The end of the city tour is within sight.

There are also other interesting places and sights worth seeing outside the city.

The Catholic answer to the Anglican Christchurch Cathedral is the **Cathedral of the Blessed Sacrament**, located on Barbados Street. It was built at the beginning of the 20th century, and at least its external appearance can hold its own when compared to the more famous church at the center of the city. On the other hand, the small church **St. Barnabas** in the suburb of Fendalton is more romantic than either of them.

The **Ferrymead Historic Park** opened its doors on a historical site indeed. The first steam-engine powered train was driven here in 1863. It is, therefore, not surprising that everything in this fascinating museum today revolves around technology and transportation. You will find more peace and quiet in a beautiful part of the city called **Mona Vale.** Here you can also see the Avon River from its best side.

Above: An idyllic spot on the banks of the Avon River in the middle of the city. Right: The Banks Peninsula is worth a visit.

For those who wish to turn their backs on Christchurch for a short time, there are two worthwhile stops quite nearby. South of a section of the city called **Cashmere**, the Dyers Pass Road ascends to **Victoria Park** and continues up the hill where the **Sign of the Takahe** (Hackthorne Road) presents itself in an unexpected medieval architectural style. Moreover, a stop here is rewarding since a good restaurant is modestly concealed behind the walls, which were completed in the middle of this century. Catering to more simple culinary tastes is the **Sign of the Kiwi.** From this 332 m high lookout, you have a wide panoramic view of Christchurch and parts of the Canterbury Plains.

BANKS PENINSULA

The most beautiful day-outing goes across the **Banks Peninsula,** southeast of Christchurch. It is best to take the Port Hills Road out of the city, which leads through a tunnel for the last few kilometers, down to the small seaport of

Lyttelton. The town stretches along the crater rim of a 12-million-year-old sunken volcano. Besides a few historical buildings, the **Timeball Station** is of interest. It signals (not only to seafarers) the exact time at 1 p.m. daily with a balloon. Via Port Levy, Pigeon Bay and Okains Bay with its **Maori and Colonial Museum**, you will arrive at the main attraction on the peninsula: **Akaroa** – a taste of France on New Zealand soil. The names of the streets and houses are reminiscent of the French interlude between 1838 and 1849. The historical **Langlois-Eteveneaux House** is dedicated to Captain Jean Langlois. Akaroa's sunny side is the sandy beach **Wainui** southwest of the harbor.

Try a taste of excellent French cuisine for lunch or dinner at Peter Anderson's **La Rue Restaurant** (6 Rue Balguerie; specialties are seafood and pheasant dishes). Some diners in this restaurant first return to Christchurch (82 km away) the next day. If you should intend this as well, you might try to find a bed for the night in **Akaroa Village Inn** (Beach Road, directly on the water).

In the winter, two other day-trip alternatives are possible on the Banks Peninsula tour. **Mount Hutt** is 104 km away, **Porter Heights** is 89 km away, both are skiing areas. In the summer, several beaches along **Pegasus Bay** are enticing to swimmers and surfers.

If your day-trip can be slightly extended, Christchurch is a haven not only for train fans. The *TranzAlpine Express* takes off each morning on a five-hour inland ride to Greymouth on the West Coast. The *Coastal Pacific* runs along the coast towards Picton and is an ideal trip combined with a whale-watching tour in Kaikoura. The route of the *Southerner* across the Canterbury Plains to Invercargill is less spectacular. However, there is one thing common to all routes: Travelers can be back in Christchurch by evening. No matter how you have spent the time around Christchurch, a home-brewed beer at the Dux de Lux is the ideal way to end the day.

CHRISTCHURCH AND ITS ENVIRONS

Accommodation

CHRISTCHURCH: *LUXURY:* **Noahs Hotel**, corner Worcester St. and Oxford Terrace, Tel: 03-3794700. **Cotswold Inn**, 96 Papanui Rd., Tel: 03-3553535. **Parkroyal Christchurch**, corner Kilmore and Durham St., Tel: 03-3657799. **The George Hotel**, 50 Park Terrace, P.O. Box 13063, Tel: 03-3794560.

Quality Inn, corner Durham and Kilmore St., P.O. Box 647, Tel: 03-3654699. **Chateau Blanc**, Cranmer Square corner Kilmore St., Tel: 03-3657698. **The Pavillions**, 42 Papanui Rd., P.O. Box 25061, Tel: 03-3555633. **The Towers**, corner Deans Avenue and Kilmarnock St., Riccarton, Tel: 03-3480613. **Windsor Private Hotel**, 52 Armagh St., Tel: 03-3661503.

MODERATE: **Alta Vada Motel**, 112 Blenheim Rd., Tel: 03-3481271. **Avenue Motel**, 136 Bealey Ave, Tel: 03-3660582.

Cashel Court Motel, 457 Cashel St., Tel: 03-3892768. **City Court Motels**, 850 Colombo St., Tel: 03-3669099. **Hagley Motel**, 13 Darvel St., Tel: 03-3487683. **Mayfair Court Motel**, 285 Hereford St., Tel: 03-3661266. **Middlepark Motel and Kowhai Lodge**, P.O. Box 11-162, 120 Main South Rd., Upper Riccarton, Tel: 03-3487320. **Northcote Motel**, 309 Main North Rd., Redwood, Tel: 03-3528417. **Windsor Hotel**, 52 Armagh St., Tel: 03-3661503

BUDGET: **Backpackers Inn the Square**, 50 Cathedral Square, Tel: 03-3665158 (central location, at the cathedral). **Bealey International Backpackers**, 70 Bealey Ave, Tel: 03-3666760. **Foley Towers Downtown Backpackers**, 208 Kilmore St., Tel: 03-3669760. **Arangi Backpackers**, 15 Riccarton Rd., Tel: 03-3483584. **Meadow Park**, 39 Meadow St., P.O. Box 5178, Tel: 03-3529176 (camping and cabins). **North South Airport Park**, corner Johns Rd. and Sawyers Arms Rd., Tel: 03-3595993 (camping and cabins; 1,5 km from the airport).

A large number of hotels and motels of all categories are situated along Bealey Avenue and Papanui Street.

AKAROA: *LUXURY:* **Akaroa Village Inn**, 86 Beach Rd., Tel: 03-3047421.

MODERATE: **Driftwood Motel**, 56 Rue Jolie, Tel: 03-3047484. **Madeira Hotel,** Rue Lavaud, Tel: 03-3047009. **Mount Vernon Lodge and Stables**, Rue Balgueri, P.O. Box 51, Tel: 03-3047471. **Waiiti Motel**, 64 Rue Jolie, Tel: 03-3047292.

BUDGET: **Akaroa Holiday Park,** Morgans Rd., off Old Coach Rd., P.O. Box 71, Tel: 03-3047471.

Onuku Farm Hostel, P.O. Box 50, Tel: 03-3047612. **Chez La Mer**, Rue Lavaud, Tel: 03-3047024.

Restaurants

Café Mainstreet, corner Colombo and Slaisbury St., Tel: 03-3650421 (vegetarian, non-smokers' Café). **The Bridge Restaurant**, 128a Oxford Terrace, Tel: 03-3669363 (dining with a view over the Avon; New Zealand lamb, expensive). **Cheers Café**, 196 Hereford St., Tel: 03-3663431 (good breakfast, open from 7 a.m.).

Dux de Lux Restaurant, Arts Centre, Montreal St., Tel: 03-3666919 (popular meeting-place with own beer-brewery and vegetarian restaurant; open daily 10 a.m.–midnight).

Sign of the Takahe, corner Dyers Pass and Hackthrone Road, Tel:03-3324052 (restaurant in an old castle with a romantic view over Christchurch, dinner between 7–10:30 p.m.; a bit outside of town).

Scarborough Fare Restaurant, Esplanade, Sumner Beach, Tel: 03-3266987 (situated on Christchurch's seafront; fairly expensive seafood). **The Homestead Mona Vale,** 63 Fendalton Rd., (ideal for a quick snack; the River Avon – and punting – in front of the terrace.

Thomas Edmonds Restaurant, corner Cambridge Terrace and Manchester St. (Tea in a Victorian pavilion at the River Avon).

Café/Bar Vesuvio, 182 Oxford Terrace, Tel: 03-3662666 (in-place, not only for up-and-coming businessmen).

Museums

Airforce Museum, Main South Rd., Wigram, Tel:03-3439532 (Mon–Sat 10 a.m.–4 p.m.; Sun 1–4 p.m.). The history of the Royal New Zealand Air Force is on display here.

Arts Centre Christchurch, corner Worcester St. and Rolleston Ave, Tel: 03-3660989 (daily 8:30 a.m.–5 p.m.). Popular cultural center with more than 150 craft workshops, plus galleries, theaters and restaurants: an absolute must.

The weekly **market** takes place on Saturdays and Sundays from 10 a.m.–4 p.m., for information, Tel: 03-3660989).

Canterbury Museum, Rolleston Ave, Tel: 03-3668379 (daily 10 a.m.–4:30 p.m.). Guided tours take place at 10:15 a.m., 1:15 and 2:30 p.m.; admission free.

Canterbury Society of Arts, 66 Gloucester St., Tel: 03-3667261 (changing exhibitions).

Ferrymead Historic Park, 269 Bridle Path Rd., Heathcote (Museum of Transport and Technology; buses No. 3G, 3H, 3J or 3K run to the Historic Park), Tel: 03-3841970.

Robert McDougall Art Gallery, Rolleston Ave, Tel: 03-3650915 (daily 9 a.m.-6 p.m.; in the Botanic Gardens; exhibition of Australasian and European painting).

Tips and Trips

Airport: Christchurch Airport is situated 11 km from the city center. The taxi fare to the airport is ca. 15 NZ$, a bus ride ca. 2 NZ$ (Bus No. 24L to the airport runs daily between 6 a.m. and 9.45 p.m. every 45 min; Sun and public holidays every hour). A shuttle-bus service connects the airport with the hotels. Airport departure fee is NZ$ 20.

Aquarium and Zoo, 155 Beach Rd., North Beach, Tel: 03-3834109 (daily 10 a.m.–5 p.m.; take buses No. 19M, 29M or 10N).

Banks Peninsula: A beautiful garden with a historic house (1853) can be visited in **Taunton Gardens** 2,5 km south of Governors Bay (daily except Mon 10 a.m.–6 p.m.). The **Langlois-Eteveneaux-House** is open daily 10:30 a.m.–4 p.m. (October–Easter until 4:30 p.m.). On Sundays, the **Akaroa Lighthouse** can be visited from 1 to 4 p.m.)

Boat-trips on the Avon: Those eager to train their muscles can hire a rowing-boat at the Antigua Boatsheds (daily 10 a.m.–5 p.m.; Tel: 03-3665885). Less strenous is *punting*, the comfortable traditional English method of moving a boat foreward with the help of a long stake – or, if you're in the lazy holiday mood, getting someone to move you along the river! (October–March daily 10 a.m.–6 p.m.; May–August 10 a.m.–4 p.m.; three boat-piers in the city center, i.e. at the Canterbury Information Office. Information: Tel: 03-3799629).

Botanic Gardens: The greenhouses are open to tbe public daily from 10 a.m.–4 p.m. Between September–April the Information Centre (Tel: 03-3661701) is open from 10:15 a.m.–4 p.m., May–August from 12 noon–3 p.m.

Canterbury Provincial Government Buildings: A guided tour through the complex in Durham Street takes place every Sunday at 2 and 2:30 p.m. (Tel: 03-3516776 or 3326184).

Car Rental: The car rental agency Maui offers a one-way service for their customers: Cars (and caravans) rented in Christchurch can be returned in Auckland on the North Island, or vice versa – an ideal way to save time (no long return journey) and money (only one-way ferry ticket between the islands). Hardy Cars, 6 Bridge St., Nelson, Tel: 03-5481681, Fax: 03-5481581 and Renny Rent-a-Car, 113 Tuam St., Tel: 03-3666790, offer short-term car-rental at reasonable prices.

Christchurch Cathedral: Tuesdays and Wednesdays the cathedral choir performs at 5:15 p.m., and the choirboys sing Fridays at 4:30 p.m. (except during school holidays). The cathedral spire can be climbed Mon–Sat 9 a.m.–4 p.m., Sundays 1–4:30 p.m.

Duty-free Shopping: Numerous duty-free shops offer their goods in the city center. Don't forget to compare prices and quality of the products – not all items prove to be a bargain. The shops deliver your duty-free shopping to the airport before boarding your flight. **International Antarctic Centre**, Orchard Rd., Christchurch, Tel: 03-3589896. Open daily 1 Oct-31 March 9:30 a.m. to 8:30 p.m., 1 April-30 September 9:30 a.m. to 5:30 p.m.

Lyttelton: *Diamond Launch Services* offer a harbor round-trip for 10 NZ$ daily at 2.45 p.m. From the middle of August until the beginning of May a ferry-service connects Lyttelton and Ripapa Island (departure daily 2 p.m.; with guided tour to Fort Jervois; price 12 -18 NZ$).

Nightlife: In Christchurch, any nightlife worth a mention takes place mainly at the weekend. One of the best known nightclubs is The Firehouse (293 Colombo St., Tel: 03-3329208; Wed–Sat from 5:30 p.m.; sometimes live music).

Rail: InterCity offers day trips by train to Greymouth (transAlpine), Arthurs Pass and Kaikoura. Information: Tel: 0800-802802, or at the Canterbury Information Center.

Skiing: Nine skiing areas are situated within the vicinity of Christchurch (1,5 to 2,5 hours by car), Mount Hutt and Porter Heights being the most interesting ones. The skiing-season on Mount Hutt runs from June to Nov; skiing equipment can be hired in all ski resorts. Agencies in Christchurch offer reasonable package tours (one day to one week).

Tourist Information

Air New Zealand Travel Centre, 156 Armagh Street, Tel: 03-3797000. Reservations: Tel: 03-795200.

Automobile Association (AA), 210 Hereford St., Tel: 03-3667626.

Canterbury Information Centre, corner Worcester St. and Oxford Terrace, Tel: 03-3799629 (weekdays 8:30 a.m.–5 p.m.; weekends, public holidays 9 a.m.–4 p.m.).

DOC: Conservation House, 1st Floor, 133 Victoria St,. Tel: 03-3799758 (in Christchurch). Old Coach Rd., Tel: 03-3047334 (in Akaroa).

Outdoor Recreation Information Centre, Worcester St., Tel: 03-3799395 (weekdays 10 a.m.–4 p.m.; Saturdays in summer 10 a.m.–2 p.m.).

Christchurch Airport Information Centre, Tel: 03-3537783/4.

Infoservice Centre, Domestic Terminal, Tel: 03-3537774, (weekdays and Sundays 8 a.m.–8 p.m., Saturdays 8 a.m.–7 p.m.).

HIGHLANDS AND PLAINS

ARTHUR'S PASS NATIONAL PARK
LAKE TEKAPO
MOUNT COOK NATIONAL PARK
DUNEDIN

Now it's time to say farewell to Christchurch. A foggy mist hovers across the Avon River. Joggers are making their first rounds in Hagley Park. Heavy rush-hour traffic rolls along Fendalton Road towards the downtown area. This is a good reason to turn your back on the big city of Christchurch, to trade in the hectic pace of the city for the vast expanses of unadulterated nature and solitude of the south.

Highway 1 offers a number of choices just a few kilometers up the road, but deciding which one to take should not be difficult. Only those in a hurry remain on Highway 1, rapidly crossing the Canterbury Plains, then meeting up again with the coast at Timaru and following the highway past Oamaru in the direction of Dunedin.

Without discrediting this coastal trip, the inland route along the Southern Alps is much more fascinating. To start this route, you turn (still within Christchurch city limits) onto Highway 73 westward towards Arthur's Pass.

The first route on Highway 1 to Dunedin will take about five hours. For

Preceding pages: Panoramic natural splendor, Mount Cook and Lake Pukaki. Left: The Church of the Good Shepherd, one of the few man-made sights on Lake Tekapo.

the inland route through the Alps, you should plan at least a few days right from the start. The scenic landscape is worth time and the effort.

The Coastal Route

Highway 1 – which, as just mentioned, leads straight through the Canterbury Plains – offers as visual excitement, a seemingly endless patterns of fields and meadows predominate in all directions. Approximately 70 million sheep of more than 20 different breeds graze New Zealand's pastureland. However, for the farmer of Canterbury province everything revolves around the Corriedale sheep that supplies both fine wool and excellent meat.

The road leads past **Burnham**, where you not only have the last opportunity to visit **Lake Ellesmere**, but also to restock your wine supply for your next dinner directly from a vineyard. The **Giesen Wine Estate** is one of the most southerly wine-growing regions in the country.

The **Rakaia River** forms the boundary to the region called Aorangi. The town of **Rakaia**, with a population of 900, comes alive just twice a year: On the *Queen's Birthday Weekend* at the beginning of June when jet boat races take place on the river, and in late summer when the fishing season opens. After all, the Rakaia River is known for its abundance of delicious salmon and trout. A tip for fishermen: A major annual salmon fishing contest takes place here the last weekend in February.

Ashburton, the "breadbasket" of New Zealand, has a population of 15,000 and much to offer throughout the year, at least for *Kiwis*. John Hall first broke the ground as early as 1853, but the origins of the city date back more than 500 years. The *moa* hunters set up camp in this region while searching for that giant flightless bird. The bird is, of course, long extinct and has become just a hazy memory. The same goes for the times when the Ashburton River could only be arduously crossed with the ferry.

Timaru lies a full 160 km from Christchurch, and it is time for a rest in the shadows of the mighty **basilica**. The monotonous drive through the plains comes to an end here. Highway 1 follows the coastline again after Timaru. A visit to **Caroline Bay** is a good introduction to the area. Here Maori once sought shelter from wind and weather with their canoes, and hundreds of years later whalers set up a camp at this site.

For those who want to take a trip into the mountains, an opportunity is offered via Highway 8 from **Washdyke** (near Timaru), as well as at **Pukeuri Junction** near Oamaru via Highway 83.

The Highland Tour

It makes no difference if you take the route through the Canterbury Plains to Mount Cook or the one to Greymouth towards the west coast – both trips start out on Highway 73 through the Canterbury Plains for the first few kilometers. As soon as the snow-covered mountains of the Southern Alps come clearer into view, the road divides.

In the direction of the west coast you continue on Highway 73, which takes you up to **Craigieburn State Forest Park,** located behind Springfield. In summer, hiking opportunities are numerous, and in winter skiing is popular. The geographical and scenic attractions of the area open up directly behind Craigieburn. Arthur's Pass National Park and Arthur's Pass Village (population: 300) will give you the initial impression of actually being in the Swiss Alps.

ARTHUR'S PASS NATIONAL PARK

In the center of South Island, approximately a three-hour drive from Christchurch, lies **Arthur's Pass National Park**. The park stretches out over the main divide of the Southern Alps and possesses all the striking characteristics of an alpine region: peaks over 2000 m high; shallow rivers with vast tributary systems, such as the **Waimakariri, Poulter** and **Taramakau Rivers**; and fantastic hiking trails and mountain-climbing opportunities. The park has a surface area of 100,000 hectares and can be easily reached by car and train from either the east or west. The overwhelming beauty of a train ride through the alpine mountain world is not easily forgotten.

The park's scenery and vegetation change dramatically from west to east. In the west you will find dense podocarpus rain forests, deep rushing rivers and a genuine bird paradise. To produce and sustain this environment, more than 5000 mm of rain falls here annually. In comparison, only 1500 mm of rain falls on the alpine highlands in the rainshadow zone of the east. Here, the vegetation is generally less lush. Graceful beech trees give way to dry tussock grass on which deer and merino sheep graze. The hiking areas are accessible without any trouble from the valleys' rivers and streams.

Arthur's Pass Village, with overnight accommodations and park headquarters, is the starting point for outdoor activities.

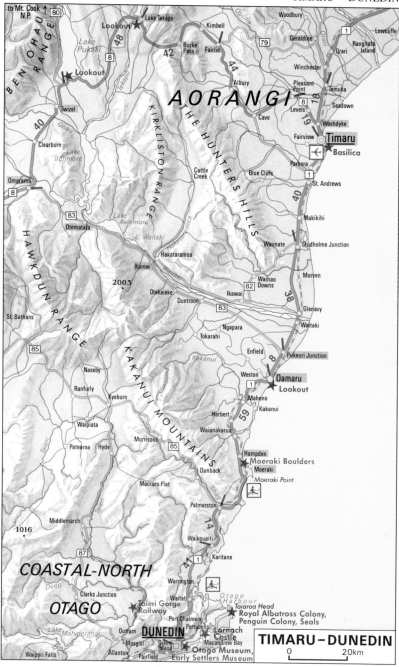

TIMARU – DUNEDIN

0   20km

The short hiking trails for less adventurous visitors will keep the average walker breathlessly busy for three or four days. There are of course tours lasting three to four days with overnights sleeping arrangements in good huts.

Two of the most popular summer routes go into the **Mingha** and **Deception Valleys** and to **Waimakariri Valley**. The first tour takes approximately two days in good weather through Mingha Valley over **Goat Pass** (1070 m), and then westward down into Deception Valley with its lush, green rain forests. Do not forget that heavy rainfall can make the river valleys impassable, so stay tuned to the weather report.

Interesting hikes have also been planned along the course of the Waimakariri River (sleeping arrangements in huts are possible). Most of the routes in this re-

gion will take up to four or five days. Several trails along the upper reaches of the Waimakariri cross over the main divide of the Southern Alps and lead back to the main road. Even travelers wishing to just take a short visit to a national park close to Christchurch will have a good time at Arthur's Pass. In the winter, you can also go skiing on a small slope at **Temple Basin**.

A few kilometers westward beyond Arthur's Pass on Highway 73 comes a stretch of particularly breathtaking scenery. To the right and left of the narrow serpentine road, steep rocky cliffs line Highway 73 until **Otira,** where the valley opens up again. It is now only about 74 km to **Kumara** on Highway 6.

On the Rooftop of New Zealand

There are a lot of ways to leave Christchurch traveling south. The most beautiful route is without doubt the one to Mount Cook. It is best to take one of the numerous side roads leading off High-

Above: The entrance to the Mount Cook National Park. Right: Fields of lupines have spread in the gentle climate of the foothills of the Southern Alps.

way 73. After getting your bearings again at the small town of **Hororata**, you travel further west on Highway 72, which takes you to **Mount Hutt.** It is a sleepy hollow in the summer, but turns into a skiier's stronghold in the winter (five tow and chair lifts). For experienced skiers, the slope on **South Face** is a special tip and definitely a big sporting challenge. The skiing season on Mount Hutt lasts from the end of May to the beginning of November. An artificial snow machine makes sure that even in the mildest of winters plenty of snow is on the slopes.

The best spot to start your ski trip with good overnight accommodations is a place called **Methven**, located on Highway 77. Here you can meet at one of the many pubs for an evening après-ski in front of a crackling fire. In the summertime, however, there is little evidence of this busy, lively atmosphere.

You will pass by Mount Somers, Mayfield and Geraldine during the next kilometers. The landscape here hardly changes: green meadows stretching up to

the horizon, soft chains of hills upon which flocks of sheep graze, sometimes thousands in number. All of this is typical New Zealand scenery. Highway 79 turns off at **Geraldine** towards Fairlie. After a further distance of 46 km comes Highway 8, which goes over the 829 m high **Burke Pass** to Lake Tekapo.

The scenery will now change. The green Canterbury Plains slowly turn into the golden brown tussock grass of **Mackenzie Country**. This region owes its name to James McKenzie, a Scotsman who tried to hide 1000 stolen sheep in this region in 1855.

LAKE TEKAPO

The most pleasant place for an overnight stay is **Lake Tekapo.** The trip from Christchurch to the shores of the lake can be made comfortably in one day.

A gas station, a take-out restaurant, a motel and a handful of houses – that is Lake Tekapo in a nutshell. This place would be of no significance whatever if it were not for its unique lake. No matter what time of day you arrive at the lake – you will be greeted by a natural color spectacle, especially if the sun is shining. The finest grained sand, produced by the glacier scouring the cliffs and then flushed into the valley by mountain rivers, causes the water to constantly change its colors; the palette is from glowing green, to dark blue, to radiant turquoise.

The next morning, an enjoyable walk along the shores of the lake up to the **Church of the Good Shepherd** can be taken. If you are fortunate, the church will be open. The view from the altar toward the mountains is quite spectacular. A bronze memorial is located next to the church and dedicated to the friendship between man and the sheepdog, of especially great significance in Mackenzie Country, with its long, hard and harsh winters.

With this in mind, you can start out on one of the most beautiful routes on South Island – the 47 km long trip from Lake Tekapo to **Lake Pukaki** takes you right through the center of New Zealand's mountain country. During the period from December to February, the route is especially rewarding because numerous fields of wild lupine transform the landscape into a flowered carpet, which ends only at the snow-covered peaks.

It is time now to set your sights straight ahead – to the northwest on the right side, **Mount Cook** will appear for the first time. Its peak majestically looms 3764 m into the clear blue skies. You will be able to select your own personal viewpoint from among the many different ones of Mount Cook along the next few kilometers. However, among the most recommendable spots is the lookout above Lake Pukaki. Behind this lake, New Zea-

Right: One of the easier ways of reaching the snowy crest of Mount Cook is by helicopter.

land's highest mountain seems close enough to touch. Nevertheless, there are still 52 km (on Highway 80) from the nearby turn-off at the south shore of the lake up to **Mount Cook Village** right below the peak. This trip is an absolute must, even if you are pressed for time. Neither should you be deterred by the fact that you have to return the same way via the narrow road.

Highway 80 follows directly along the shores of Lake Pukaki. When half way around, you will have reached **Glentanner Park.** This spot has two advantages. For one, it provides good overnight accommodations (not too cold in bad weather) overlooking the entire mountain range. For another, you can start out the next morning on a breathtaking helicopter ride around Mount Cook.

As an alternative, flights are offered in small planes from the airport near **Mount Cook Hermitage**. Whether you choose helicopter or plane, keep in mind that the weather is usually the best in the early morning hours. Around 10 a.m., the clouds start forming and blow in from the west coast. Therefore, you should plan your flight as early as possible (after about 7 a.m.).

MOUNT COOK NATIONAL PARK

This park located in the heart of the Southern Alps is without a doubt the great shining jewel in the crown of New Zealand's national parks. The spectacular Mount Cook, the highest peak in the country, is called *aorangi* by the Maori, meaning "cloud-piercer." Mount Cook is surrounded by 18 peaks, all of which are over 3000 m high. A challenge for hikers and mountain climbers are: Mount Sefton (3157 m), Mount Tasman (3498 m), Mount Dampier (3440 m), Mount Haast (3138 m), and Douglas Peak (3085 m), to name a few.

Not quite as high but still as tremendous is the **Tasman Glacier.** The glacier

is the largest in the country: 27 km long, it has an average width of 1.6 km, and is 600 m thick. It is slowly working its way down to the valley.

Whether it is winter or summer, the dramatic character of this landscape will unfold in its entirety when you approach **Cook Village** from the shores of the glacial Lake Pukaki. On clear days, the view here reaches all the way westward to Mount Cook and Mount Tasman. Cook Village is quite well equipped to accommodate visitors. You will find a wide range of lodging and camping accommodations, along with mountain tour guides.

The vicinity around the village is well-suited for short walks, and easy trails wander through beech forests or to the **Blue Lakes** at the edge of an old glacier moraine. **Glacier Lookout,** located on **Old Ball Hut Road**, offers a grand view overlooking the Tasman Glacier. If you dare to head straight for the heart of the mountains, a regular ski-plane will fly you to the eternal snows. In winter, skiers often fly up and spend the rest of the day

skiing down the slopes into the valley. Helicopter skiing is also available during the peak of the tourist season.

A number of extended tours begins at Cook Village. The one-day tour to **Sealy Tarns** rewards you with a spectacular panoramic view of the mountains. On the Old Ball Hut Road you will come to one of the first cabins in the park, with a view of Mount Cook and the Tasman Glacier. The alpine character of the park sets limits to the number of overnight accommodations along the trails. There are, however, places to stay overnight at **Hooker Hut** under the south flank of Mount Cook, and at **Mueller Hut** and **Liebig Hut**. All three huts lie right in the heart of the highest mountain peaks and are favorites among mountain climbers. You should check with the officials at park headquarters regarding the danger of avalanches in the wintertime.

For those who would rather refrain from the hikes lasting a few days, but still want to participate in that unforgettable mountain experience, **Kea Point** is the

answer. The two to three-hour round-trip hike starts at Hermitage Village and awards yet another spectacular view of Mount Cook, **Mueller Glacier** and the ice masss of Mount Sefton from the lookout point at the end of the hike.

From **Glencoe Lookout** (the path begins behind the hotel), you will be back within 30 minutes. When heavy clouds hang over the mountains, you should consider paying a short visit to **Mount Cook Village** and, in hopes that the weather will change, spend the night below in **Twizel**.

The area around Twizel is electrifying in the true sense of the word. The **Upper Waitaki Power Development Scheme**, a large intricate canal and power plant system, annually produces a great share of New Zealand's energy requirements (even the lights for North Islanders go on from here). A positive side effect for

Above: The Moeraki Boulders, volcano by-products for geologists, provisions lost by gods for the Maori.

sports enthusiasts is the man-made **Lake Ruataniwha,** where a rowing center for the country has been established.

At the hang-gliding paradise **Omarama**, the paths part. Those who want to spend more time in the mountains should travel via **Lindis Pass** towards **Cromwell** and **Queenstown**. Visitors wishing to return to the coast and those wanting to take in the big-city atmosphere of Dunedin should turn left onto Highway 83.

Via **Otematata** on **Lake Aviemore** (fishing and boating area) and **Kurow**, after approximately 120 km, you will reach **Pukeuri Junction**, putting you on Highway 1 again. Whether you take the coastal route or the inland route, both head in the direction of Dunedin.

The Moeraki Boulders

A pleasant walk along Thames Street in **Oamaru** will provide all the evidence necessary as to the city's fine qualities. Most of the buildings (many give the impression of being too massive) are made

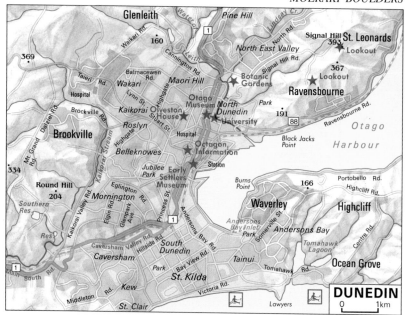

out of the white limestone typical of this region. Many banks, churches and hotels, mostly constructed at the end of the last century, illustrate the ideal utilization of this stone. Throughout New Zealand, the *Oamaru stone* has found its place – for example, in the town hall and post office in Auckland, at the custom's house in Wellington and in the town hall of Dunedin.

At the end of Thames Street, you should not immediately follow Highway 1, but rather turn left for a short visit down to the old business district at the harbor. Here, between Harbour Street and Tyne Street, a unique and very photogenic scenery with old storage houses, dilapidated shops and pubs that have long been closed has been maintained. You can almost hear the hearty laughter of whalers behind the boarded-up windows of the Northern Hotel, as it must have resounded back in the 1880s. From the lookout point **Cape Wanbrow** (at the end of Tyne Street), you have a beautiful view of Oamaru and the bay.

There is hardly reason to make any stops the next few kilometers. At the earliest, beyond **Hampden** where the mountain range reaches to the water, you should take the turn-off to the **Moeraki Boulders** along the coast. Numerous round boulders, some of which are up to four meters in diameter, lie lazily along the beach. The rational explanation given by geologists for this natural phenomenon is quite simple. These boulders are rock bubbles that were formed more than four million years ago as a result of volcanic activity.

The Maori legend tells the story a bit differently and it is, as in many cases, much more poetic: The canoe of the gods, called *waka atua*, stranded on the shore after a long journey from *hawaiki*. The storage baskets were spilled onto the land and still can be admired as boulders today. Even though the region has been declared a state reserve, its days seem to be numbered. Erosion caused by the strong surf and gusty winds is taking a hard toll on the rocks, as well as a large

175

number of thoughtless tourists who leave their graffiti signatures painted on the boulders.

A small café is located above the beach, ideal for lunch and providing an ocean view. Afterwards, the last coastal stretch for an evening arrival in Dunedin will take about an hour (80 km).

DUNEDIN

A view of **Dunedin** and the wide bay at **Otago Harbour** can be had from **Pine Hill**, a part of the city of Dunedin. The road winds steeply downhill and leads directly to the Octagon, center of the capital of Otago province.

If you are fortunate enough to arrive on a Sunday in late summer, you will be able to enjoy things very typical to Otago at the **Octagon**: The bagpipe contest (there

Above: A pretty row of houses on Tudor Street in Dunedin. Right: Bagpiping in full regalia is a competitive sport on Sundays on the Octagon.

is even a New Zealand bagpipe band championship) is as much a part of Dunedin as the whiskey brewery on Willowbank Street, the Victorian buildings and, of course, the kilt.

When Captain Cook thoughtlessly sailed past the spot on February 26, 1770, he left it up to the Scottish settlers to build a city. The Scots came in 1848 via the vessels *John Wickliffe* and *Philip Laing*, hoping to find work, fortune and happiness. For many, their dreams came true as early as 1861. The gold rush transformed Dunedin, the Edinburgh of the South as it is sometimes referred to, into a prosperous boomtown.

The city, which numbers 110,000 inhabitants, owes its significance today primarily to **Otago University.** At the end of February, when approximately 15,000 students flock to the city for the winter semester, almost every store lures shoppers with signs reading "Welcome Back Students," or with special offers on anything from haircuts to second-hand furniture. Moreover, there is a colorful food festival on the grass at **Woodhaugh Park**, located at the end of George Street. In this manner, Dunedin demonstrates that it is everything but a city stagnating in its "ancient" heritage. The blend of progress and tradition, young and old results in a mixture that is hard to beat.

Even when there are many reasons to celebrate, only one beverage is drunk: the beer labeled *Speights*. After all, New Zealand's oldest brewery has its headquarters here on Rattray Street. Guided tours are offered weekdays at 10:30 a.m.

A sweet alternative is a tour to the **Cadbury chocolate factory** (open Monday through Thursday). Cadbury chocolate is, of course, not only popular with children.

From the Octagon to the University

A good place to start a city tour is at the eight-cornered – appropriately-named – Octagon, restored in 1989. The **Robbie Burns Statue** in the middle of it calls to mind the famous Scottish author and the city's roots. Across from the statue, **St Paul's Anglican Cathedral** towers into the sky. **Stuart Street** begins at this point and is full of diversity. A row of historical houses lines the street at the upper end, providing photographers with ample subject matter; and at the other end, it meets the **train station**, although few remaining trains roll over the railroad tracks every day. The train station, with its colorful windows, delicate ceiling ornamentation and intricate floor mosaics (allegedly composed of 725,760 stones), is without equal in all of New Zealand. It is quite natural that the construction materials originated in Oamaru.

Also worth seeing is the **Early Settlers Museum** on Cumberland Street, especially because of the role it plays in presenting a comprehensive understanding of the Otago province, and because of the care and diligence put into maintaining its collection. The museum

shows that Dunedin was always a little ahead of its time in New Zealand. For example, the first gas street lamps were lighted in Dunedin; the city residents rode the first public transportation system here; the first daily newspaper issued was the *Otago Times*, and it still exists today; the first hydropower station was put into operation in Dunedin; and the first ship carrying frozen meat destined for Europe was set to sea from here in 1882.

The most lively section of town is the **University District** located between George, Union and Castle Streets is full of life. Founded in 1889 on the idyllic Leith River, the main building houses the oldest university in New Zealand. A walk is also worthwhile here and can be continued through **Logan Park** and the **Botanical Garden**. Before you stop off at one of the small cafés in the University District for lunch, take a look at the **Olveston House**, 42 Royal Terrace. Behind its historical walls you will see how settlers furnished their homes, and a fine art collection.

It is only a few minutes from **Royal Terrace** to the center of present-day Dunedin. It is this continous shift between old and new, between past and present that makes the particular charm of the "city-on-Otago-Harbour."

OTAGO PENINSULA

The vicinity around Dunedin is also attractive. A day-trip across the **Otago Peninsula** should be included in your plans. The destination of this trip is the **albatross colony** on Taiaroa Head, 30 km from Dunedin. The only mainland brooding colony of these giant seabirds in the world is located here. Tours of maximum 17 people begin at the Royal Albatross Centre ($ 15, daily except Tuesday morning from November 25 to September 16, Tel. 03-4780498). An alternative are the nearby **penguin and seal colonies** (turn

Above: Otago Peninsula, near Penguin Beach, where sometimes penguins and seals inadvertently entertain visitors.

off to the right from Harrington Road at the Penguin Place sign; the necessary key is located there). Twilight Tours offer an afternoon tour (departure 2 p.m., lasting until 9 p.m.) covering the city – panorama mountain, steepest street in the world, Otago museum – and giving historic insights into Dunedin. For an extra fee visitors are taken to an **albatross colony**, a **cormoran's breeding ground**, a **seal colony**, and the **breeding place of yellow-eyed penguins**. Further attractions on the peninsula are the historical **Fort Taiaroa** (entry permit required); **Larnach Castle**, built in 1871 and the only one in New Zealand (open daily from 9 a.m.); **Portobello Marine Aquarium**, open only on weekends; and **Glenfalloch** with its beautiful gardens and pathways. Since overnight accommodations on the peninsula are limited, you will probably want to return to Dunedin in the evening, where you could take in one of the regularly-scheduled bagpipe concerts. The picture of an "Edinburgh of the South" is then complete.

178

CANTERBURY PLAINS
SOUTHERN ALPS / DUNEDIN
Accommodation

ARTHUR'S PASS: *MODERATE:* **Alpine Motels**, Tel: 03-3189233. *BUDGET:* **Mountain House**, P.O. Box 12, Tel: 03-3189258.

ASHBURTON: *MODERATE:* **Regency Motel**, 820 East St., Tel: 03-3088266.

DUNEDIN: *LUXURY:* **Cargill's Motor Inn**, 678 George St:, Tel: 03-4777983: **Leisure Lodge Motor Inn**, Duke St., Tel: 03-4775360.
MODERATE: **Adrian Motel**, 101 Queens Drive, Tel: 03-4552009 (4 km outside of town, near St. Kilda Beach). **Canongate Motel**, 20 Canongate, Tel: 03-4777972. **Leviathan Hotel**, 65 Lower High St., Tel: 03-4773160.
BUDGET: **Pavolva Backpackers**, 1 Vogel St., Tel: 03-4792175. **Aaron Lodge Motel and Caravan Park**, 162 Kaikorai Valley Rd., Tel: 03-4764725. **Law Courts**, corner Stuart and Cumberland St., Tel: 03-4778036. **Elm Lodge**, 74 Elm Row, Tel: 03-4741872.

LAKE TEKAPO: *MODERATE:* **Lake Tekapo Motor Camp**, Lake Side Dr., Tel: 03-6806825. **Lake Tekapo Alpine Inn**, Highway 8, Tel: 03-6806848. *BUDGET:* **Youth Hostel**, P.O. Box 38, Tel: 03-6806857.

MOUNT COOK: *BUDGET:* **Youth Hostel**, corner Bowen and Kitchener Drives, Tel: 03-4351820. **Glentanner Park**, Tel: 03-4351855.

MOUNT HUTT / METHVEN: *MODERATE:* **Aorangi Lodge**, 38 Spaxton St., Tel: 03-3028482. **Koromiko Lodge**, State Highway 77, Tel: 03-3028165. *BUDGET:* **Mount Hutt Accommodation**, 177 Rakaia Gorge Rd., Tel: 03-3028508.

TIMARU: *MODERATE:* **Aorangi Motels**, 400 Stafford St., Tel: 03-6880097.
BUDGET: **Selwyn Holiday Park**, Selwyn St., Tel: 03-6847690. **Elizabeth House**, 14 Elizabeth St,. Tel: 03-6884685.

TWIZEL: *LUXURY:* **Mackenzie Country Motor Inn**, Wairepo Rd., Tel: 03-4350869. *BUDGET:* **Basil Lodge**, P.O. Box 30, Tel: 03-4350671.

OAMARU: *BUDGET:* **Oamaru Gardens Holiday Park**, 30 Chelmer St., Tel: 03-4347666. **Alpine Motel**, 285 Thames St., Tel: 03-4345038.

OMARAMA: *BUDGET:* **Omarama Holiday Park,** P.O. Box 34, Tel: 03-4389875.

Restaurants

DUNEDIN: **95 Filleul Restaurant**, 95 Filleul St., Tel: 03-4777233 (Victorian flair with open fireplace; expensive). **High Tide Restaurant**, 27 Kitchener St., Tel: 03-4779784 (a bit outside of town; great view across the harbor). **The Palms Café**, 84 High St., Queens Gardens, Tel: 03-4776534 (relaxed atmosphere, good cappucino).

OAMARU: **Club 45**, Rippon St., Hillderthorpe, Tel: 03-4313899 (special location: 45 km north of Oamaru on Highway 1 directly on the 45th parallel; jazz and blues from the 1930s; open for dinner from 6 p.m.; closed Mondays and Tuesdays).

Museums

DUNEDIN: **Early Settlers Museum**, 220 Cumberland St., Tel: 03-4775052 (weekdays 8:30 a.m.–4:30 p.m.; Saturdays 10:30 a.m.–4:30 p.m.; Sundays 1:30–4:30 p.m.). **Otago Museum**, 419 King St., Tel: 03-4772372.

Tips and Trips

DUNEDIN: Scottish goods from bagpipes to kilts can be purchased at **The Scottish Shop**, 187 George St., Tel: 03-4779965.
The Otago Excursion Train Trust runs railway trips from the station in Dunedin to the **Taieri River Gorge** with the *Taieri Gorge Train*, October–March 3:30 p.m., April–May 2:30 p.m. Tel: 03-4774449.

MOUNT COOK / GLENTANNER PARK: Helicopter-flights daily with The Helicopter Line, Tel: 03-4351801 (from 96 NZ$).

Festivals and Special Events

DUNEDIN: *Anniversary Day* is celebrated on March 23.

TIMARU: A buoyant *Beach Carnival* takes place at Caroline Bay from the end of December until the beginning of January.

Tourist Information

ARTHUR'S PASS: **Visitor Information**, Main Rd., Tel: 03-3189211.

ASHBURTON: **Information Centre**, corner East and Burnett St., Tel: 03-3081064 (Mon–Fri 9 a.m.–4:30 p.m., Sat 10 a.m.–4 p.m., Sun 10 a.m.–1 p.m.)

DUNEDIN: **Visitors Centre**, 48 The Octagon, P.O. Box 5457, Tel: 03-4743300, (weekdays 8:30 a.m.–5 p.m., weekends 9 a.m.–5 p.m.). **DOC**, 77 Stuart St., Conservation House, Tel: 03-4770677.

METHVEN / MOUNT HUTT: **Information Centre**, corner McMillan and Alford Forest Rd., Tel: 03-3028749 (Mon–Fri 8 a.m.–5 p.m.; Sun, public holidays 11 a.m.–1 p.m.).

MOUNT COOK NATIONAL PARK: **Visitor Centre**, Bowen Dr., Tel: 03-4351818.

OAMARU: **North Otago Promotion and Information Centre**, Severn St. (opposite the police station), Tel: 03-4341656 (open Mon–Fri 9 a.m.–5 p.m.)

TIMARU: **Information Centre**, 14 George St., Tel: 03-6886163 (Monday–Friday 8:30 a.m.–5 p.m.).

TWIZEL: **Information Centre**, Wairepo Rd., Tel: 03-4350802 (Mon–Fri 9 a.m.–4 p.m.; weekends 10 a.m.–3 p.m.).

SOUTH ISLAND

Nelson
Wellington
Nelson Marlborough

West Coast Canterbury
Christchurch

Timaru

Southland
Dunedin

Invercargill

Stewart I.

THE SOUTHERN REGION

CATLINS
STEWART ISLAND
FIORDLAND NATIONAL PARK
MILFORD SOUND
QUEENSTOWN

The region designated South Otago begins south of Dunedin. Soft rolling hills dominate the countryside for the next 80 km until you reach Balclutha on Highway 1, leaving no doubt about the fact that this is fertile farmland. Stops along the way are not necessary, unless one failed to tank up on fuel and provisions in Dunedin.

Balclutha is situated on the largest river in New Zealand (at least when it comes to volume of water, and that's how the residents prefer to see it). The 338-km long **Clutha River** begins at Lake Wanaka and flows into the Pacific Ocean. Lengthwise, it is surpassed only by the 354-km long Waikato River on North Island.

For many years, the city served only as a traffic junction. In 1852, the ferry connection across the river was initially put into operation. 14 years later, traffic rolled across a bridge for the first time; and today traffic generally whizzes by Balclutha when heading for Invercargill, another 137 km via Gore on Highway 1. Unfortunately, many of these travelers miss one of the most unexplored and thrilling landscapes in New Zealand, the **Catlins**.

Preceding pages: Mitre Peak on the Milford Sound. Left: Matinal mood at the ferry dock of Te Anau Downs.

The highway through the Catlins is a part of the **Southern Scenic Route**, which encompasses the most fascinating landscapes in the south up to Milford Sound.

THE CATLINS

Many New Zealanders shake their heads when the name Catlins is mentioned. "Never heard of it!" is often the answer. Therefore, the trip on Highway 92 is all the more rewarding (turn off from the main road in Balclutha at High Street).

Even though the drive takes you over paved streets for the first stretch, dusty roads twisting along the craggy coast and leading through dense woods are more typical of the Catlins. Altogether, there are approximately 45 km of unpaved road on the way to Fortrose via Highway 92. If you take any side roads, reckon with thick dust clouds and therefore poor visibility.

At **Port Molyneux** (you will scan the area in vain for the seaport mentioned in the name), there is a splendid view of the coastline from the cemetery. **Kaka Point**, a popular vacationing spot with beautiful beaches and good surfing conditions, is located only 3 km further south of Port Molyneux.

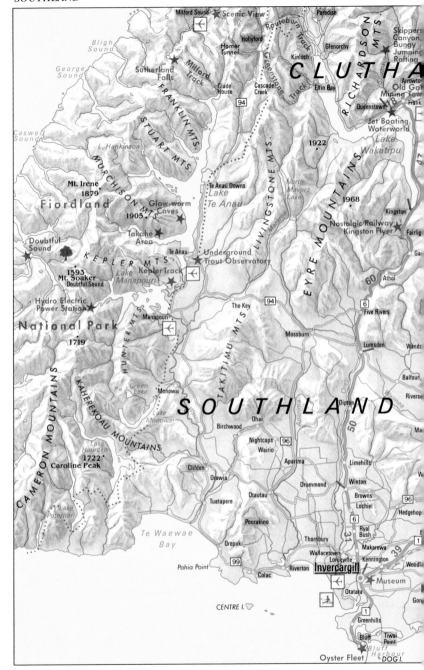

SOUTHLAND

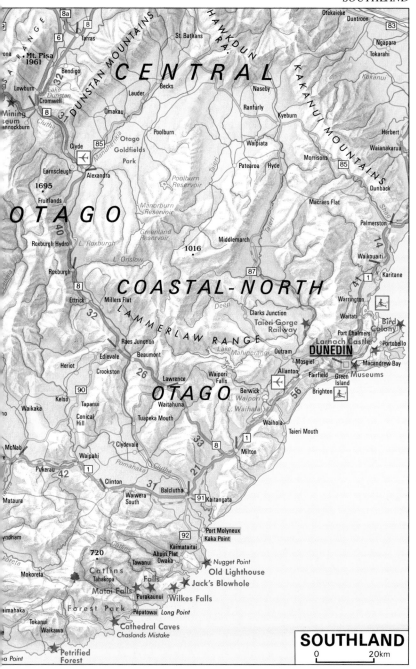

SOUTHLAND

0   20km

185

Kaka Point's prime attraction is **Nugget Point** (turn left, then 8 km). The road winds steeply around a few hills and ends at a small parking area. From here it is about a ten-minute walk along the coast (the path up to the new lighthouse is a dead end). The precipitous crags and sheer cliffs shoot out from the ocean at a height of up to 120 m and are crowned with New Zealand's oldest **lighthouse** (built in 1870). If you are fortunate, you may be able to observe seals, sea lions and dolphins splashing in the bay.

Those who spend more time traveling in the Catlins will soon discover that problems sometimes arise when looking for a place to stay overnight. Therefore, it is recommended that visitors take whatever accommodations are available and close by – for example, the campsite in **Kaimataitai**. You can also travel back via Karoro Creek Road to **Ahuriri Flat**

Above: Nugget Point in the Catlins, the "end of the world". Right: Shucking oysters, hard work for the pleasure of others.

and further on into the heart of the region at **Owaka**, where you will find overnight accommodations ranging from comfortable hotels (*Catlins Inn*) to simple campsites. On this stretch of road, another stop is worthwhile, and not just for railroad enthusiasts: **Tunnel Hill** can be easily reached via a short trail off of Highway 92. It leads to a now out-of-service railroad tunnel, which was carved out of the cliffs by hand in 1893.

The **Catlins State Forest Park** and the actual **Catlins Coast** begin just past Owaka. The paved road ends after a few kilometers and the trip becomes a dusty adventure.

Keep in mind when planning your itinerary that your pace will decrease rapidly, especially if you get caught behind one of the numerous logging trucks. The many one-way bridges (this single-lane traffic is typical of New Zealand) will leave no option for you but to stop and wait. The slow tempo and pauses will at least allow you to enjoy the region at your leisure. One after the other, nature's

highlights appear. Just 9 km past the Catlins River, you can turn off to the left towards **Wilkes Falls**; or walk around **Jack's Blowhole** (a one-hour round trip from Jack's Bay parking lot – really only worth walking in stormy weather and at high tides).

If you would like to venture on a longer hike, the best place to start is in the **Catlins River Valley**. The starting point for the walk is **Tawanui Camp**, centrally located to the south (campsites with toilets are available). The walk leads to **Frank's Creek**, the longest stretch with 2.5 hours hiking time); to **Wallis Stream** and **The Wisp**. Taking a good five hours, the trail guides you four times across the river spanned by suspension bridges, takes you through dense forests, and reveals a great variety of bird species.

Less strenuous and therefore recommended for almost everyone is a trip to **Purakaunui Falls.** You turn left onto a narrow road off of Highway 92 and after a comfortable ten-minute walk you will witness the Purakaunui River plunge down about 20 m over several terraces. For visitors who never tire of the sight of waterfalls, the **Matai Falls** are located in the **Table Hill Scenic Reserve** directly on the road (a 20-minute walk).

Past the Tahakopa River you will reach **Papatowai** (gas station, campsite and coffeeshop). The road climbs up to **Florence Hill**, and from this point there is a fantastic view of the coast. Down below you will see **Tautuku Bay** with its long, sprawling sandy beaches and the **Rainbow Islands**, from whose blowholes gushes white frothy spray.

Just before reaching **Chaslands**, you can take a short trip at low tide to **Cathedral Caves** (a 40-minute walk; the tides are posted at the turnoff on Highway 92).

Below the MacLennan Range, the highway curves towards the south. Beyond the Waikawa River, the road is again paved. Before reaching **Fortrose**, there are two other interesting stops to be recommended: **Curio Bay**, where at low tide you can see the remains of a petrified forest, and **Waipapa Point**. Although the

187

next sign directs the traveler to Invercargill, the destination should in fact be Bluff, which comes after a turn left before entering the city of Invercargill.

Land's End and Sometimes Oysters

The small town of **Bluff** is situated not only at the "end" of New Zealand, it actually seems to be at the end of the world. Two particular circumstances give this town with a population of 3000 its uniqueness: Bluff is the departure point for trips to Stewart Island; and it is the home of New Zealand's oyster fleet, which harvests ocean rock oysters (and not cultured ones). Gourmets throughout the country eagerly await the fresh ocean delicacy each year at the beginning of March. Many even embark on the long journey south from as far away as Auckland; and not without good reason. With the same regularity that the fishing fleets set out to sea, the labor union calls strikes for higher wages and better working conditions for the fishermen. It is, therefore, usually on smaller private boats that the oysters are first brought ashore. This has no detrimental effect to their taste.

The boats *Miro* and *Bargara*, owned by the private enterprise Fowler & Roderique, are sure to set out to sea. They harvest and bring in anywhere from 30 to 100 sacks of oysters to Bluff each day. To safeguard the oysters in their natural habitat, there is a yearly limit of approximately 1000 sacks per boat. At **Fowler & Roderique**, not only can you personally experience the shucking of the oysters, but also you can buy them fresh for dinner. For those who hesitate cooking their own oysters, there are always fresh oysters and chips, a Bluff specialty, available at various take-out restaurants.

An interesting place to stop is the shop **Foveaux Souvenirs** on Gore Street, owned by Dawn Bragg. It almost resembles a museum. In the past years, Dawn has accumulated an impressive collection of unusual and unique souvenirs and buttons from the former USSR – under the loose heading of "Perestroika was here". The former Soviet fishing fleet uses Bluff as a base and its sailors seem to feel right at home at Dawn's.

The best well-known resident of Bluff is the journalist Peter Arnett. Working for the American news network CNN, he was the last newscaster to report live from Baghdad during the Gulf War in 1991. He was in fact born in this little town. Even though Arnett has now become an American citizen, for Bluff he is still the city's most famous offspring.

A less attractive side of Bluff lies on the other end of the harbor. Aluminum is melted 365 days of the year at the large industrial complex on **Tiwai Point**, which negatively affects the air in the area figuratively and literally.

On the east end of the town you'll come to **Stirling Point**, where William Stirling founded a whaling station in 1836. Today, a sign with the words "Land's End" marks the end or the beginning (however you consider it) of Highway 1. To Cape Reinga on North Island it is a 1401 km drive; and Stewart Island across Foveaux Strait is only a stone's throw away. Just the same, the strait can prove difficult to cross. The number of ferry connections to the island have been increasingly cut down due to their unprofitability, and sometimes they even stop completely as early as Easter. The 27 km ride to Stewart can also be a rough one, and stormy weather has very much contributed to the island's isolation during the past 150 years.

STEWART ISLAND

"Paradise" is written on the hood of the rusty bus that takes you on a bumpy, jolting drive from Stewart Island Airport to the town of **Oban**. This outpost is truly a paradise for those searching for solemn beauty and pristine nature.

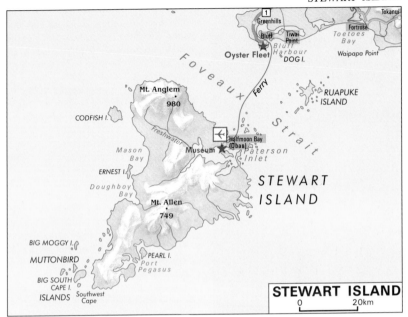

STEWART ISLAND
0   20km

One thousand years ago, Polynesian settlers named this idyllic spot *rakiura*, meaning "land of the glowing heavens", owing to the *aurora australis* (or southern lights) that lights up the clear skies with a radiant glow. The Europeans named the island after William Stewart, the first officer on the British marine ship *Pegasus*, who was the first to chart the island on a map in 1809.

At the same time, the Norwegians used the island as a base for their whale and seal hunts. Among the island's 500 residents, there are still Norwegian descendants earning NZ$ 50 million annually from the abundant ocean floor.

Since the introduction of electricity in 1988, comfortable tourist accommodations have multiplied. There are now clean, warm lodges for the self-sufficient traveler and many rooms to rent in private homes which also provide delicious meals.

The densely-wooded island, with its **Mount Anglem** (980 m), is lined with beaches and spits on which seals bask in the sun. Hiking trails lead past lush giant ferns, virgin beaches enchant you with their azure blue waters, and the peacefulness of nature surrounds everything. On a boat tour, you can observe dolphins and penguins romping playfully in the water; with a little bit of luck, New Zealand's official Kiwi bird will be standing in flocks on the shore.

From the main city Oban, located on Halfmoon Bay, you can tour half of the island in three to four days via a number of trails skirted with giant ferns. There are only about 20 km of road on Stewart Island, but considerably more foot trails. **Paterson's Inlet** to the north is especially interesting.

More than 20 small islands located in this area give the appearance of floating in the water. It goes without saying that those who visit Stewart Island should have a passion for solitude for even the active diversion of the six-hole golf course and the most southerly bar in the world cannot change the reality of these remote environs.

Invercargill and the Way to Fiordland

Besides Bluff (via the ferry), **Invercargill** is the next departure point for trips by airplane to Stewart Island. Located 30 km from Bluff, Invercargill's history also has its beginnings in the days of the whalers. Later on, a flourishing flax industry provided the city with an economic boom. In the meantime, everything revolves around agriculture and sheep breeding. Since the whaling days everything here has calmed down, however. The city cannot and will not deny its Scottish past. Many streets bear the names of Scottish rivers: Forth, Tay, Dee and Esk.

The city owes its fame partly to its location. Invercargill, with a population of 55,000, is the southernmost city of New Zealand, the third largest on South Is-

Above: Tussock grass is characteristic of the landscape near Te Anau. Right: Seal taking it easy on the banks of the Fiordland National Park.

land, and only Stewart Island lies between it and the Antarctica. The **Southland Centennial Museum and Art Gallery** on Gala Street is worth strolling through. It has a vast collection of objects on exhibit regarding the history of Southland. One highlight of its bounty of exhibits is information on the sub-antarctic island environment and on the *tuatara*. The ancestors of this giant lizard have been extinct for more than 135 million years. A central green spot in the city is **Queen's Park.** It is beautiful and relaxing, even if it can hardly compare with the verdant wilderness of Stewart Island.

At Invercargill the highway divides: Highway 1 curves along the east coast and then heads again towards the north; Highway 6 proceeds past **Winton,** **Lumsden** and **Mossburn** (152 km, stops along the way are quite unnecessary), then to Te Anau, the entrance to Fiordland National Park. If time allows, there is an interesting alternative route via Highway 99 along the coast past **Clifden**, and from there further on through lonely backlands directly to Manapouri on **Manapouri Lake**. This route is part of the **Southern Scenic Route**, previously mentioned, and stops at the seaport of **Riverton** (*paua* shells are available here!), the bush-walk area of **Pourakino** and the calm **Colac Bay** (the most beautiful beach in the vicinity is **Wakapatu Beach**) are rewarding. Relatively unexplored hiking areas can be found at **Lake Hauroko** and **Lake Monowai**. On the **Dusky Track** from Lake Hauroko, you can travel a total of three days until you reach **Loch Maree Hut** (16 hours of straight hiking; 32 km have to be covered by boat on the lake; starting point is near Hauroko Burn Hut). From here, the hike to **Dusky Sound** to the southwest will take six hours (overnight accommodations available at **Supper Cove Hut** with 12 beds). In the northern direction, you will need three days to reach the west arm of Lake Manapouri.

Dusky Track can turn dangerous in bad weather and heavy rainfall, and it is an outdoor challenge even if ventured upon in good weather. It should not be taken lightly. Therefore, it is recommended to register at the DOC before starting the hike and sign the visitors' books in the huts along the way. Information and maps can be obtained at the DOC office in Te Anau.

Fiordland: Pure Nature as Far as the Eye Can See

Lake Manapouri and nearby **Doubtful Sound** increasingly have become "rivals" of Milford Sound, although they have not achieved its level of touristic importance. This could be due basically to the arduous approach to Doubtful Sound. The sound can only be reached on a reserved boat tour. Most visitors come to Manapouri after a day-trip in Te Anau. From here, they cross the lake to the shores of the West Arm. Afterwards, a hydro-power plant (through a tunnel you can reach the engine room located 200 m below the water's surface) and **Wilmot Pass** (670 m) "black" any direct access to the lake itself. The road continues through dense beech forests down to **Deep Cove**, where you can take a boat tour (usually a short one) on the **Sound of Peace and Serenity**, one of the largest pure-water reservoirs in the world. From Manapouri, the tours of the sound start at 8:30 a.m. in the summer and 10:30 a.m. in the winter (the tour lasts about six hours). The town itself offers overnight accommodations of varying classes of comfort; it has a post office and stores.

The undisputed center of Fiordland is **Te Anau** (21 km). On the shores of **Te Anau Lake** (53 km long and up to 276 m deep) everyone lives from and for tourism. The town, which has a population of 3000, is an ideal starting point for trips to Milford Sound, as well as hikes through Fiordland National Park.

Therefore, park headquarters on the **Te Anau Terrace** is the most important address for every visitor.

FIORDLAND NATIONAL PARK

The **Fiordland National Park**, which spreads out over a vast area of 1.2 million hectares in the southeastern section of South Island, is the most varied and spectacular park with regard to scenery in the entire country. It is also said to be the rainiest spot in the world! Although there are more than 7 m of precipitation annually, it should also be mentioned that extensive periods of sunny weather have also been reported. Whenever it rains heavily, otherwise undemanding roads become difficult to pass. Weatherproof clothing and insect repellent should not be missing in your baggage (or backpack). The swarms of sandflies that buzz around in the early morning or evening are not dangerous, but they can be very annoying and spoil your good mood!

A broad spectrum of wonderful hiking trails are among the incentives for a tour into Fiordland. Regardless of whether you are just taking a ten-minute stroll on one of the marked paths, or whether you intend to courageously venture out into the wilderness, there is something for everyone here. Majestic peaks tower high above the rampant green rain forests in the west and the beech forests in the east. After the nightly rainfall, the clear rivers can suddenly be transformed into roaring and raging waters. Most visitors are attracted to the glacier fjord Milford Sound with its overwhelmingly beautiful landscape. Good or bad weather has no effect on the splendor of the region. When it rains cats and dogs, the awe-inspiring waterfalls plunge down the fjord walls; and when the sun shines, you will stand speachless in front of the sheer face of the steep cliffs rise out of the water at the height of one kilometer.

Hikers and campers just might have trouble making decisions as to what to do because the choices are manifold here. The world-famous (and rightly so) **Milford Track** is not exactly deserted, but the four-day tour with up to six hours of walking each day from Lake Te Anau to Milford Sound is magnificent but not easy. Although the trip can be undertaken without guides, you do need a tramping permit. It is almost impossible to enter the track without the expensive permit since the entrance on both sides is accessible only by water, and therefore easily controlled by the DOC.

The number of tramping permits is limited to 10,000 per year. This restriction made by the DOC has made it possible for nature to recover and regenerate after a period of strain and stress, so that the trail is again an enjoyable experience for all.

Another excellent trail leads to **Hollyford Valley**, which stretches out for approximately 70 km between Milford Road and the Tasman Sea. This long and strenuous trip (especially after rainfall) offers beautiful views across the **Darran Mountains**, the **Hollyford River** and **Lake McKerrow**. Guided tours are available in the summertime. The heavily-traveled **Routeburn** and **Greenstone Tracks** also begin on Milford Road. The newly-cleared **Kepler Track** takes you through wooded highlands to the west side of Lake Te Anau in three to four days. The track starts out at the suspension bridge at Te Anau. There are three huts along the way, each with 40 beds: **Moturau**, **Iris Burn** and **Mount Luxmore**. It is also possible to hike just parts of the track – for example, the relatively easy walk along the river to Iris Burn or the slightly more difficult climb to Mount Luxmore, where you can be picked up by a helicopter for the return trip.

For a truly adventurous experience in the wilderness surrounded by unspoiled nature, Fiordland National Park is ideal.

MILFORD SOUND

Those who wish to stay someplace where the scenery is beautiful should go

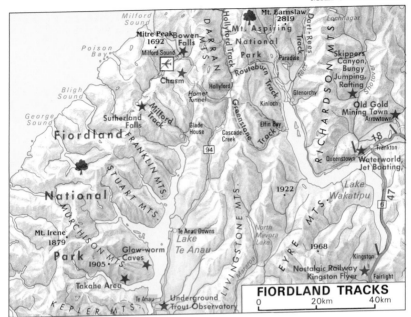

FIORDLAND TRACKS

0   20km   40km

to one of the numerous motels on the lake's shoreline. Visitors looking for adventure in the evening can start off to the **Te Ana-au Caves** at 8:15 p.m. (first departure at 2 p.m.). These glowworm grottoes were discovered in 1948 by Lawson Burrows, and can be only reached via water. The Te Ana-au Caves are located at the edge of the takahe area, where about 100 takahes still live. For many years, it was believed that these flightless birds were extinct.

After sundown, Te Anau has little else to offer. This has its positive side because the motto *carpe diem* applies to every new day here. An early start on the trip to Milford Sound guarantees a rewarding and unforgettable outdoor experience (in nice weather). An added advantage of early rising is avoiding the crowds of tourists who roll out daily from Queenstown to Milford. The Southlanders have given this rush the nickname "traffic tide." Between 8 and 10 a.m., the masses flow in. Around 3 p.m., they pour back out for the return trip.

So enjoy the 119 km long early approach from Te Anau. Stops are worthwhile at the **Te Anau Downs**, where hikers can start off to the Milford Track, the **Mirror Lakes**, **Lake Fergus**, with fascinating views of mountains, glaciers and raging mountain rivers, as well as to the entrance of **Homer Tunnel** (often the weather divide!), where you will meet up with the cocky *kea* (do not feed!). If you treasure your vehicle, it is best to keep on driving. If you stop, you are certain to receive a lasting memento since the *keas* relish pouncing on windshield wipers and rubber stripping, tearing them into tiny pieces in a flash with their sharp beaks. Beyond the unlit tunnel, the road descends down to the ocean. After traveling approximately 15 km, you will have reached the destination of your dreams: Milford Sound.

However, to ensure that your dreams do not turn into nightmares, be warned that at Milford Sound solitude and serenity are long gone because there are approximately 2000 visitors daily in the

193

summertime, and annually a total of about 250,000 visitors.

By the year 2000, the authorities would like to double the number, and preparation for this goal has already begun. The extension and reinforcement of the infrastucture were started in 1990/91. These measures will help cope with the growing number of tourists. However, this part of New Zealand will surely lose a piece of its unspoiled character in the process.

The absolute landmark of Milford Sound is the sharply protruding **Mitre Peak**, the highest peak in the world when measuring its direct elevation from sealevel at 1692 m. A rewarding excursion is the boat trip through the sound (various departure times all day long).

The tranquility and diverse wildlife, including numerous sea lion and seal colonies, can only be truly appreciated and

Above: A boat ride gives a particularly interesting and dramatic view of the mountains surrounding Milford Sound.

experienced from the water. The tours last approximately two hours.

The sound was carved out of the cliffs during the ice age about 1.5 million years ago. It is 16 km long and was given its name by John Grono, a seal hunter. He came to the sound in 1823, leaving behind the name of his Welsh birthplace, Milford Haven.

After returning from the boat ride, you can go by foot to **Bowen Falls** via a narrow path leading away from the boat dock. The falls plummet down a rock face over 160 m high.

Milford Sound is particularly fascinating in good weather. If the weather is poor (which it is quite often), you will hardly be compensated with the numerous waterfalls that cascade down the mountain sides.

Those who have the time and wish to enjoy the area in peace and quiet (which is actually possible), should stay overnight in Milford Sound. The selection of accommodations range from simple dormitories to luxurious hotels.

But be careful! In the evenings, as well as in the early morning hours, the sandflies can be a veritable torment. The bites of these small insects are not dangerous, but very unpleasant – particularly because they attack their victims in swarms of hundreds. In the future when you hear the words "Milford Sound" you will inevitably think of the sandflies as well as of beautiful landscapes.

To assist you in planning your travel itinerary, the following information could be of importance. It takes about 2.5 hours from Queenstown to Te Anau, and from Te Anau to Milford Sound approximately three hours. If you make a few stops along the beautiful plains covered with tussock grass, the trip will take a little longer.

Back at Te Anau, Highway 94 proceeds to **Mossburn**, where you take a left turn and head for **Five Rivers** and Highway 6. At **Kingston**, you will have reached not only the southern edges of **Lake Wakatipu** but also the train station of the nostalgic *Kingston Flyer,* an old fashioned steam-locomotive, which chugs along to **Fairlight** in 45 minutes during the summer months.

For the next 40 km, the road closely hugs the lake's shoreline. There is time enough to reflect on a Maori legend that tells of a sleeping giant who was burned on the present site of the lake, although his heart kept on beating. This is the mythological explanation for the changing water level of **Lake Wakatipu**. The so-called "breathing lake" rises and falls approximately 12 cm in five- minute periods. Scientists explain this phenomenom as the result of changing atmospheric pressure across the water's surface, which measures almost 300 sq. km.

Giants' hearts evidently beat differently, and so it is with the rhythm of city life in Queenstown for the visitor who has just arrived from the solitude and the magnificent impressions of nature in Fiordland.

QUEENSTOWN

Queenstown, located on the shores of Lake Wakatipu, is the tourist center of South Island. After the solitary experience in the wilderness, many travelers enjoy the change of pace to the activity between The Mall and the lake's shore.

One of the first settlers in Queenstown was the pioneer William Gilbert Rees, who provided many mountains and valleys in the area with their English names. In 1863, the government declared the area a township, and Rees was forced to tear down the foundation walls of his farm. At about the same time, a certain William Fox appeared on the scene and discovered the "richest river in the world," the **Shotover River**: From then on everything revolved around gold and panning it out of the riverbed.

Queenstown's main attraction in the 1990's is its location, which implies a broad selection of outdoor sports and activities. These range from hiking (over ten well-kept trails in the vicinity), paragliding, golf (one of the most beautiful 18-hole golf courses in the world is located in **Kelvin Heights**, a section of Queenstown), skiing, mountain biking, white-water rafting, to the comparatively passive sport of jet-boating.

Not exactly new, but still the number one challenge of an odd kind is bungee jumping. With a special rubber rope *(bungee)* tied to the ankles, courageous daredevils can jump from bridges and freefall until they are caught up by the bungee. Two bridges famous for bungee jumping are the **Skippers Canyon Bridge** (height: 75 m) and the **Pipeline** (100 m) are a bit out of the way but easily reached and conveniently combined with a white-water rafting tour or jet-boating; at **Kawarau Bridge** (directly on Highway 6 on the way to Cromwell), where jumpers can fall to depths of 50 meters.

Alan J. Hackett, who has bungee-jumped from the Eiffel Tower, is the in-

ventor of this typical New Zealand sport. The rubber rope can be adjusted to exact lengths (upon request) so that the jumper's freefall is stopped just as he touches the water's surface with his hands. It might be added that accidents and injuries seldom occur during this breathtaking thrill. *Bungy* jumping is now being offered in many larger cities in the country.

Jet-boating, in comparison, has already become a classic sporting activity which hardly any Queenstown visitor misses out on. In the 1950s, a farmer by the name of Hamilton designed and developed this boat powered by a gas turbine enabling it to skim over the water. His purpose for the boat was to explore remote rivers and search for new pastureland.

Today, the boat is a big tourist attraction. The most popular tour takes the visitor on Shotover River through **Skippers**

Above left and right: Jet boating on Shotover River and bungy jumping from Kawarau Bridge. Right: Tandem Skydivers.

Canyon. Caution is advised: There are over 100 enterprises offering the tours and they are all quite different. Some plan the tour over the Kawarau River only, which is less exciting. By the way, those who wish to take their vehicles to Skippers Canyon should take special care when driving through the canyon along the narrow and unpaved road.

Involving less technical machinery, but all the wetter an adventure is whitewater rafting on a nearby section of the river (degree of difficulty: up to 5). The 170 m long **Oxenbridge Tunnel** and the **Cascade** are especially thrilling.

A trip less exciting due to the absence of rocky gorges, but still one of the most beautiful trips in the vicinity of Queenstown, is *jet-boating* on the **Dart River**. To reach it, you take a bus over an unpaved road from Queenstown to **Glenorchy**, a sleepy village nestled on the north end of Lake Wakatipu, where **Mount Earnslaw** (2819 m) dominates the heavens, snow-capped practically all the year round.

You can take a boat to the borders of **Mount Aspiring National Park.** The landscape is virtually untouched. Only the small town of **Paradise** still carries traces of the gold rush days. At that time, particularly the Chinese believed that their fortune lay buried in the Dart River. They were unfortunately mistaken: Gold was discovered in another river, and the Chinese returned home after years of generally hard times and much disappointment.

Penetrating deeper into the national park, you will come to the **Rees Dart Track**. In about five days of hiking, which is not always the easiest, you can circle the entire Earnslaw Range. The daily hiking time will amount to about nine hours. The Rees Saddle should only be attempted in good weather. A trip from **Dart Hut** along **Dart Glacier** to the **Cascade Saddle** is then also worthwhile. Being equipped with insect repellent is wise because of the sandfly plague.

The **Routeburn Track** also begins at Glenorchy. *Burn* is an old Scottish word

meaning river. This track is among the most popular hikes in New Zealand, following the course of the river. Its popularity is due in large part to the fact that you can hike towards Milford in three to four days. To reach the sound itself, you have to cover about 30 km of ground, starting at the trail's end on the road from Te Anau – hitchhiking is best.

The third track in the Lake Wakatipu area is called **Greenstone Caples Track**. Starting point for the track is usually on the west side of the lake at **Elfin Bay**, which can be reached on the road from Glenorchy. An alternative would be to turn off the Routeburn Track at **Lake Howden** and hike back either along Caples or Greenstone Rivers towards Lake Wakatipu. You will need three to four days for the entire track. The most difficult part of the hike is the climb to **McKellar Saddle**. An ideal spot to set up your tent for a few days of peace and quiet is the area along the mouth of the river. There is also excellent trout fishing in the waters of the Greenstone and

Caples Rivers. One only needs the appropiate permit from the DOC.

Attractive in Summer and Winter

Queenstown (no one wishes to be quoted as to which queen's city it is) not exactly only offers numerous attractions for the active vacationer, but is also interesting and entertaining for those who like a more relaxed and slower-paced schedule. A popular tour, due partly to its nostalgic character, is the one aboard the *T. S. S. Earnslaw* on Lake Wakatipu. The steam boat first broke the water on February 12, 1912, and it sets out on the lake several times daily (no trips in June). The most preferred tour is the one at 2 p.m., with a stop at the **Walter Peak Sheep Station** (lasting short of three hours). The largest farm in the Wakatipu

Above: The old T. S. S. Earnslaw on Lake Wakatipu. Right: Making one's way down the Yellow Brick Road, goldfields near Wakatipu.

area has a stock of approximately 25,000 sheep and 2000 cattle. The evening cruise of the *Earnslaw* begins at 6 p.m. (lasting 1.5 hours) and frequently affords fantastic lighting conditions and effects – not only for photographers.

After returning to **Steamer Wharf**, a look into the underwater world can be quite interesting. The **Queenstown Waterworld** offers the visitor the opportunity to take an eye-to-eye look at trout, salmon (in season), eels and ducks. The best view of the city itself is from **Bob's Peak**. At the end of Brecon Street, a cable ride takes you up to the peak's lookout at an elevation of 446 m.

Helicopter rides have advanced over the decades into one of the basic tourist attractions in Queenstown. They offer the kind of view no platform however high can offer, and with the last effort. The most popular flights are over the city, to Lake Wakatipu, to Skippers Canyon, to the Remarkables and to Milford Sound. However, the latter trip will cost more than NZ$ 400.

The Remarkables are better experienced with both feet on the ground, or rather on snow. This skiing area was opened in 1986. It has three chair lifts, one of which opens up slopes suitable for even the best of skiers (*Sugar Bowl Lift:* cost of a day pass is about NZ$ 45).

Even better known is the **Coronet Peak Ski Area.** This area encompasses 280 hectares of land and has everything from slopes for beginners to deep-snow ski runs (a day pass costs about NZ$ 45 as well).

During the 1991 season, 21 snow machines were in operation. By and large one can count on snow between June and October on Coronet Peak and the surrounding area.

On the way home from Coronet Peak, there seems to be only one place to meet in the winter, at **Arthur's Point.** Both ski teachers and ski "bunnies" congregate here after finishing up on the slopes.

In Queenstown itself, everyone gathers at **Eichardt's Tavern** in winter and summer. Parts of this building at the end of The Mall date back to the year 1871. This august age in no way spoils the atmosphere. In fact, there is no better spot to go out for a beer or to play a round of billiards than at Eichardt's. It is the in-place for all outdoor experts (and many who think they are). Every evening the wildest adventure stories make the rounds (frequently with live music).

It is better to go next door to satisfy your hunger. Either at **Westy's** (at The Mall, open at 6 p.m., usually live music), or at **Chicos** (The Mall, open at 6:30 p.m.), or at **The Cow**, a pizza and spaghetti house (Cow Lane, open from noon until 3 a.m.).

For those who want to dance the night away, the **Dolphin Club** is the appropriate place, located at 54 Shotover Street and open from 9 p.m. to 3 a.m..

By now you will realize that Queenstown is just a bit different than the rest of New Zealand.

Where Gold Diggers Romped

On the way from Queenstown to Wanaka, a small road turns off at **Lake Hayes** (15 km) to the gold-rush town of **Arrowtown.** It has been quaintly restored and offers the opportunity to relive the old days between pubs, shops and the post office. The most popular subject for photographs is the sign reading "Reward – $500" (located on the main street) where you can add your own name to the notorious "wanted list."

A quick look at the map, and you will discover an inviting short cut at nearby **Crown Terrace**. The unpaved Highway 89 leads to Wanaka in a mere 54 km. Caution is advised, however. The scenery is beautiful, but the road is in terrible condition. Travelers driving a rented vehicle should check in advance as to whether or not this route can be traveled without objections from the insurance company. Many rental agencies specifically prohibit the use of this road in their contracts. If you do find yourself on this

road, a good stop-over for lunch is the **Cardrona Hotel** (varying business hours during the year), which has preserved a touch of the gold rush era. In contrast, the nearby **Cardrona Ski Field** is relatively new, and is considered a good spot especially for beginners (located 69 km from Queenstown). However, there are few overnight accommodations available.

On the other hand, if you continue from Arrowtown on Highway 6, you will soon pass by **Kawarau Bridge** on the left side. This is your last chance for *bungy* jumping into the depths below the bridge. The highway follows the course of the Kawarau River and the tracks of the gold diggers. The landscape is barren and brown, but still a heaven on earth for a few adventurous and lucky souls.

Tourists can follow the footsteps of the gold hunters along the **Otago Goldfields Heritage Trail,** formed by 17 towns between Dunedin in the east and Glenochry

Above: Arrowtown recalls some of the more pleasant aspects of the gold rush.

in the west. Information can be obtained at the DOC offices in Dunedin, Alexandra and Queenstown. The small **Gold-mining Museum** in the Kawarau Gorge gives practical visual instructions on the subject and offers visitors the chance to look for gold.

At **Cromwell**, the landscape suddenly changes to green again. In the "Orchards of the South," as they are widely known, numerous vegetable and fruit stands flank both sides of the road. The prices are higher than in the north, but there is no better place to restock on travel provisions, especially if you are planning to journey back to the west coast at one, long fell swoop. The road divides at Cromwell. Highway 8 leads beyond the Clutha River in the direction of **Lindis Pass** – a lovely tussock grassland, especially enchanting at dusk. There is another 33 km to be traveled to **Omarama**. Lake Pukaki, with its view of Mount Cook, is still 40 km away. Wanaka, the next main destination, is another 50 km down Highway 6.

SOUTHERN REGION
CATLINS AND ITS ENVIRONS
Accommodation

CATLINS: *MODERATE:* **Catlins Inn**, 21 Ryley St., Owaka, Tel: 03-4158350. **Chaslands Farm Motor Lodge**, Owaka, Waipati Rd., R.D.2, Tel: 03-4158501. **Rosebank Lodge**, 265 Clyde St., Balclutha, Tel: 03-4181490.

BUDGET: **Catlins Coast Accommodation**, Progress Valley R.D.1, Tokanui, Tel: 03-2468843. **Papatowai Motor Camp,** Tel: 03-4158063 (28 km south of Owaka).

Restaurants

GORE: Table Talk Café, 113 Main St., Tel: 03-2087110 (one of the few lunch-stops on the route to Invercargill).

Tips and Trips

CATLINS: Fergus Sutherland and his Catlins Wildlife Trackers, Dunedin, P.O. Box, Tel: 03-4552681, offer two-day guided tours in the Catlins – with a very friendly family flair.

SOUTHERN SCENIC ROUTE: The **DOC** (Dunedin, Owaka, Stewart Island, Invercargill and Te Anau) and the **AA** (Dunedin and Invercargill) supply information and leaflets on the most important sights and on road conditions along your chosen route.

Tourist Information

GORE: Visitor Information, Ordsal St., Tel: 03-2089908.

OWAKA: **Catlins Forest Park Visitor Centre**, corner Campbell and Riley St., Owaka, Tel: 03-4158341.

STEWART ISLAND / BLUFF
Accommodation

STEWART ISLAND: *LUXURY:* **Stewart Island Lodge**, Halfmoon Bay, Tel: 03-2191085. *MODERATE:* **Stewart Island Holiday Homes**, Elgin Terrace, Tel: 03-2176585. **Shearwater Inn**, Halfmoon Bay, Tel: 03-2191114.

BUDGET: **Homestay Accommodation**: Anne Pullen, Tel: 03-2191065. Michael Squires, Tel: 03-2191425. Andy and Jo Riksem, Tel: 03-2191230 (all P.O. Box 103, Halfmoon Bay). **South Sea Hotel**, Tel: 03-2191059.

BLUFF: *MODERATE:* **Bay View Hotel**, Gore St., Tel: 03-2128615. **Foveaux Hotel**, Gore St., Tel: 03-2127196.

BUDGET: **Property Arcade Backpackers**, 120 Gore St., Tel: 03-228074.

Restaurants

BLUFF: **Captain's Retreat**, Gore St. (Southland's best fish restaurant).

STEWART ISLAND: Annie Hansen's Dining Room, Elgin Terrace, Tel: 03-2191059 (delicious fish dishes in a rural atmosphere; open most evenings between 6–7 p.m. only).

Tips and Trips

Adventure: Paul and Joan Pasco, P.O. Box 168, Bluff, Tel: 03-2127254 arrange hunting-, fishing- and diving-tours on and around Stewart Island.

Bus: H & H Bus Service runs between Bluff and Invercargill every 1,5 hours (Mondays–Fridays). Connection with the Steward-Island Ferry: the bus to Bluff (ferry to Steward Island) leaves at 7:45 a.m. from Invercargill (Kelvin St.), and returns from Bluff at 4:30 p.m. after ferry arrival.

Connections to Stewart Island: Southern Air flies three times daily from Invercargill to Stewart Island. (Flying time ca. 20 minutes, the fare is 140 NZ$ return; Information: Tel: 03-2189129).

The ferry from Bluff runs twice daily (times are subject to weather conditions; the fare is 80 NZ$ return). **Trout**: A small consolation for luckless anglers: A trout farm on Stewart Island opens its doors to the public. Tel: 03-2191085.

Festivals and Special Events

BLUFF: The *Oyster Festival* is celebrated every year in April with plenty of oysters and festivities. The actual oyster-season starts at the end of February/beginning of March.

Tourist Information

STEWART ISLAND: Information Centre, Halfmoon Bay, Tel: 03-2191130. **BLUFF: Foveaux Souvenirs**, Gore St., Tel: 03-2128305.

INVERCARGILL
AND ITS ENVIRONS
Accommodation

INVERCARGILL: *LUXURY:* **Kelvin Hotel,** 16 Kelvin St,. Tel: 03-2182829.

MODERATE: **Aachen Motel**, 147 Yarrow St., Tel: 03-2188185. **Coachmans Inn**, 705 Tay St., Tel: 03-2176046. **Bavarian Motel**, 444 North Road, Tel: 03-2157552, Fax: 03-2157592

BUDGET: **Invercargill Caravan Park**, 20 Victoria Ave, Tel: 03-2188787. **Southern Comfort Backpackers**, 30 Thompson St., Tel: 03-2183838. **Invercargill Caravan Park**, 20 Victoria Ave., Tel: 03-2188787, has cabins as well.

LORNEVILLE: *MODERATE:* **White House Hotel**, Riverton Highway, Tel: 03-2358116 (Highway 96).

LUMSDEN: *BUDGET:* **Mossburn Country Park**, Five Rivers Rd., R.D.3, Tel: 03-2486030.

WINTON: *BUDGET:* **Central Southland Lodge**, 232 Great North Rd., Tel: 03-2368413.

Restaurants

INVERCARGILL: Ainos Steakhouse and Restaurant, Ruru Street, Waikiwi Shopping Centre, Tel: 032159568 (the speciality here is South-

land lamb, closed Sundays). **Donovan's,** 220 Banfield Rd., Tel: 03-2158156 (speciality of the house: lamb in whiskey sauce; expensive; open 5 p.m.–1 a.m.). **Homestead Restaurant,** corner Avenue und Dee Street, Tel: 03-2183125.
RIVERTON: Rivertonian Restaurant, 102 Palmerston St., Tel: 03-2348734 (a last chance to savor fresh Bluff oysters on your way to Fiordland; open daily from 6 p.m.; closed Mondays and Tuesdays).

Museum
INVERCARGILL: Southland Centennial Museum and Art Gallery, Gala St./Queens Park (open Mondays–Fridays 10 a.m.–4:30 p.m.; Sundays and public holidays 1–5 p.m.), Tel: 03-2189753.

Tourist Information
INVERCARGILL: **Visitor Centre,** Queens Park, Tel: 03-2146273 (open Mondays–Fridays 9 a.m.–5:30 p.m.). **Department of Conservation (DOC),** State Insurance Building, Don St., Tel: 03-2144589.
LUMSDEN: Information Centre, Old Railway Station, Tel: 03-2487334 (Mondays–Fridays according to season from 9/10 a.m.–4/5 p.m.).

TE ANAU / FIORDLAND
Accommodation
TE ANAU: *LUXURY:* **THC Te Anau,** Lakefront, Tel: 03-2497411. **The Village Inn,** Mokoroa St., Tel: 03-2497911.
MODERATE: **Edgewater XL Motels,** 52 Te Anau Terrace, Tel: 03-2497258. **Lakeside Motel,** 36 Lakefront Dr., Tel: 03-2497435. **Luxmore Resort Hotel,** Milford Rd., Tel: 03-2497526.
BUDGET: **Fiordland Resort Hotel,** P.O. Box 68, Tel: 03-2497511. **Te Anau Motor Park,** P.O. Box 81, Tel: 03-2497457. **Te Anau Mountain View Cabin and Caravan Park,** Mokonui St. and Te Anau Terrace, P.O. Box 171, Tel: 03-2497462.
MANAPOURI: *BUDGET:* **Lakeview Motels & Motor Park,** Manapouri-Te Anau Rd., P.O. Box 3, Tel: 03-2496624.
MILFORD SOUND: *LUXURY:* **THC Milford,** Tel: 03-2497926.
BUDGET: **Milford Lodge,** Tel: 03-2498071.
Restaurants
TE ANAU: Henry Family Restaurant, 64 Te Anau Terrace, Tel: 03-2497411 (lovely sea-view). **Jailhouse Café,** Tel: 03-2498083 (good breakfast from 7 a.m.). **Our Great Te Anau Restaurant,** 1 Te Anau-Manapouri Rd., Tel: 03-2497457.
Tips and Trips
Boat Trips on Milford Sound: The *Red Boats* (belonging to the THC Hotel) depart at 10:30 a.m.

and 11 a.m., 1, 1:30 and 3:30 p.m. (trip to the open Tasman Sea; duration of trip ca. 2 hours; the fare is 35 NZ$).
Bike Tours: Explore the Sound in a slightly unusual way with *Milford Sound Adventure Tours* (Te Anau, Tel: 03-2497227): Outward journey by bus, return journey – downhill! – 40 km on a mountain-bike.
Kepler Track: The Te Anau Motor Park, Tel: 03-2497457, runs a shuttle-bus service to the track; the bus runs daily at 8:30 a.m., 10 a.m. and 4:45 p.m. from Te Anau to Rainbow Reach; 10 a.m., 3 p.m. and 5 p.m. from Rainbow Reach to Te Anau. Luggage may be left in the Motor Park.
Milford Track: Information and booking for individual hiking tours along the track: Te Anau Travelodge, P.O. Box 185, Te Anau, Tel: 03-2498514. A maximum of 40 people per day are allowed to start on the track, starts daily except Sundays (1996/7: 1300 NZ$). Once you've booked your accommodation in a hut, this is binding – you can't change your mind and turn up at a different hut, and/or at a different date. The so-called Independent Walk must be booked in advance (and permit requested) at the DOC, P.O. Box 29, Te Anau, Tel: 03-2498514. Fee NZ$ 200 with transportation, NZ$ 90 without transportation (1995). Reduced prices for children.
Warning for Hikers: Along the tracks in Fjordland National Park many rivers and lakes are contaminated by Giardia-bacteria.
Tourist Information
TE ANAU: Fiordland Travel, Te Anau Terrace, Tel: 03-2497416 (open daily 7:30 a.m.–9 p.m. in summer, 8 a.m.–4 p.m. in winter).
DOC, Fiordland National Park, Visitor Centre, Te Anau Terrace, Tel: 03-2498514, Office hours 9 a.m. to 4:30 p.m.
DOC, Clifden Road, Tuatapere, Tel: 03-2266607.

QUEENSTOWN AND ENVIRONS
Accommodation
QUEENSTOWN: *LUXURY:* **Holiday Inn Queenstown,** Sainsbury Rd., Fernhill, Tel: 03-4426600. **Nugget Point Club,** Arthurs Point Rd., Tel: 03-4427680. **Queenstown Parkroyal Hotel,** Beach St., Tel: 03-4427800. **THC Queenstown Resort Hotel,** corner Marine Parade and Earl St., Tel: 03-4427750. **Lakeland,** Lake Esplanade, Tel: 03-4427600. **Sherwood Manor Motor Inn,** Frankton Rd., Tel: 03-4428032. **The Lodges,** 6 Lake Esplanade, Tel: 03-4427552.
MODERATE: **Alpine Sun Motel,** 14 Hallenstein St., Tel: 03-4428482. **Amber Motor Lodge,** 1 Gorge Rd., Tel: 03-4428480. **Contiki Lodge,** Sainsbury Rd., Fernhill, Tel: 03-4427107. **Lakeside Motel,** 18 Lake Esplanade, Tel: 03-4428976.

Mountain View Lodge Motel, Frankton Rd., Tel: 03-4428246. **The Mountaineer Hotel**, corner Rees and Beach St., Tel: 03-4427400.
BUDGET: **FAB Accomodiation**, 42 Frankton Rd., Tel: 03-4426095. **Bungi Backpackers**, corner Sydney and Stanley St., Tel: 03-4428725. **Pinewood Motel**, 48 Hamilton Rd., Tel: 03-4428273. **Queenstown Motor Park**, 51 Man St., Tel: 03-4427252 (cabins and camping, spacial grounds, very clean). **Youth Hostel,** 80 Lake Esplanade, Tel: 03-4428413.
ALEXANDRA: *BUDGET:* **Alexandra Holiday Camp**, Manuherikia Rd., P.O. Box 7, Tel: 03-4488297.
ARROWTOWN: *BUDGET:* **Arrowtown Caravan Park**, 47 Devon St., Tel: 03-4421838.
CLYDE: *LUXURY:* **Olivers Lodge**, Central Otago, P.O. Box 38.
BUDGET: **Clyde Camping Ground**, Whitby St., Tel: 03-4492713.
CROMWELL: *BUDGET:* **Sunhaven Motor Camp**, Alpha St., Tel: 03-4450164.
FRANKTON: *BUDGET:* **Frankton Motor Camp**, Yewlett Crescent, Tel: 03-4427247.
GLENORCHY: *BUDGET:* **Glenorchy Holiday Park**, 2 Oban St., Tel: 03-4429939.

Restaurants

QUEENSTOWN: Millies, 24 Beach St., Tel: 03-4427309 (New Zealand fish and meat for the whole family; central location). **Minami Jujisei**, Rees St., Tel: 03-4429854 (Japanese food; a favourite not only with Japanese visitors). **Nugget Point Restaurant**, Arthurs Point Rd., Tel: 03-4427630 (New Zealand cuisine around a romantic open fireplace; a bit out of town; expensive). **The Stonewall Café**, Eureka House, The Mall, Tel: 03-4426429; Snacks. **Treetops of Queenstown**, Arawata Terrace, Sunshine Bay, Tel: 03-4427238 (international cuisine, expensive). **Upstairs Downstairs Restaurant**, 66 Shotover St., Tel: 03-4428290 (international and New Zealand cuisine in Victorian decor; expensive; from 6 p.m.).
ALEXANDRA: Fruitlands Gallery, State Highway, 8 km to the south, Tel: 03-4487838 (in a 19th-century pub; too good and too expensive for just a short stop; open 11:30–2:30 a.m.).
CLYDE: Olivers Restaurant and Lodge, 34 Sunderland St., Tel: 03-4492860 (one of the culinary highlights of Central Otago; expensive).
TARRAS: The Merino Shop, Central Otago, Tel: 03-4452872 (teas, snacks and a souvenir-shop selling sheepskin products; part of Bendigo Station).

Tips and Trips

Bungy Jumping: The agency A.J. Hackett, P.O. Box 488, Tel: 03-4421177 offers this test of courage to those raring to plunge from great heights, suspended from a rubber rope. You can jump off the Skippers Suspension Bridge (75 m) and the Kawarau Suspension Bridge (50 m); the price per jump is ca. 90 NZ$.
Car Rental: Hardy Cars, 6 Bridge St., Nelson, Tel: 03-5481681, Fax: 03-5481581.
Dart River: The agency Dart River Jets (P.O. Box 76, Tel: 03-4429992) offers a perfect mix of *Jet Boating* and experiencing nature; excursions twice daily (8:15 a.m. and 2:15 p.m.) on a 5,5 hour trip along the Dart River near Glenorchy (more than 100 NZ$).
Fiordland: Fiordland Travel, Steamer Wharf, Tel: 03-4427500, arrange the broadest spectrum of trips, from Doubtful and Milford Sound to a cruise on the *T.S.S. Earnslaw* (special prices for multiple bookings or groups).
Helicopter Flights: Organized by The Helicopter Line, Tel: 03-4423034 (for reservations and information throughout the country, Tel: 09-3774406.) The *Helicopter Line Plus* package-arrangement combines rafting, jetboating, bungy-jumping and a picnic.
Rental Skis: Bill Lacheny Sports, The Mall, Tel: 03-4428438 (opposite the bus stop to Coronet Peak and The Remarkables).
Skiing- and Snow-Info: Coronet Ski Area and The Remarkables: Mount Cook Line, P.O. Box 4644, Christchurch, Tel: 03-482099.
Wine: Blackridge (near Alexandria), the southernmost wine-growing estate in the world, is open to visitors. Tel: 03-4492059.
Whitewater-Rafting: The boats of Kiwi Discovery, 37 Camp St., Tel: 03-4427340 brave the rapids of the Shotover River every day (duration ca. 4,5 hours). A four-day tour explores the Landsborough River.

Festivals / Special Events

QUEENSTOWN: An extensive *Winter Festival* is celebrated during the first week of August. At the end of October, the *Alpine Ironman* is elected after a hard winter-triathlon.
ALEXANDRA: The *Eastern Arts and Crafts Festival* takes place at eastertime with handicraft displays and special events.
OTAGO: *Goldfields Celebrations* take place in the Otago region every year, in the middle of Nov.

Tourist Information

QUEENSTOWN: Information Centre, corner Shotover and Camp St., Tel: 03-4424100 (Mondays–Fridays 7 a.m.–9 p.m.; weekends 7 a.m.–6 p.m.). **DOC**, 37 Shotover St., Tel: 03-4427933.
ALEXANDRA: Information Centre, 22 Centennial Ave., Tel: 03-4489515 (Mon–Fri 9 a.m.–5:30 p.m.). **DOC**, 45 Centennial Ave, Tel: 03-4488874.
GLENORCHY: DOC, Mull/Oban St., Tel: 03-4429937.

THE WILD WEST

WANAKA
MOUNT ASPIRING NATIONAL PARK
WESTLAND NATIONAL PARK
PAPAROA NATIONAL PARK

WANAKA

The situation in **Wanaka** can be compared to that of Queenstown. A difference between the cities in favor of Wanaka is, that for many visitors, with a population of 1500 and located on the shores of a beautiful lake, Wanaka has been spared the hustle and bustle of large tourist crowds. The only time it gets a bit hectic is when scores of skiers come for a few weeks in the winter. Excellent heli-skiing is possible in the Harris Mountains, and there are prepared slopes at Cardrona Ski Field and Treble Cone Ski Field running down into the valley.

According to an old Maori legend, Te Rakaihautu dug out **Lake Wanaka**. With the earth from his diggings, the Maori giant created the surrounding mountain range. This occurred long before the first white settlers arrived in 1857. At the beginning of this century, the Wanaka Station, with more than 100,000 sheep, was established on the hilly pastureland.

The road from Wanaka to the Matukituki Valley leads not only across great pastureland, but also to Mount Aspiring

Preceding pages: Huge ferns like these are among the oldest plants on earth. Left: On the way to the ascent of the great Franz Josef Glacier.

National Park. After traveling six kilometers, you come to the trail up to **Roys Peak** on the left side. This trail is easy to climb and takes you through meadows up to an elevation of 1581 m. From here you have a wonderful view of the snow-covered **Mount Aspiring** (3027 m). The same is true of the view from **Glendhu Bay**, reached after traveling another 10.5 km. You come to the town of Mount Aspiring, one of the many starting points for trips into the national park, by way of an unpaved road with several river crossings. (Caution is advised when traveling during spring – rivers can swell around midday and become impassable).

MOUNT ASPIRING NATIONAL PARK

Mount Aspiring National Park, just like Fiordland National Park, stretches across the main divide of the Southern Alps. Its classic alpine landscape will make every mountain enthusiast's heart flutter. Experienced mountain climbers and hikers can begin their tours either on **Haast Road** heading to the west coast, in the wide river valleys on the upper end of Lake Wakatipu, or in the valley of the Matukituki River. The scenery is overwhelming whether you decide to take one of the short day-outings off of Haast

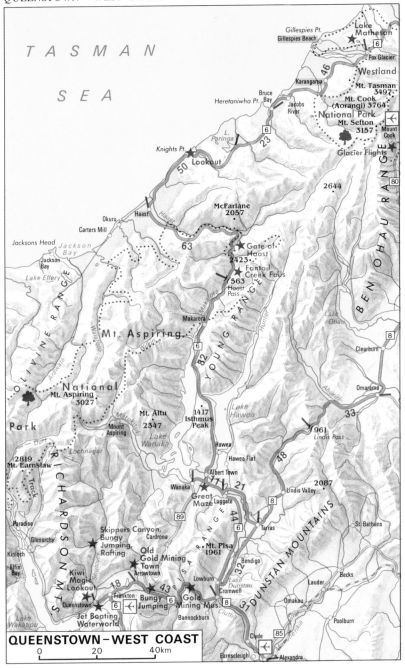

T A S M A N

S E A

Gillespies Pt.
Gillespies Beach
Lake Matheson
Fox Glacier
Westland
Karangarua
Mt. Tasman 3497
Bruce Bay
Jacobs River
Heretaniwha Pt.
Mt. Cook (Aorangi) 3764
National Park
Mt. Sefton 3157
Mount Cook
Glacier Flights
L. Paringa
Knights Pt.
Lookout
50
23
46
2644
McFarlane 2057
Haast
Okuru
Carters Mill
63
Gate of Haast
2423
Fantail Creek Falls
563
Haast Pass
Jacksons Head
Jackson Bay
Jackson Bay
Lake Ellery
Makarora
Hunter
Lake Ohau
82
Clearburn
Mt. Aspiring
National
Mt. Aspiring 3027
Park
Mt. Altu 2347
Mount Aspiring
1417 Isthmus Peak
Lake Hawea
Omarama
33
961
Lindis Pass
2819 Mt. Earnslaw
Lochnagar
Lake Wanaka
Hawea
Hawea Flat
48
Albert Town
Wanaka
Great Maze
Luggate
89
6
Lindis Valley
8
2087
St. Bathans
Paradise
Glenorchy
Skippers Canyon, Bungy Jumping, Rafting
Cardrona
Mt. Pisa 1961
Bendigo
Tarras
Becks
Kinloch
Elfin Bay
Kiwi Magic Lookout
Old Gold Mining Town
Arrowtown
Lowburn
Lake Dunstan
32
Lauder
Omakau
18
43
Frankton
Bungy Jumping
Gold Mining Mus.
Cromwell
8
31
Poolburn
Queenstown
Jet Boating Waterworld
Bannockburn
Clutha
85
Clyde
Lake Wakatipu
Earnscleugh
Alexandra

QUEENSTOWN–WEST COAST

0   20   40km

Road towards Wanaka and the west coast, or if you undertake one of the many three to four-day tours. Colossal glacial slopes covered with beech forests merge into high mountain meadows, and finally reach up to magnificent mountain peaks with elevations of more than 2000 m. This region is perfect for hiking and camping, and on the larger tracks you will find cabins owned by the park service. Many of the longer hikes over alpine passes and saddles should only be attempted in the summer months. You can obtain more information at the park headquarters in Wanaka or at the ranger stations in Makarora and Glenorchy.

The favorite trail in the park is the two to three-day **Routeburn Track**, with a starting point at either Milford Road or the lower Dart River above Glenorchy on the upper end of Lake Wakatipu. This track takes you past impressive beech forests, high alpine landscape and lakes. During the summertime, the huts are usually filled to capacity. Fantastic trails roam through the West Matukituki Valley, and from here across the Cascade Saddle to the Dart and Rees Rivers, or to the east arm of the Matukituki. In these valleys, the meadows and rivers teeming with trout are surrounded by alpine highlands. The West Matukituki is also the main approach to **Mount Aspiring,** the "Matterhorn" of New Zealand (recommended only for experienced mountain climbers).

Haast Road is the starting place for a series of enchanting day-tours and some rather difficult trails in the river valleys of the **Wilkin** and **Makarora**. Check with the ranger station in Makarora or park headquarters for appropriate information before starting out on these hikes.

Another popular route is the **Rees Dart Track**. It is a relatively easy four-day tour, guiding you up one valley and down another. It can be combined with a brief trip to the river valleys of the Routeburn and Greenstone, which then take you

back to Glenorchy at the upper end of Lake Wakatipu.

During the summer, commercial minibuses offer a regular daily service to and from the starts and final destinations of the most popular trails. In summer, the weather can be unpredictable – heavy rains and even snow at higher elevations are possible. Never underestimate the large alpine rivers. They may appear safe, but their cold temperature and strong currents can quite literally knock you off your feet.

Over Haast Pass to the West Coast

After completing a relaxing tour on the lake with the **Pink Lake Cruises** and casting one last glance from the lookout on Chalmers Street, you will probably bid Wanaka farewell. However, a quick stop at **The Maze**, located at the end of town, might be fun. It is a rather interesting challenge, a labyrinth approximately 1.5 km long, and many a visitor has gone twice the length before reaching its exit.

The drive to the west coast is less confusing. The road runs between Lake Hawea and Lake Wanaka. Below **Isthmus Peak** (1417 m) you will see both lakes simultaneously. The road continues until shortly before **Makarora,** where you will find a DOC office, a tea room and a wonderful one-hour hike to the **Blue Pools**. This section was been improved.

Do not expect too much from **Haast Pass.** With an elevation of 563 m, it is the lowest and at the same time the most southerly of the four passes over the main divide of the Southern Alps.

After leaving **Central Otago** you come to **Westland**, a remote, lonely region even for New Zealanders. The narrow landstrip running along the coast is no wider than 50 km at any spot. Between Haast and Westport, only 35,000 *Coasters* reside in this expanse of 430 km. Many *Kiwis* consider these people

rather reserved and odd. They love their coast more than anyplace else, even if rain is a part of everyday life. At Franz Josef Glacier, the average annual precipitation is 4.9 m of falls annually. Raingear is absolutely necessary for a west-coast trip. One aspect is common to all of the otherwise quite different places on the west coast: Their prime was achieved during the days of the gold rush, which began on **Greenstone Creek** in 1864.

From Haast to Greymouth

Lined with numerous waterfalls, Highway 6 squeezes through the **Gates of Haast** and downriver towards the west coast. You will meet up with a New Zealand superlative here: the site of the country's longest single-lane bridge, clocking in at 732 m. Not quite as long, but more unusual is another one-lane

Above: The western coastline as seen from Knights Point. Right: Suspension bridges are frequent along hiking trails in the west.

bridge, located in Greymouth: the drivers of vehicles have to share the one lane with the railroad as an additional thrill.

Haast Beach is anything but a superlative, although it is an ideal starting point for a tour of the west coast. A gas station, a store, a hotel, a DOC bureau, and a beach littered with driftwood is all you will find here. Although the Haast-Jackson Bay Road continues in a southerly direction, our itinerary leads north from now on. The road is narrow, bordered by giant ferns and dense rain forests. It curves along the coastline up to **Knights Point**, which boasts wonderful panoramic perspectives. The nearby lakes of **Moeraki** and **Paringa** can be reached from the road and are under the protection of the DOC. It takes about 70 km of driving through untamed country to arrive at Fox Glacier.

Fox Glacier is second only to Franz Josef Glacier as a favorite place to stay overnight on the west coast, especially for travelers who left Wanaka the same morning. Both spots are ideal starting points for Westland National Park.

WESTLAND NATIONAL PARK

No other national park of New Zealand offers quite the variation in landscapes than Westland's 117,000 hectares. On the west side of the park you will find sprawling sandy beaches and serene lakes, on the east side snow-capped mountains and meter-thick glaciers, and in between a 20 km narrow strip of lush rain forest. Altogether, there are 60 glaciers located in the park. The most spectacular ones are without a doubt Franz Josef and Fox.

The 14,000-year-old ice masses of **Fox Glacier**, about 13 km southeast of the Fox region (access via unpaved road), are best seen from the mouth of the glacier or from a helicopter. The mouth itself, up to four meters high, is quite overwhelming. The ice slides from an elevation of about

3000 m from the base of Mount Tasman's peak (3498 m) into the valley below, and can best be explored from the **Valley Walk** (20 minutes) beginning at Glacier Valley Viewpoint. The **Cone Rock Track** (a 2.5 hour hike starting from this spot) will also lead you up into the mountains, and from the peak at an elevation of 500 m, providing a spectacular view of the ice masses. Originally, Fox Glacier was named Albert Glacier after Queen Victoria's spouse. But in 1872, the politician and explorer William Fox gained the upper hand in the name game, probably because he painted a famous picture of the ice walls.

One of the greatest hiking challenges in Westland National Park (and possibly in New Zealand) is the track along the **Copland River** which begins 30 km south at Karangarua. After the climb along the river, you can hike from Copland Pass across to Mount Cook, and then continue hiking on the other side of the Southern Alps. For this hike it is imperative to have good mountain equip-

ment and alpine-climbing experience.

The other side of Westland National Park, covered with green and facing the ocean, is located around **Lake Matheson**. The lake is famous for the reflections in its water and has become a favorite postcard motive throughout the country. To experience this phenomenon first hand, you should travel the 6-km stretch to the lake in the early morning or late evening hours. Needless to say, that total lack of wind is essential. Both trails are worthwhile just the same. To the jetty you will need about one hour, and from that classic spot with its "View of Views" – Mount Cook and Mount Tasman almost close enough to touch – you can be back within two hours.

It is another 16 km to the coast and **Gillespies Beach**. This drive is worthwhile, particularly if you then take the two-hour **Gillespies Trig Track** or the three-hour **Seal Colony Walk.**

It seems that almost every town in Westland can afford its own glacier. Just 24 km north of Fox Glacier, **Franz Josef**

Glacier's ice masses jut up right behind the last houses. Franz Josef is considered the more beautiful of the two. A 6-km long, unpaved road goes to the lower reaches of the 13-km long glacier with ice up to 300 m thick in some places. The parking lot serves as hunting grounds for a few *keas* who have their eyes on anything that can be taken apart or dismantled.

In the mythology of the Maori, the glacier is called *nga roimata o Hine hukatere*, meaning "the tears of the avalanche maiden." The legend tells of the adventurous Hine who convinced her lover Tane to climb a mountain, whereby he was killed in an accident. The gods froze Hine's tears of mourning and thus formed the ice of the glacier.

The **Glacier Valley Walk**, taking about two hours, leads up to Glacier Viewpoint. Warm clothes and caution along the track are recommended. A beautiful view can be had from **Sentinel Rock**.3Crossing rivers in the park requires utmost caution. The waters are ice-cold and frequently torrential. Sandflies are also a summer nuisance in Westland National Park. The best time to travel is between May and July, due to the frosty nights bringing clear air the following day. This period of the year is also noted for minimum rainfall.

Between 1901 and 1965, the glacier end of Franz Josef retreated more than 1500 m. Shortly after the construction of St James Anglican Church in 1931, the glacier could still be seen through the altar window during the church service. By 1953, the white ice mass had disappeared from view. Now the glacier's future looks rosy again. In the past few years, it has grown more than one kilometer.

The town of **Franz Josef** is the departure point for the most spectacular glacier tour by helicopter. This sightseeing flight is a must in good weather, especially since you will be flying over and around Mount Cook, Mount Tasman, Mount Sefton and the Fox and Tasman glaciers.

White Heron and Big Gold

From here the coast loses its rough character and rugged charm, the landscape levels off gradually as Highway 6 continues through the wooded inland region for long stretches. A short outing along the coast to **Okarito** at **The Forks** is worthwhile. A special stone commemorates the year 1642. At that time, the Dutch explorer Abel Tasman saw the shores of present day New Zealand for the first time.

During the gold rush in the middle of the 19th century, more than 1500 people lived in Okarito, providing the economic wherewithal for the upkeep of a number of banks, hotels and pubs. Today, just a few canoeists stroll about on their way to or from boating trips and bird-watching excursions on Okarito Lagoon.

The same would have been the case for **Whataroa** if it had not been for a certain bird: the great white heron. It was believed that these birds were practically extinct, but now there is a breeding ground for the heron on New Zealand once again. More than 50 pairs of birds are now nesting on the **Waitangitaona River** near Whataroa. From the beginning of November until the end of January (the best time is in November/December), you can enter the breeding grounds, but only with a permit and for just 2.5 hours on the outings, organized since 1988 by the White Heron Sanctuary Tours. By way of Mount Herkules and along Lake Ianthe you will come to **Ross** with the only tavern far and wide, where the **Historic Goldfields Walkway**, along with the small **Gold Museum** on James Street, take you back to the town's days gone by.

In 1907, the *Honorable Roddy* was found here – a gold nugget weighing approximately 99 ounces, the largest found

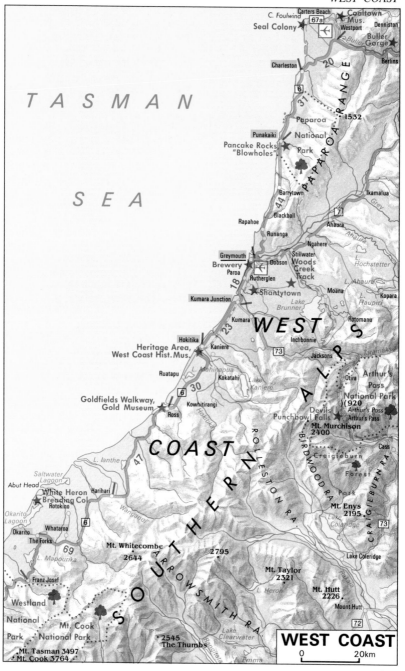

Map Labels

TASMAN

SEA

C. Foulwind
Carters Beach
Coaltown Mus.
Seal Colony
Westport
Denniston
67a
Buller Gorge
Buller
Berlins

Charleston

6
31
20
1532

Paparoa

Punakaiki
National
Pancake Rocks "Blowholes"
Park

44

Barrytown

Blackball
Ikamatua
7
Rapahoe
Ahaura
Runanga
Ngahere
Grey
Greymouth
Stillwater
Brewery
Dobson
Woods Creek Track
Paroa
Hochstetter
Rutherglen
L. Ahaura
18
Shantytown
Moana
Kopara
Kumara Junction
Lake Brunner
L. Haupiri
Rotomanu
Kumara
WEST
23
Inchbonnie
Rotomanu
Hokitika
Kaniere
73
Jacksons
Heritage Area, West Coast Hist. Mus.
L. Mahinapua
Arthur's Pass
Ruatapu
Kokatahi
Otira
National Park
6
30
Lake Kaniere
ALPS
(920)
Arthur's Pass
Goldfields Walkway, Gold Museum
Kowhitirangi
Devils Punchbowl Falls
Arthur's Pass
Ross
Mt. Murchison 2400
Cass
COAST
47
L. Ianthe
Craigieburn
Saltwater Lagoon
ROLLESTON RA
BIRDWOOD RA
Forest
Abut Head
White Heron Breading Col
Harihari
Mt. Enys 2195
CRAIGIEBURN RA
Rotokino
Okarito Lagoon
Wanganui
Lake Coleridge
73
Okarito
Whataroa
6
Lake Coleridge
The Forks
69
L. Mapourika
Mt. Whitecombe 2644
2795
Mt. Taylor 2321
Franz Josef
L. Heron
Mt. Hutt 2226
Westland
SOUTHERN
ARROWSMITH RA
Mount Hutt
National
72
Park
Mt. Cook National Park
2545 The Thumbs
Lake Clearwater
Mt. Tasman 3497
Mt. Cook 3764
L. Emma

WEST COAST

0   20km

in New Zealand to date. In modern times, the town's livelihood has switched to dealing in opossum pelts, which are tanned at the local factory and sold (NZ$ 20 and up).

Hokitika gained attention not only because of its gold, but also because of the greenstone (a kind of jade). With a population of 3500, the town is the smallest on the west coast. The customs house, clock tower and the statue of a former New Zealand prime minister, Richard Seddon (who served from 1893-1906), are of interest here.

All three sights are located in the **Hokitika Heritage Area**. The town is situated along the railroad track of the *TranzAlpine Express*, which shuttles daily to and from Christchurch on the east coast. For visitors interested in a west-coast souvenir, a greenstone charm or gold

Above: The white heron, pride of New Zealand, is threatened with extinction. Right: The Pancake Rocks near Punakaiki, battered by the sea.

nugget from one of the jewelry shops in Hokitika would be appropriate.

At **Kumara Junction**, a side-trip along Highway 73, which takes you over Arthur's Pass to Christchurch, is of interest. You do not need to go as far as Christchurch, but instead turn left before Jacksons and drive the scenic road to Moana at **Lake Brunner**. The lovely countryside and the remote location of the lake have helped preserve the idyllic surroundings. Since there are hardly any places to stay overnight, it is advisable to head back towards the coast to **Greymouth** (population: 12,000) in the evening. Greymouth does not have much to offer the visitor as far as sightseeing is concerned. Even the harbor, once a bustling place to be, has quieted down.

If you have continued further along the coast at Kumara Junction, you will probably stop in **Shantytown**, a gold-digger village restored as an open-air museum. Visitors are invited to try their hand at panning for gold here. Another opportunity to retrace the footsteps of the gold diggers through tunnels and gorges is along the **Woods Creek Track** (17 km away). A flashlight is an absolute necessity to complete the 45-minute trail.

The stretch between Westland National Park and Greymouth is an ideal day trip.

PAPAROA NATIONAL PARK

New Zealand's youngest national park was established in 1987. The park's main attraction is the **Pancake Rocks of Punakaiki**, which indeed really do look like stacked pancakes rising up directly from the shoreline. Wind and waves have carved away at the soft sedimentary rock for centuries, forming bizarre and fantastic shapes. At high tide and with strong surf, white spray shoots out of various blowholes along the shore. The best view can be had from **Dolomite Point** (10 minutes from the information center).

The mountains of the Paparoa Range reach down to the coast and sometimes drop off, forming cliffs 300 m high. Via the **Pororari Gorge Track** you reach the beach, which is a lovely picnic area in the shadow of weather-beaten limestone walls. The **Inland Pack Track** runs through the section of park heading inland. Many a gold digger and his horse once traveled here.

You will need about three days for this 25 km long trail and can start from Punakaiki (among other places) or at Fox River to the north. Good campsites have been established at three different locations along this trail.

Along the Whitebait Coast

A stop at **Charlestown** has its own special thrill. North of the city (once with a population of 12,000) you can visit **Mitchell's Gully**, a goldmine still in operation today. On the way to Westport, the landscape along the rugged west coast smooths out as one goes along. Almost everyone seems to be on the road from September 1st to November 14th because of whitebait season. The tiny young of five different fish species appear in huge schools in sections of the rivers closest to the coast. They are caught with nets and considered a delicacy. The popularity of the whitebait has led to a substantial decline in numbers during the past few years.

Westport itself is similar to Greymouth as far as its lack of attractions is concerned. Town life revolves primarily around the harbor and the shipping of cement and coal (**Coaltown Museum** on Queen Street). On hot days you can cool off in the water at **Carters Beach**. Further south, beyond **Cape Foulwind**, is the seal colony of Tauranga Bay.

Highway 67 travels in a northerly direction to Karamea and then to the start of Wangapeka Track and Heaphy Track, which both end at Golden Bay. Most travelers remain on Highway 6, following it through the wild **Buller Gorge** towards Nelson, 230 km away.

WANAKA / THE WEST COAST

Accommodation

WANAKA: *LUXURY:* **Aspiring Lodge**, corner Dunmore and Dungarvon St., Tel: 03-4437816. **THC Wanaka**, Helwick St., Tel: 03-4437826. **Wanaka Motor Inn**, Mt. Aspiring Rd., Tel: 03-4438216.

MODERATE: **All Seasons Motel**, State Highway 6, Tel: 03-4437530. **Bay View Motel**, P.O. Box 11, Tel: 03-4437766. **Brookvale Manor**, 35 Brownston, Tel: 03-4438333. **Lakeview Motel**, 68 Lismore St., Tel: 03-4437029. **Mount Aspiring Motel**, State Highway 6A, Tel: 03-4437698. **Pembroke Inn**, 94 Brownston St., P.O. Box 149, Tel: 03-4437296.

BUDGET: **Pleasant Lodge Holiday Park**, Glendhu Bay Rd., P.O. Box 125, Tel: 03-4437360 (3 km out of town). **Wanaka Bakpaka**, 117 Lakeside Rd., Tel: 03-4437837. **Wanaka Youth Hostel**, 181 Upton St., Tel: 03-4437405. **Wanaka Motor Park**, Brownston St., Tel: 03-4437883.

BLACKBALL: *BUDGET:* **The Blackball Hilton**, Tel: 03-7234705 (20 km northeast of Greymouth; romantic "gold-digger" flair, reasonable prices).

FRANZ JOSEF: *LUXURY:* **THC Franz Josef**, State Highway 6, Tel: 03-7520719. **Westland Motor Inn,** State Highway 6, P.O. Box 33, Tel: 03-7520728 and 729.

MODERATE: **Callery Lodge**, Cron St., Tel: 03-7520738. **Glacier Gateway Motor Lodge**, Highway 6, Tel: 03-7520776. **Glacier View Motel,** Tel: 03-7520705.

BUDGET: **Pavolva Backpackers**, Cron St., Tel: 03-7520738. **Franz Josef Holiday Park**, Tel: 03-7520766. **Youth Hostel**, 2 Cron St., Tel: 03-7520754.

FOX GLACIER: *MODERATE:* **A1 Motel**, Lake Matheson Rd., Tel: 03-7510821. **Hasley's Motel**, P.O. Box 23, Tel: 03-7510833. **Lake Matheson Motels**, Tel: 03-7510830. **Pinegrove Motel**, P.O. Box 26, Tel: 03-7510898 (36 km south of Fox Glacier).

BUDGET: **Glacier Holiday Park**, Lake Matheson Rd., P.O. Box 37, Tel: 03-7510821. **Golden Glacier Inn**, State Highway 6, Tel: 03-7510847. **Ivory Towers**, Sullivans Rd., Tel: 03-7510838. **Fox Glacier Backpackers Inn**, State Highway 6, Tel: 03-7510847.

GREYMOUTH: *LUXURY:* **Ashley Motel and Motor Inn**, 70-74 Tasman St., Tel: 03-7685135. **Charles Court Motel**, 350 Main South Rd., South Beach, Tel: 03-7626619.

MODERATE: **Ace Tourist Motel**, State Highway 7, Omoto Rd., Tel: 03-7686884. **Duke of Edin-**

burgh Hotel, Guiness St., Tel: 03-7684020. **Ora-Nui Motel**, 108 High St., P.O. Box 257, Tel: 03-7685716. **Willowbank Motor Lodge,** State Highway 6, P.O. Box 260, Tel: 03-7685339. (2 km out of town).

BUDGET: **Noah's Ark Backpackers**, 16 Chapels St., Tel: 03-7684868. **Greymouth Seaside Holiday Park**, Chesterfield St., Tel: 03-7686618. **Youth Hostel,** 15 Alexander St., Tel: 03-7684951.

HOKITIKA: *MODERATE:* **Teichmann's Central B&B**, 20 Hamilton St., Tel: 03-7558232. **Goldsborough Motel**, 252 Revell St., P.O. Box 201, Tel: 03-7558773. **Hokitika Motel**, 221 Fitzherbert St., Tel: 03-7558292.

BUDGET: **Hokitika Holiday Park**, 242 Stafford St., Tel: 03-7558172. **Kokatahi Hotel,** 18 km out of town, at the Lake Kaniere Scenic Rd., Tel: 03-7558490.

IKAMATUA: *BUDGET:* **Ikamatua Hotel**, Grey Valley, Tel: 027-23555 (situated 20 km south of Reefton).

LAKE BRUNNER: *LUXURY:* **Lake Brunner Lodge**, Kumara, Inchbonnie Rd., Tel: 027-7380163.

MAKARORA: *BUDGET:* **Haast Pass Tourist Services**, Tel: 03-4438372.

OKARITO: *BUDGET:* **Youth Hostel**, Tel: 03-7534082. (Keri Hulme, a New Zealand writer of international recognition, has lived here).

PUNAKAIKI: *BUDGET:* **Punakaiki Motor Camp**, Highway 6, Tel: 03-7311894. Punakaiki Beach Hostel, Webb St., Tel: 03-7311852 (right on the beach).

WESTPORT: *LUXURY:* **Ascot Motor Lodge**, 74 Romilly St., Tel: 03-7897832. **Buller Bridge Motel**, Esplanade, P.O. Box 187, Tel: 03-7897519.

MODERATE: **Black & White Hotel**, 198 Palmerston St., Tel: 03-7897959. **Blue Tasman Motel**, Carters Beach, P.O. Box 114, Tel: 03-7898059. **Buller Court Motel**, 235 Palmerston St., Tel:03-7897979. **Westport Motel**, 32 Esplanade, Tel: 03-7897575.

BUDGET: **Bazils Hostel**, Russell St., Tel: 03-7896410. **Seal Colony Tourist Park**, R.D., Carters Beach, Tel: 03-7898002. **Tripinns**, 72 Queen St., Tel: 03-7897367.

Restaurants

WANAKA: Capriccio Restaurant, 123 Ardmore St., Tel: 03-4438579 (New Zealand specialities; expensive). **First Café**, Ardmore St. **Te Kano**, Brownstown St. (vegetarian food; a bit outside of town).

Barrows Tavern and Pembroke Inn, both on Ardmore St. (the best place for a beer after a day of skiing). **Relishes Café**, Shop 1, Ardmore St., Tel:

03-4439018 (you can choose between wholefood and "normal" cuisine; situated at the lakeshore; good lunch-stop). **Rafters**, Wanaka Motor Inn, Mt. Aspiring Road, Tel: 03-4438216 (open from 6–9 p.m.; closed Fridays). **Ripples Restaurant**, Pembroke Mall, Tel: 03-437413 (New Zealand specialities; expensive; closed in June).

FOX GLACIER: Fox Glacier Tearooms and Takeaway, Tel: 03-7510868. **McSullys Café**, Main Road.

FRANZ JOSEF: D.A.'s Restaurant, Tel: 03-7520721.

GREYMOUTH: Café Collage, Upstairs, 115 Mackay St., Tel: 03-7685497 (in the town center). **Pizzeria Bonzai**, 31 Mackay St., Tel: 03-7684170 (Mondays–Fridays from 11 a.m.–10 p.m., Saturdays and Sundays from 5–10 p.m.).

HOKITIKA: El Jebel, New World Shopping Mall, Revell St., Tel: 03-7558818 (New Zealand's only fondue-restaurant).

WESTPORT: Cristy's Restaurant, 18 Wakefield St., Tel: 03-7897640 (good place for whitebait; open daily from 6:30 p.m.).

WHATAROA: White Heron Tea Rooms, Main Rd. (Lunch and snacks at the roadside; open from 8 a.m.–8 p.m.).

Museums

HOKITIKA: West Coast Historical Museum, Tancred St., Tel: 03-7556898, (open to the public Mondays–Fridays from 9:30 a.m.–4:30 p.m., Sundays and public holidays in summer from 10 a.m.–4 p.m.).

Tips and Trips

Bus Connection to the West Coast: The *West Coast Express* runs along the west coast from Nelson to Queenstown and back; the five-to-six-day journey is ideal for independent travelers planning individual routes.
Information: Paradiso, 42 Weka St., Nelson, Tel: 03-5488817.

Skiing: A day-pass for the Treble Cone Ski Area costs 50 NZ$, a pass for the Cardrona Ski Area 45 NZ$ per day.

Heli-Skiing: from Harris Mountain Heli-Ski, P.O. Box 177, Wanaka, Tel: 03-4437930.

Wanaka: Whitewater rafting on the Clutha River and Windsurfing on Lake Wanaka is organized by Good Sports, P.O. Box 86, Tel: 03-4437966.
Memorable aerial impressions can be savored on various flights from Wanaka, i.e. on the flight over the Mount Aspiring region. For travelers with plenty of time and a sense of adventure: take a one-way flight to the Milford Sound, move on from there by hitchhiking or take the bus to Queenstown. Informa-

tion: Aspiring Air, Wanaka Airport, P.O. Box 68, Tel: 03-4437943.

Westport: Blackwater rafting (an exciting underground adventure by boat through tunnels and caves) and *abseiling* in the Buller Gorge from Norwest Adventures, 41 Domett St., Tel: 03-7896686. Whitewater rafting, jetboating and riding are offered by Buller Adventure Tours, Tel. 03-7897286.

Whitebait: Informations and fishing permits are available from The Fisheries Officer, Ministry of Agriculture and Fisheries, P.O. Box 162, Greymouth, Tel: 03-7686268.

Festivals / Special Events

WANAKA: The *Harris Mountains Heli-Skiing Powder 8's* is in the second week of August.
Great fun is the *Wanaka Snow Festival*, celebrated during the last week of August.

WESTPORT: The *Buller Whitebait Festival* is celebrated from the middle to the end of October with plenty of fish.

HOKITIKA: The *Wildfoods Festival* takes place evey year in the middle of March.

Tourist Information

WANAKA: **DOC** and **Information Centre**, Mount Aspiring National Park, Ardmore St., Tel: 03-4431233. **AA**, Bruce Ecroyd Auto Services Ltd, Tel: 03-4437868.

FOX GLACIER: DOC, Westland National Park, Main Rd., Tel: 03-7510807.

FRANZ JOSEF: DOC, Westland National Park, Main Rd., Tel: 03-7520796.

MAKARORA: DOC, Mount Aspiring National Park, Haast Pass, Highway, Tel: 03-4438365.

GREYMOUTH: Information Centre, Regent Theatre Building, at the corner of McKay and Herbert St., Tel: 03-7685101 (Monday–Friday 9 a.m.–5 p.m.).
DOC, intersection of Johnson and Swainson, Tel: 03-7680427.
AA, 84 Tainui St., Tel: 03-7687109.

HOKITIKA: Westland Visitor Information Centre, 23 Weld St,. Tel: 03-7558322 (Mondays–Fridays from 9 a.m.–5 p.m., Saturdays from 9 a.m.–1 p.m.). **DOC**, Corner Sewell and Gibson Quay, Tel: 03-7558301.

KARAMEA: Information Centre, P.O. Box 94.
DOC, P.O. Box, Main Rd., Tel: 03-7826852.

PUNAKAIKI: DOC, Paparoa National Park, Main Rd., Tel: 03-7311893.

WESTPORT: Tourist Information Centre, 1, Brougham St., Tel: 03-7896658 (daily 9 a.m.–5 p.m., closed Sundays in winter). **DOC**, Russell Street, Tel: 03-7897742 and 7743. **AA**, Carters Beach Motor Camp, Tel: 03-7898002.

NEW ZEALAND TODAY

The New Zealander is undergoing a change from living in a welfare state to a more limited, economically realistic way of life. After 50 years of ease, he is learning to work again. The first settlers – the Polynesians much more than the Europeans who came 150 years ago – were individualists, perhaps adventurers, motivated by nothing but ambition to set out to conquer oceans and seek their fortunes, whatever that might have been, in a new world. They chose jungle-covered islands lashed by stormy seas as their future home. The land here was among the newest on earth, its mountainous region formed late in the Cenozoic era, less than five million years ago, and constantly modified by continuous earth movements and volcanic eruptions.

By the time of human settlement, the islands presented a benign environment with a balanced climate providing ideal conditions for plant growth. The Maori people who migrated from the Pacific islands had evolved into a sophisticated society based on collective ownership, strong family ties and a moral code rooted in deep spirituality. This culture inevitably had to clash, and still does today, with the lifestyle of the later European settlers and their ambitions for material wealth. The fact that both sides were unwilling to make compromises contributed to a series of bloody battles in the early 19th century, resolved only when the Maori were persuaded to sign the Treaty of Waitangi, guaranteeing their rights to land and human dignity, which still did not stop the whites from continuing to take over the best Maori land.

Cultural compromises have never been made, however, and most educated New

Zealanders now believe that none should be made on the Maori side since the dignified tradition of living together in harmony inherent to their culture has much to offer modern society. At the same time, there has been a slow realization on the part of the whites that the terms of the Treaty of Waitangi have only been paid lip service to over the decades. There is a inclination to put past sins right, but it is likely to take a fundamental cultural adjustment on the part of the Pakeha (non-Maori) majority before this is converted to action.

Most European immigrants who came to New Zealand 150 years ago were craftsmen from the English middle class. With their strong will to survive, they adapted to the lack of comforts combined with hard conditions. They cleared land and carved out farms and communities. As soon as the new machinery of government would allow, provisions for social and economic security were enacted. In 1877, universal free education was introduced. In 1893, women were granted the right to vote by New Zealand, the first country in the world to take such an obvious step.

The new nation prospered on exports of wool to Europe, until the late 19th century when gold was discovered. This brought a rush of immigration from Europe, America, Australia, and even China, adding new cultural elements. The wealth of the golden era encouraged large groups of organized, but adventurous people to come from northern and central Europe to become agricultural and industrial workers, their job security and good wages ensured by strong trade union agreements endorsed by a benevolent government.

The world-wide economic depression of the early 20th century had sobering effects on a nation whose wealth depended upon exporting agricultural produce to Europe, and brought a fresh determination by the government to protect its

Preceding pages: Limestone landscape at the foot of Fox Glacier. Sheep are a major New Zealand export in good times. Right: A demonstration against cuts in social benefits.

people from hardship. Free health care and education, retirement pensions and low-cost housing provisions were introduced. Workers' rights to good wages for shorter hours of work were strengthened, and the unemployed were well compensated. In addition, every New Zealander had the right to a private home on a small piece of land. The result has been low-rise towns and cities which sprawl. Auckland, the largest city, today spreads over 101,615 hectares – the size of Paris.

The spirit of adventure moves New Zealanders to travel widely, and migrate in numbers, especially to Australia. The outcome is that in spite of quite a healthy birthrate, the national population has remained at about three million for nearly 20 years.

Adventurism has brought a willingness by New Zealanders to volunteer in Great Britain's wars. Between 1939 and 1945, nearly every family was affected by such participation, and more than 10,000 of New Zealand's soldiers died. There is now a reaction to the past in the form of a strong peace movement, which colors the national foreign policy. This is seen particularly in that the country has declared itself a nuclear-free zone.

Dependence on an agricultural economy means New Zealanders are acutely aware of the value of their environment. When it began to be tainted by fall-out from French nuclear testing in the Pacific, there was public outcry. The anti-nuclear policy has caused rifts with foreign powers like Great Britain and the USA because they can no longer use New Zealand as a port for their nuclear-powered ships.

It was also war in Europe that brought the last great Golden Age for New Zealand. The post-1945 rebuilding of Europe brought a great demand for New Zealand foodstuffs, wool and timber, and the payments made New Zealand rich.

The booming farm profits were invested exclusively in making the agricultural sector even more efficient, in the belief that the demand for its products would last forever.

By the 1960's however, the European economies had been rebuilt to the extent that they could produce all they needed, and steps had been taken to unite Europe in a common market. The biggest blow for the agriculture of New Zealand came at the beginning of the 1970's when the main market for goods, England, joined the EEC.

Suddenly New Zealand had no market for all the food and other agricultural goods it was so good at producing. It had failed to invest in diversifying the economy, and was forced to borrow to belatedly correct the problem and cover government spending.

The loans were at high interest rates, and together with a high-cost structure of production in New Zealand meant that the products of the new industries were still too expensive to be competitive internationally. The prices for agricultural

Above: New Zealand's agriculture is looking to a difficult future. Right: Hongi, the traditional Maori way of greeting.

exports began to fall. The government's social welfare payments began to rise as more agriculture-related workers became unemployed. The stable structure of the rural towns began to collapse, causing more unemployment, and people start to the cities in search of jobs, or more convenient amenities with which to live life on welfare.

The conservative National Party initiated desperate measures to save the social-welfare state from total destruction. But these subsidies, protective duties and price and wage freezes could not prevent the national per capita income from plummeting. An increasing number of businesses went bankrupt, which put more and more people out of work.

Finally, just before national bankruptcy, a new Labour Party government began an economic experiment, which resulted in every New Zealander personally feeling the financial pressure on the nation.

It began by dismantling all the paternalistic protective measures. State enter-

prises were privatized and had to survive without taxpayer subsidies. The subsidies for agriculture, protective duties and import restrictions were dropped.

A lot of farmers, who had financed everything with credits and subsidies, were suddenly faced with economic ruin. The immediate result was even more unemployment, and the standard of living fell threateningly close to that of a third-world country.

But inflation is now down to a very low level; internal costs have been controlled. New Zealand produce is currently going out to world markets at prices that make it attractive to buyers.

Maori Heritage

New Zealand is the homeland of Maori people. Legend tells us that the Maori navigator Kupe came to New Zealand in A. D. 750, followed by the ancestors of present-day Maori in what is termed the "Great Migration" of A. D. 1350. The Maori name for New Zealand is *Aotea-roa* (the land of the long white clouds), as it appears at first sighting on the horizon.

The Maori people are unique and their tradition and culture are still a living part of everyday life. Their knowledge has been orally passed down for generations through the family and the tribe. Geneology is of paramount importance for a Maori since it gives identity and pride in one's being. Also of great significance is the land which provides the foundation for life, and the *wairua*, the spiritual well-being which promotes the harmonious unity of body and spirit.

There are still many different Maori tribes living within ancestral tribal regions. Although they are one people, tribally there are some traditional differences, which still prevail today with regard to ritual, language, arts and manners. These differences are not easily detected by visitors, nor is it simple to distinguish which tribes the Maori belong to. The influences of Western civilization have been absorbed by the Maori without the loss of their heritage, tradition or identity.

Rotorua is known as the center of Maori culture. Here the traditional steam *hangi* is still a regular method of cooking used by the Maori people, despite the electrical conveniences they possess. The *hangi* of the village is a pit of bubbling hot thermal spring water, with wooden planks placed above it. The pots of food are placed on the planks and then covered with towels or woven mats. Because space is limited, each family usually puts the meat, vegetables and potatoes in its own container, which are then heated by the rising steam. Cooking time is two to three hours.

The steam *hangi* is the traditional method of cooking used by the Maori living in a thermal region. The ground *hangi* (*umu*) is another traditional method used by Maori not in a thermal region or on special occasions such as Christmas, New Year, Easter, etc.

Above: Ornamented carvings in a marae, a Maori meeting house. Right: Haka, a facial gesture that means business in Maori.

The *hakari* (feast) is an important part of Maori tradition. It is customarily the correct way to express goodwill and hospitality to visitors. Only the most succulent food is offered to guests. Most popular are *kumara* (sweet potato), *karengo* (seaweed), *tuna* (eel), raw fish, pork, mussels in the shell, *rewena* (Maori bread), *titi* (Maori chicken), *hangi*-cooked lamb, chicken, pork, ham, potatoes, and pumpkin.

Another important part of the Maori culture is music. For example, the action song, where the words are interpreted with hand movements. The *wiri*, or shaking of the hands, gives life to each movement. Even today, the Maori still record important events, memorable occasions, famous people and achievements in their songs.

The *whai korero* (traditional formal speech) is used to greet visitors. The ritual and protocol of the Maori ancestors is respectfully adhered to and followed by the *patere*, the monotone chant which is traditional for the Maori. The *pukana* (facial expressions) during the chant give added emphasis to the extended greeting.

The hand game, in which two players try to catch each other in the same hand action by anticipating their opponents next move, helps sharpen the reflexes and reactions. The stick game is used to improve timing and coordination of movement, essential when using the longer spear-like weapons in battle.

The *haka* is a sequence of movements performed by men. In former times it was used prior to battle. *Haka* provoked the warriors into an aggressive frame of mind, stirring their anger and courage. It also created a ferocious and intimidating challenge to the enemy. As a psychological ploy, it is a living reminder of the skills and tactical strategies used successfully in earlier times by the Maori.

The legend of Hinemoa and Tutanekai is the inspiration to the love song *Pokarekare Ana*. It relates the love that gave Hinemoa the strength to defy her family and tribe, and swim from the shores of Rotorua to the small island of Mokoia in the dark of night guided by the sound of her lover's flute, to join Tutanekai there. The haunting love song, like the *haka*, shows the complexity of the Maori heritage.

Very often a *poi* is used by Maori women to depict a variety of sounds and images. A *poi* is a ball attached to a short or long piece twine.

The "short" *poi* is twirled and beaten against the palm and back of the hand to convey the sound of tramping feet, or the movements of small birds and insects.

The *poi waero* is the single long poi, the traditional form, which in former times was only used by maidens of high rank. The more modern double and quadruple "long" *poi* depicts large birds in flight, clouds or steam rising from the many hot pools and geysers of the region.

Another, funny-looking tradition is the *hongi*, a gentle pressing together of the noses. Although it may appear unusual,

the significance of the greeting is that of respect and friendship. The pressing of the noses signifies the joining of the "breath of life".

As you can easily see, the Maori recognize the need to allow enough time for genuine expression of profound feelings.

The Maori clothing is often the same design as that of earlier times. The *piupiu* is the traditional flax "skirt" worn by both women and men. The *pari* (bodice) and *tipari* (headband) are woven by the traditional *taniko* (finger weaving) method, although Gobelin weaving is now often used.

Other garments are the *rapaki* (short skirt) worn by young men, *tapeka* (shoulder to waist band) worn by men, and *kaitaka* (long gown) worn by the women. Most traditional garments are adorned with the feathers of native birds and specially dyed and woven threads.

The Maori are part of New Zealand's history, who in retaining their culture and traditions want to actively participate in its future as well.

TRAMPING IN NEW ZEALAND

Every visitor to New Zealand should participate at least once in that hiking activity the *Kiwis* call "tramping." Choosing which trail to follow can present the innocent newcomer with quite a dilemma: Thousands of miles of trails crisscross the twelve national parks and three maritime parks that make up approximately 20 percent of the country's total area. The following five tracks undoubtedly are among the most beautiful and popular of them all.

Milford Track
Fiordland National Park

The Milford Track on South Island has justly become famous for its scenery, but is the only hike in a national park where you have to pay a track fee. For those who want to walk the trail independently, the cost is around NZ$ 160, covering hut fees and boat trips at Lake Te Anau and Milford Sound. The guided walk, with meals provided, costs up to NZ$ 1300. At the height of the summer season, booking in advance with the Department of Conservation or tourist agencies is a prerequisite to the tramp itself.

Despite this somewhat complicated preamble, "the Milford" is still very rewarding. It's a beautiful walk through deep glacial valleys, with magnificent views and delightful side-trips to attractions like the Sutherland Falls, the third highest waterfall in the world.

For independent walkers, everything starts at the Te Anau Downs jetty, about 30 km from the town of Te Anau (location of park headquarters). After an inspiring two-hour trip across the lake, the track starts at Glade House and follows a well-marked route through beech forests

Right: Finding a few hours of solitude in the wilderness of the Milford Sound in the Fiordland National Park.

and grassy flats to the scenically-situated Clinton Forks Hut. On either side, the sheer walls of Clinton Canyon rise up to over 2000 m. The lower reaches of the Clinton River have good stocks of trout, but if you intend to do some fishing you need to get a license from the park headquarters.

The next day, the route turns up the west branch of the Clinton through superb beech forest. Along the way there is a short side track to Hidden Lake which is a nice spot for a lunch-time break. After about four or five hours, the valley narrows approaching to Mintaro Hut, tucked into the cliff walls of McKinnon Pass and near a small lake of the same name. The track over the pass zigzags about 1,5 km to the summit at 1150 m. On a fine day there are amazing views across ranges of mountains and down the Clinton and Arthur Valleys. The best way is to take the left track about 20 minutes after leaving the top. This runs through thick jungle with small waterfalls.

Once down at the head of the Arthur River Valley, leave your pack at the public shelter and visit Sutherland Falls (two-hour round trip). The longer one of the tracks offers better views of the entire three-stage drop of the waterfalls, which plummet a total of 580 meters to the valley floor from Lake Quill. Afterwards, it's an easy stroll to Dumpling Hut for a well-earned rest.

The final day is a six-hour walk down the Arthur Valley. You will have to keep track of time if you want to connect with the launch at Milford Sound at 2 p.m. The best place to stop for lunch is at the picturesque Gate Falls.

In conclusion, don't get to the pick-up point at Sandfly Flat too early since it has been quite aptly named by fly-bitten predecessors. The idea is to walk onto the jetty just as the launch is pulling in, ready for a restful cruise across the spectacular Milford Sound. (Note: Guided hikers use separate refuges).

Travers-Sabine Valleys
Nelson Lakes National Park

Throughout recent years, the Travers and Sabine Valleys have become the most popular area in the Nelson Lakes Park for hiking and camping, and with good reason.

The tracks here are very pleasant, relatively easy and yet with a wide variety of mountain and valley terrain and extensive vistas of peaks rising above 2000 m on either side of the long glacial valleys. Most of the tracks in this area also pass through lovely South Island beech forest.

The usual way of approaching this four-day, twin-valley trip is to start at the mouth of the Travers River, where it runs into the head of Lake Rotoiti. The second approach is from Lake Rotoroa. From the Lakehead Hut, the track winds its way through the lower reaches of the delightful Travers Valley. It passes through a mixture of grassy open flats and beech forest with great views of the St. Arnaud Range to the east.

The well-marked track follows the left bank of the river for most of the way to the John Tait Hut (five hours), halfway up the valley. There are also several side-trips to huts in the Travers Range to the west, Lake Angelus, Mount Hopeless and the Cupola Hut.

Above the John Tait Hut, the track becomes more dramatic, circumventing a gorge, but soon dropping down again to the river flats before reaching the Upper Travers Hut with it's fantastic view of the east face of Mount Travers (this section takes about three hours).

The Travers Saddle crossing (1800 m) to the Sabine Forks Hut can mean a long day, depending on the weather and track conditions: It takes between six and nine hours. Bring along water and watch the weather carefully. In summer, it's perfectly accessible to the average tramper. On a clear day, the panoramas from the saddle to both the east and the west are absolutely breathtaking.

After the saddle, the track drops relatively quickly to the bushland below. The

most interesting feature of this section is the East Sabine Gorge, a three-meter wide chasm, plunging to a depth of 35 m. Luckily there's a good bridge here. Just before this gorge, you will see a good campsite on a grass terrace. If you're sick of crowded huts at the height of summer, you can pitch your tent here and enjoy some solitude.

However, if you've still got plenty of steam, continue on down to the Sabine Forks, where there are two huts. The new one is at the start of the west branch of the Sabine, and the older one on the east branch. Both have wood/coal stoves if heat is what you need.

The next day, a comfortable, well-beaten track taking four or five hours guides you down to the Sabine Hut through beech forests and occasional clearings. From the Sabine at the head of

Above: Mount Aspiring provides photo-graphic inspiration in the evening sun. Right: The view across Lake Wanaka to the Mount Aspiring National Park.

Lake Rotoroa, you can either continue marching around the east side of the lake for six or seven hours, and thus bring the hike to its conclusion; or take one of two alternative routes back to Lake Rotoiti. The first possibility is to return to the Travers Valley via Lake Angelus and the Angelus Hut.

The other alternative is to walk out to the Mount Roberts parking lot on Lake Rotoiti, via the Speargrass Hut. Both will add a day or two to your hiking schedule, so it's advisable to plan your provisions accordingly.

Routeburn Track
Mount Aspiring National Park

After the Milford Track, the Routeburn Track in the Mount Aspiring National Park is the most popular walk in any of the national parks. The trick is to try to avoid the high summer season between December and the end of January when the huts are likely to be literally teeming with hikers, particularly from overseas.

This three-day trip can be approached from either end – from the Milford Road or from the head of Lake Wakatipu via Queenstown. Transportation is readily available to either starting point during the summer. Perhaps the best approach is from Glenorchy, a delightful town at the head of Lake Wakatipu. The track winds its way through silvery beech forest, alongside the clear-flowing Routeburn River with crystal pools.

You should reach the first hut at Routeburn Falls in three to four hours, maybe longer if it's a very hot day and you stop for a bracing swim along the way. The hut is in a splendid position, high above the valley with peaks all around, and has flush toilets! When the hut is full during vacation periods, you can stop at the lower hut at Routeburn Flats, or camp nearby.

The next day, the clearly-marked route leads across the more exposed mountaintops with extensive, romantic vistas of snow-covered peaks, passing the mysterious Lake Harris.

The 1227-m high Harris Saddle is very exposed, so don't underestimate the risk of rapid weather change, particularly in the spring and autumn. On a fine day, however, the two-hour walk from the top down to the striking Lake Mackenzie is pure delight. There are panoramic, dramatic views of the Darran Mountains and the Hollyford Valley, which lies hundreds of meters below.

After a night at the hut at Lake Mackenzie (good swimming here), it's an easy four-hour walk out to the Milford Road. However, if the weather's great and you feel like more, have lunch at Lake Howden, and then head down the Greenstone Valley, a select place for trout fishers. Two days of hiking should bring you back to Greenstone Track. Transportation is easily available from here back to Glenorchy.

The other possibility is to cut down a side track from Lake Howden Hut to the Hollyford Valley. But don't forget insect repellent to deal with the sandflies if you choose this path.

Lake Waikaremoana Track
Urewera National Park

Following the lake edge for much of the time, this four-day walk is a hiking classic. Since the track is very popular during the summer holiday period, it is advisable to carry tents. What makes the Waikaremoana Track so inviting is its superb mixture of magnificent views of the large lake and huge areas of untouched jungle country with an extensive bird world. The track can be started from either end, although most people leave from Onepot Bay, just off Highway 38. Camping sites are available here, close to an old rebout dating back to the mid-19th century.

The first part of the walk from this end is a stiff climb of four or five hours up the Panekiri Bluff (1177 m). However, there are excellent views of the lake below and

Above: An abandoned farm adds to the forlorn ambience along the track in the Westland National Park.

the vast expanse of jungle that makes up this 212,000 hectare park. Once you get to the top of the ridge, the going gets easier until you reach the Panekiri Hut, which is perched on a ridge dropping some sheer 600 m down to the lake below.

The next section of the track is less strenuous. It follows the ridge for some distance before a steep descent down through an increasingly luxuriant forest landscape. This is a dramatically steep drop of over 300 m to the Waiopaoa Hut, which is almost hidden in dense lowland bush. Now you can think about swimming, or fishing for brown or rainbow trout since the rest of the trail will give you ample opportunity to take a well-deserved break at the delightful lakeside bays and inlets.

The next day, it's about a four-hour walk to Marauiti Hut – passing the Korokoro Falls along the way. The lakeside track continues through a mixture of jungle and bushland, with many good campsites such as Te Kopua Bay, which also offers good fishing at the right time of the year.

After lazing around at Te Kopua Bay, an energetic two or three hours of hiking will take you past more sandy bays and rocky points to the Te Puna Hut, which boasts an interesting view of Panekiri Bluff in the distance.

The next day you can either decide to spare your feet and only go to Wanganui Hut, which takes about two hours, or even walk out to the road if you're in a hurry (half a day).

A real jungle experience is waiting for you in Urewera National Park. If you've brought a tent and a good book, then it's possible to remain as long as the food or your fishing luck lasts. That's assuming the weather stays on the sunny side, because there's a reason why this is called the land of the mists!

Tongariro Crossing
Tongariro National Park

The classic North Island walk can be started from the "Chalet" hotel beneath Mount Ruapehu, or from an access road off state highway 47. If you park on the access road, don't leave valuables inside. There is a theft problem in this area. The Mangatepopo Hut is just 15 minutes from the end of the access road. Note that bacteria has been found in the water at this hut, so it is definitely recommended that you boil it before drinking.

From Mangatepopo, the clearly-posted track winds its way up the valley of the Mangatepopo towards the saddle between Mount Tongariro and Mount Ngauruhoe. The terrain becomes increasingly barren and volcanic the further up the valley you go. On your right are the huge black lava flows from the most recent eruptions of Ngauruhoe. Also keep your eyes open for the soda springs on your left at the base of Tongariro.

If you are in good shape, you should make the saddle in about one hour. Then you have to decide whether to try climbing to the summit of the active volcano, Mount Ngauruhoe (2290 m). If you are fit and have started early, it is possible and certainly fascinating to get to the top and look down into the huge crater of an active volcano, a round-trip climb of three hours. Many people just make the summit a day-trip destination from the hut. The important thing is not to get overtired and ruin the rest of the hike to Ketetahi Hut. But get advance information about possible eruptions!

After the saddle, the track crosses a stark, treeless plateau scattered with volcanic debris, slinks up and over a small ridge, and skirts the Red Crater (still active) and the Emerald and Blue Lakes with their startling colors. This is a fascinating volcanic landscape, pitted with craters and hot springs. Another plus on a fine day is the extensive view to the east across wide tussock plains to the jungle-covered Kaimanawa Ranges. From the Red Crater area, it is also possible to take a detour to the summit of Tongariro (1968 m), taking about one hour each way.

In summer, it gets very hot in this area between Tongariro and Ngauruhoe, so be sure to take a sun hat, sun glasses and water. But be warned, this is also an alpine crossing and covered with snow in winter. It can get freezing cold and snow.

After skirting Blue Lake, the track turns through a small pass and opens up on the northern slopes of Mount Tongariro. Here there are superb views of Lake Taupo and the country to the north. After six or seven hours of walking, you can bask in the luxuriance of the natural hot springs close to Ketetahi Hut (it is not advisable to put your head under the water, as there is a risk of meningitis). Now refreshed, you can go back to the hut for another tasty meal.

The walk out to the road (and your waiting car) should only take an hour or so the next day.

SPORTS IN NEW ZEALAND

After the Olympic Games in Seoul in 1988 a quip made the rounds in New Zealand that went: "The *Kiwi* athletes can only make it to the top sitting down." Mark Todd won the gold medal in military riding, Ian Ferguson and Paul McDonald were Olympic winners in the two-man kayak over a distance of 5000 m. Only the surfer Kendall Bruce was lacking the sitting position in his triumph in the Division II. In their hearts, however, the New Zealanders were extremely proud of their small Olympic team. Besides the three gold medals, it also brought home two silver and eight bronze medals. With this, New Zealand was almost as successful as its favorite rival, Australia (three gold, six silver, five bronze medals). Moreover, as the *Kiwi* experts had immediately calculated, in

Above: A sport with a future, cycling is gaining popularity in New Zealand. Right: The old tradition of lawn bowling lives on.

relation to population only the German Democratic Republic (as it existed at that time) had brought forth more Olympic champions per capita.

New Zealand is a sports-loving nation. More than anywhere else in the world, sporting activities take a central position in the daily lives of the people. Top athletes enjoy great respect in the society. Much has been speculated on the reasons for the virtually fanatic interest in any type of physical training. Some talk of the pioneer spirit of a young nation or the lack of a sufficiently developed cultural life. Others see the main motive in an untamed natural environment that invites participation in outdoor experiences of all kinds, or in an unbridled people, who have contributed to the development of the country with great physical labor. Finally, there is still the close relationship to the mother country of modern competition sports, Great Britain, where most Caucasian immigrants have their roots. Probably all of these aspects have contributed to New Zealand's sports craze. On the average, every resident indulges in more than three different sporting activities, and it is quite frequent that even top athletes pursue different sports in summer and winter. If need be, the enjoyment of variety is placed before success through specialization.

The athletic tradition in New Zealand is closely tied to that of Great Britain. The most popular sport is rugby. The three million New Zealanders have produced a host of excellent rugby players so that the national team, the *All Blacks* (attired totally in black), was undefeated for years. The *All Blacks* were an export hit and political issue, but not only in a positive sense. With their regular guest performances in South Africa, they provoked numerous boycott actions by Black African countries at Olympic games, world championships and Commonwealth games. This had no detrimental effect upon their popularity at home.

There was not one seven-year old who couldn't tell how the *All Blacks* came to their first victory in Australia, nor one eight-year old who was unable to name the captains of the team for at least the last 50 years. On weekends and every evening during the week, hundreds of people play touch, a gentler form of rugby, at various parks, and there are numerous fans among women as well. In every city, there are now touch playing divisions, in addition to the official rugby leagues that mobilize entire city districts.

In contrast to the *All Blacks*, the *All Whites* are true orphans. New Zealand's national soccer team, which once qualified for the world championships, stands in the long shadows cast by the rugby stars. The image of being a sport for spoiled rich boys still sticks to soccer, whereas rugby supposedly challenges the "real man".

Still other typically British sports enjoy unbroken popularity. Lawn bowling is at the top of the list. The game is played with solid wooden balls, which are additionally weighted on one side, and therefore follow a curved path on the short grass when they are rolled towards the smaller white ball called *jack*, their goal.

Primarily, thousands of older *Kiwis* play this game in more or less stylish clubs, properly attired in the typical bowling uniform: the women in white skirts, blouses, jackets and hats; the men wear shorts which are at least knee-length or long pants, absolutely in white. Only seldom does the club's manager tolerate deviations from the dress code, but the visitor is gladly led into the clubhouse where the trophies are displayed and a plaque with the names of all past presidents and club masters is hanging.

The most prominent bowler of New Zealand is a women by the name of Millie Khan. At the Commonwealth games in Auckland in 1990, where bowling was included in the official program along with nine other sporting events, she won the silver medal before a crowd of 10,000 spectators in a dramatic women's final.

No less British is croquet, a game in which balls are driven with a wooden mallet through a series of wickets placed on the lawn, according to a set of complicated rules. It also tends to be associated with the upper class, lawn parties and genteel people under parasols. The high prize money allows some New Zealanders to tour the country as professional croquet players. While the ignorant spectator is gladly initiated into the art of lawn bowling upon inquiry, the croquet specialists seem to guard the rules of their game like state secrets.

Naturally, criquet has also preserved the status it holds in all former British colonies. On the weekend, the beaches are just teeming with private criquet matches. The games of the national team can last up to five days, and are frequently covered in full length and live on television and radio without any trace of boredom arising from the local spectators. Criquet stars, with regard to fame and fortune, can hold their own with rugby players.

If it seems as if primarily men's sports have been mentioned so far, this is no coincidence. For a long time, sports have been solely a man's field in New Zealand, but this has changed in the last few years due to the success of a handful of committed women.

At the top of the list is Susan Devoy, several times world champion in squash and presently listed number one in the field. As Susan Devoy climbed to the throne, the New Zealanders suddenly discovered not only a love for squash but also for athletic women. Devoy has covered title pages of newspapers and magazines, and is highly regarded not only in her home town of Rotorua. When she ran from the south of South Island to Northcap in 1990, she collected millions of New Zealand dollars and donated the money to those suffering from muscular

Above: In Winter, rugby is still the most popular spectator sport. Right: Something different, wood-chopping competitions in summer.

dystrophy. New Zealand spectators tremble just as much with the women's netball team, which has stood for years unchallenged among the world's top teams and not only for lack of competition. Netball was originated in the Netherlands and is a variation of basketball. In New Zealand, it is the number one sport among women.

Since hardly any of the most popular sports activities in New Zealand are included in the Olympic program, these individualists of the South Pacific do not really care if they achieve world renown or not. The most important thing is their reputation at home, and sometimes they strive for direct comparison to their Australian neighbor and archrival in all matters of social intercourse.

A further example of this is the coast-to-coast race from the west coast of South Island over Arthur's Pass and the New Zealand Alps to Christchurch – New Zealand's own special triathlon.

Besides running and biking, the contestants must cover a large section of the course by canoe. Thousands of spectators flank the streets when the first exhausted competitors bike over the goal line after the twelve-hour ordeal. A victory in this race rates, of course, higher than a triumph as *Iron Man*, the great triathlon on Hawaii.

It is certainly not only the diverse forms of the top sports that find supporters and fans in New Zealand. First and foremost at the other end of the world, the saying "do it yourself" holds true. Take golf, for example: In the northern hemisphere, golf is more or less still a game for the elite, whereas in New Zealand it is a genuine sport of the people. The green fees seldom cost more than those of a squash court, and many clubs are open to visitors, even those who are not advanced enough in their skills.

Last but not least, New Zealand is a land of water-sports enthusiasts. Nowhere else in the world are top-rated

yachtsmen more popular than here. The large, beautiful yachts that participate in the races around the world are trimmed to top form by able and powerful sponsors. It's no wonder that almost every New Zealander is a hobby sailor. Thousands of boats are anchored in the yacht harbor at Auckland, and tourists can reasonably rent yachts everywhere. Sailing trips along the coast lasting a few days are very popular, along with outings to the Marlborough Sound in connection with diving courses.

The motto generally appears to be: the more extreme, the better! Even tramping has been cultivated into a national sport. Those who take pride in their abilities venture on hikes through the national parks taking several days. At many places, clever entrepreneurs offer full-scale survival training in the jungle. Overnight stays are in tents or modest cabins. Luxury is a taboo.

Who was it then that jokingly said: "New Zealanders prefer to pursue sports sitting down"?

237

FARMING: THE FOCAL POINT

Kiwis used to give visitors a special welcome: When they landed, the inside of their aircraft was sprayed with an antiseptic spray. For New Zealanders, this way of welcoming visitors is an embarrassment, and where possible it is now being phased out. But no insult is intended by the action. The spray is to destroy things such as insects or viruses in the aircraft, which may harm the livelihood of a nation that depends heavily on farming. New Zealand's gross annual farm production is worth more than NZ$ 7 billion, and it provides 54 percent of the nations's export income. It is thus vital for the country's economic well-being and worth a little spray.

The New Zealand farmers get a good deal of assistance from mother nature in

Above: Seasonal workers bring their houses with them in the warm seasons. Right: Quality-checking the world-famous New Zealand wool in Wanaka.

their work. The climate provides a range of temperatures from sub-tropical in the north to cool in the south, where frost may be experienced for two months of the year in the farming areas.

Most of New Zealand, apart from the high mountains, was originally forested. Starting at about the middle of the 19th century, it was cleared by settlers to provide arable land. Some 23 percent of the land remains forested, much of it as protected wilderness, and some of it as renewable forest.

Agriculture today dominates a total of 17,746,000 hectares of land, consisting in 82,063 separate farms. They usually are single units of land owned by a family that lives there in a cottage-style house. In contrast to the clusters of houses and villages in Europe, the New Zealand farming districts are characterized by seemingly isolated houses with their own neat gardens, surrounded by about 200 hectares of farmland.

Each farm is subdivided by post and wire fencing into "paddocks," which enables efficient management of animals or crops.

New Zealand farms support (1991 figures) 64 million sheep, 8 million cattle, 1.3 million goats, 600,000 deer and 400,000 pigs. The moderate climate means there is no need to keep the animals in stalls.

Some 89,000 hectares of land are used for fruit and vegetable production, and 1,265,000 for tree farming.

Although only a relatively small proportion of the arable land provides particularly rich soil, the land is capable of heavy production. Pastures are green most of the year, and the best farms can support 25 sheep or three to four dairy cows per hectare. Only in some southern regions is supplementary feed, notably hay and silage made in summer, necessary during the winter.

The present generation of farmers has three special agricultural colleges avail-

able – in Hamilton, in Palmerston North and in Christchurch where one can learn scientific methods of farming, animal husbandry, economics and other aspects of their field. The colleges are also centers of world-famous research in agricultural science and technology.

With this education and family learning acquired through generations, the farmer is able to best utilize the resources of the land. This may involve the use of special hybrids of grasses or clovers suited to soil, climate and animal type. An additional consideration in the choice of pasture is how it affects the flavor of the meat of animals that graze on it. Most New Zealanders prefer the sweet taste of young mutton raised on green grass. Some Japanese, for instance, seem to prefer it clover-fed. But the Japanese insist on free-range grass-fed New Zealand beef, which has little fat in the grain of the meat.

Although sheep may all appear to be the same woolly grazing animals, there are many different variations. The sheep producing the rack of lamb for the Canadian restaurant trade are vastly different from those which produce cutlets displayed in the refrigerators of British supermarkets.

Airfreight is employed to a large degree to convey produce in the freshest condition possible to markets nationally and internationally. There is still a large trade in frozen meat by surface shipping, however. In 1882, the first shipment of frozen meat was sent to Britain in a sailing ship with a steam engine to drive the cooling plant.

Large quantities of fruits and vegetables are also exported by sea in special containers, on voyages timed to the day to ensure that the produce is properly ripe upon arrival. The kiwi fruit is New Zealand's most famous agricultural export, but apples still remain the number one international bestseller. Last but not least, New Zealand wines have been attracting increasing attention, to the point of becoming serious competition to the European ones.

TRAVEL PREPARATIONS

Climate and Best Time to Travel

The most significant difference to the European and American climates is that the seasons of the year in the southern hemisphere are opposite to those in the northern hemisphere. Summer is from November to March with warm temperatures, and winter is from June to August with cooler temperatures.

The climatic conditions on North Island and South Island vary substantially from each other. North of Auckland, the landscape has a subtropical character. Night frost is seldom during the entire year. In the southern part of North Island, snow falls regularly at elevations above 1000 m in the winter, just as it is a part of daily life in winter in most regions of South Island. Here the temperatures frequently sink below freezing, especially at the higher elevations in the Southern Alps.

One exception is the area around Nelson and Golden Bay, where even in winter a relatively mild climate prevails with plenty of sunshine the year round.

In summer, temperatures rise throughout the country to 20 – 25 °C. However, the evenings cool off considerably everywhere. The wind usually blows from a westerly direction. For water-sports enthusiasts this means the rougher west coast has ideal surfing conditions. The calmer east coast is more suited to diving and sailing. Rain must be reckoned with at all times in New Zealand.

The best time to travel is from the end of November to the end of March – despite New Zealand's school vacation period and the sandfly nuisance. An exception to this is when you are traveling on the west coast, where the period from May to June has the clearest mountain weather and less rain. Snow skiers on South Island will certainly get their money's worth during the months of June, July and August.

Travel to New Zealand

Travel to New Zealand can commence from Europe via Asia or from America. The flight route chosen depends upon the airline and the preference regarding stopovers along the way. The flight route from Europe is about 19,500 km long, and you are in the air approximately 26 hours. It is important to remember that travel routes can be very busy between the months of November and March. Therefore, early reservations are strongly recommended (up to six months in advance). The majority of passengers enter New Zealand for the first time at Auckland (and Christchurch). The capital city Wellington is primarily of significance for domestic flights. Air New Zealand flies twice weekly (Wednesdays and Saturdays) from Frankfurt via Los Angeles to Auckland (on Saturdays, the only airline flying direct). Depending on the season, the tariff varies. An advantage flying this way: For a minimal additional charge, different South Sea stop-overs can be worked in (for example, Hawaii, Tahiti, Cook Island, Fiji, Samoa and Tonga).

London: Air New Zealand, Elsmore House, 77 Fulham Palace Road, London, Tel: 081/741-22999

Los Angeles: Air New Zealand, 1960 E. Grand Ave., El Segundo, CA 90245, Tel: 001213/615-1111

Sydney: Air New Zealand, 7th Flr. Commercial Union Bldg. 80 Arthur St. Sydney, Tel: 02/965-4111

Calgary: Air New Zealand, Tel: 604/276-7446

Belfast: British Airways, 9 Fountain Centre, College Street, Tel: 240-522

Dublin: British Airways, Tel: 686-668

Chicago and **New York**: Air New Zealand, Tel: 1-800-282-1234 (toll free from the USA).

Lufthansa, together with Air New Zealand, flies the Asian route (stop-over in Singapore among other places is possible). Singapore Airlines flies the same route five times a week. In addition, Aerolineas Argentinas, Canadian Airlines, Cathay Pacific, Continental Airlines, Garuda Indonesia, Malaysain Airlines, Qantas, Thai International, and United Airlines fly to New Zealand. Flight costs depend primarily on the departure date. The expensive peak season is from December to the end of February. For those who have time and are looking for reasonable price, flights from London or from one of the Asian metropolises, such as Bangkok or Singapore, are often less expensive but more roundabout. The problem of jet lag can best be overcome by eating lightly, drinking little alcohol during the flight and staying awake until the first night in New Zealand – this is the quickest way to get accustomed to the new rhythm of day and night.

Entry Formalities

Tourists from Australia, Canada, the Republic of Ireland, the United Kingdom, the United States and most Western European countries require neither a visa nor a health/ vaccination certificate when staying less than three months in New Zealand. Travelers must be in possession of a passport that is valid at least three months longer than the planned return date from New Zealand.

Upon entry in New Zealand, a paid return flight must be presented. "Sufficient financial means" must also be available. This point is often left to the discretion of the customs official. A general guideline is approximately NZ$ 1000 per month. Generally, the visitor to New Zealand with a well-groomed appearance can count on the "generosity" of the immigration officer.

Should you wish to stay in New Zealand longer than three months, your normal tourist visa can be renewed once for a period of three months. For stays beyond this period of time, or a work permit, you should check at a New Zealand embassy or consulate for the necessary

formalities before starting out on your trip.

Australia: New Zealand High Commission, Commonwealth Avenue, Canberra ACT 2600, Australia, Tel: (6) 273-3611, Fax: (6) 273-3194.

Canada: New Zealand High Commission: Suite 801, Metropolitan House, 99 Bank Street, Ottawa; ONT KIP 6G3, Canada, Tel: (613) 238-5991, Fax: (613) 238-5707.

United Kingdom: New Zealand High Commission: The Haymarket, London SW1Y 4TQ, United Kingdom, Tel: (71)930 8422 (Chancery), Fax: (71) 839 4580.

United States: The New Zealand Embassy: 37 Observatory Circle NW, Washington, DC 20008, USA, Tel: (202) 328 4848, Fax: (202) 667 5227.

For those who wish employment in New Zealand, it is best to contact an immigration officer in the country itself. Due to the high unemployment rate, working permits are issued only very infrequently.

Currency

There are no entry or export regulations for New Zealand or foreign currencies in the form of bills, coins, travelers checks or other forms of legal tender.

As in many other countries, the US$ is the most common foreign currency. However, most European currencies can be exchanged almost anywhere in the country. Travelers checks can be recommended. Moreover, it is advisable to carry a credit card, especially when you plan to rent a vehicle. Practically all common credit cards are accepted, especially Visa, MasterCard/Eurocard and American Express.

The New Zealand dollar (NZ$ 1 = 100 cents) comes in the following denominations: coins in 1, 2, 5, 10, 20, and 50 cents, as well as NZ$ 1 and 2. NZ$ bills come in 5, 10, 20, 50 and 100 denominations. The inflation indirectly caused the

NZ$ 1 and 2 bills to be slowly replaced by the respective coins.

Customs

Next to personal items (such as clothing, camera, etc.), travelers over the age of 17 can bring the following into the country: tobacco (200 cigarettes or 250 g of tobacco or 50 cigars); alcoholic beverages (4.5 liters of wine or 4.5 liters of beer and a bottle of liquor with a maxiumum of 1.125 ml); plus other articles at a value of NZ$ 500.

Information

Information, maps, lists of travel agents in English-speaking countries and in New Zealand, brochures (from accommodations to trips for the handicapped) are supplied free of charge by the Tourist Information of New Zealand (NZTI).

Offices of the NZTI Overseas Services: **Vancouver**: Suite 1260, 701 West Georgia St., BC V7Y 1B6, Tel: (001604) 6842117, FAX: 6841265; **London**: New Zealand House, Haymarket, SW1Y 4TQ, Tel: (004471)9730363, FAX: 8398929; **Tokyo**: Toho Twin Tower Bldg, 2FL, 1-5-2 Yurakuch, Chiyodaku, Tel: (00813) 5089981, FAX: 5012326; **Sydney**: Prudential Fin. House, 84 Pitt St., NSW 2000, Tel: (00612) 2315737, FAX: 2350737; **Singapore**: 13 Nassim Rd., Singapore 1025, Tel: (0065) 235996, FAX:2352550; **Hongkong**: 3414 Jardine House, 1 Connaught Place, Tel: (00852) 5260141, FAX: 8452915; **Los Angeles**: 501 Santa Monica Blvd. #300, CA 90401, Tel: (001213) 3957480, FAX: 3955453; NZ Marketing Representative **Buenos Aires**: Marcelo T. Alvear 590, 10th Fl., Tel: (00541)3120664, FAX: 111219.

TRAVELING IN NEW ZEALAND

Air

Together with Mount Cook Airlines, New Zealand Airlines has connections between 24 cities in the country. As a result, these two airlines have the most closely-woven network of air routes. The third most significant airlines is Ansett New Zealand.

Besides the regular tariffs (for example, Auckland – Christchurch: one-way flight approximately NZ$ 350), there is a large selection of special rates and air passes. Air New Zealand offers a "Visit New Zealand Special." When traveling with this airlines, the passenger receives a 30% reduction on domestic flights. Mount Cook Airlines offers the reasonable "Kiwi Air Pass." During the period of one month, any route of this airline can be flown in one direction. The pass, which connects all significant regions, must be purchased outside of New Zealand before arrival in the country.

Bicycle

Increasingly popular is traveling in New Zealand by bike. It is relatively easy to take a bicycle along on your trip. Air New Zealand and Lufthansa offer this service generally without additional cost (check when making your flight reservations and note total weight). It is important that your bike is properly wrapped.

The best time to travel weatherwise is from mid-October to March. With regard to traffic on the roads, the vacation period of December/January should be avoided.

Warning: New Zealand is not an easy country to bike in. Climbs and strong winds, rain showers and lonely nights between two destinations are not unusual (light weather-proof clothing that lets your skin breathe is important).

More information can be obtained at: Bicycle Association of New Zealand, Box 2454, Wellington, Tel: 04-84389; Auckland, Tel: 09-3489233.

Bus

Without a doubt, bus travel is the *Kiwis'* favorite form of inland transportation. The companies InterCity, Mount Cook Landline and Newmans offer a close-knit network which covers even remote regions, such as the West Coast between Westport and Haast, as well as the East Cape on North Island.

There are a number of reasonable offers for tourists, called travel passes. Mount Cook Landline has a "Kiwi Coach Pass" with which you can travel anywhere along their routes for seven to 33 days. The seven-day pass is valid, for example, for a total of 11 days. This provides the opportunity of making a few stop-overs without losing valid travel time on the bus (cost: NZ$ 420 for seven days; NZ$ 900 for 33 days).

Intercity offers a "Travelpass" (8, 15 or 22 days) with which buses, trains and ferries belonging to their company can be used (Cost: about NZ$ 400 for 8 days; NZ$ 650 for 22 days. The pass must be purchased before your arrival in New Zealand.) Furthermore, Newmans offers a "Coach Pass."

Especially suited for individualists and backpackers, due to the numerous opportunities to get on and off the bus in the vicinity of the national parks, is the "alternative" bus company, Kiwi Experience, 36 Custom Street, Auckland, Tel: 09-3661665.

Car Rentals

All international automobile-leasing agencies (Hertz, Budget and Avis) have representatives at the airport in Auckland. You can reserve a vehicle before arriving in New Zealand at one of these offices in your own country (minimum age: 21; international drivers' licenses and those of the 128 countries of the 1949 convention, plus Switzerland, are recognized; ask about others). These well-known companies do have their price, however.

Substantially more reasonable are a few agencies where international reservations are not possible and which have no offices at the airport. These agencies can be found for the most part in downtown

Auckland (ACE Tourist Rentals, 51-53 The Strand, Parnell, Tel: 09-3033627; Low Cost Self Drive P.O. Box 78-094, Tel: 09-3033928; Dollar Save Car Hire, P.O. Box 34266, Tel: 09-4809881, FAX: 09-4191695).

Hardy Cars, low budget rental cars, head office: 6 Bridge St., Nelson, Tel: 0064-3-5481681, FAX: 3-5481581.

A possible disadvantage: Should you have trouble returning the vehicle shortly before your departure, problems can still be clarified at home with the international agencies. This is hardly possible with the New Zealand rental firms.

Caution should be taken with the small print. Different auto-leasing agencies prohibit travel on certain unpaved roads. These roads, on which there is no damage/collision coverage, are listed on the back of the leasing contract.

A few agencies have an ideal offer (for example, MAUI and Hardy Cars). They allow the return of a vehicle (even campers) on a one-way basis. Whoever rents a vehicle in Auckland can return it at the airport in Christchurch (or the other way around).

The advantage of this arrangement: You avoid the long return trip and have time for other side-trips. You can also save a certain amount of money because you need only travel on the ferry between Wellington and Picton once. (Information available at MAUI, Leisure Port, Richard Pearse Drive, Mangere, Auckland, Tel: 09-2753013, or 530-544 Memorial Avenue, Christchurch, Tel: 03-584159 or Hardy Cars, address and phone see above.

The fees for renting a vehicle on a daily basis are between NZ$ 60 and NZ$ 100. When renting a vehicle for more than 28 days, you will usually receive a better rate. Some tourists like campers (with two to six beds). The rental rate for these vehicles runs to more than NZ$ 100 per day. Hardy Cars offer them for NZ$ 136-146 for four persons. The price depends on the season as well. In the peak season, the rate rises along with the demand. The advantage of a camper is that you can stay overnight wherever you like. On the other hand, New Zealand has an almost unbroken network of motels and camping grounds (both quite reasonable, with the opportunity of supplying your own provisions), so that with a "solid" instead of "mobile" roof over your head, you are still right in the middle of nature. Remember, for rentals between November and March reservations have to be made in advance.

Generally you have to reckon with narrow and unpaved roads outside of the big cities. Your speed with be considerably slower than you may have anticipated. This should be considered when deciding on whether to rent a car or a camper.

Gas is a bit more reasonable than in Europe, but more expensive than in the USA. An insurance policy should be taken out if you have none at home (about NZ$ 11 per day). Finally, extra caution is advised for the first few kilometers because New Zealanders drive on the left-hand side of the road.

Helpful information and maps, along with extensive camping and hotel guides, are offered by the Automobile Association (AA). Members of European automobile clubs receive the information free of charge. Offices can be found in all larger cities (main office: AA, Box 1053, 342-352 Lambton Quay, Wellington, Tel: 04-4738738).

Ferry

The ferry between Wellington, North Island, and Picton, South Island, proves time and again to be a bottleneck for most tourists since it is the only connection for vehicles between the two islands. The ferry runs up to four times daily. Adults are charged about NZ$ 40 for a one-way fare, children pay half-price and vehicles (according to length) cost between NZ$ 115 and NZ$ 150.

It is essential to make early reservations, especially during the months of December, January and February. Otherwise it can come to day-long waits in line – above all for campers. A possible inconvenience for visitors is having to set a specific date for traveling with the ferry. Changes in the travel itinerary are then not always possible.

Hitchhiking

Although it has become more difficult, you can still get around by hitchhiking. New Zealand's hospitality and curiosity about visitors from other countries assure that hitchhikers are successful. For this reason it is sometimes helpful when hitchhikers attach an emblem of their national flag onto their backpack or luggage. Patience is called for, due to the low volume of traffic.

New Zealand also now has travel-sharing centers (Travel Share Centre, 18 Heather Street, Ground Floor, Parnell, Auckland, Tel: 09-3773027, FAX: 09-3734713).

Train

Although the New Zealand railroad network is not extensively developed, it still offers several beautiful routes. The *Overlander* travels daily between Auckland and Wellington (one-way trip costs approximately NZ$ 110). A bit more reasonable is the *Northerner,* which travels the same route nights.

The *TranzAlpine Express* crosses the Southern Alps between Christchurch and Greymouth daily (one-way ticket costs about NZ$ 90). The *Bay Express* runs between Wellington and Napier (daily, approximately NZ$ 60); the *Coastal Pacific* is the ideal connection to the ferry on the route from Picton to Christchurch (daily, about NZ$ 60); and the *Southern Express* (about NZ$ 80) travels from Christchurch south to Invercargill. All routes can also be traveled with the "Intercity Travel Pass."

PRACTICAL TIPS

Accommodations

The range of overnight accommodations in New Zealand is extraordinarily diverse considering the population. The categories as listed in the Guideposts are divided up as follows:

Budget: under NZ$ 10 – NZ$ 40 for a bed (usually backpacker hostels/dormitories, caravan parks, camping sites or cabins). *Moderate:* NZ$ 70 – NZ$ 150 for a double occupancy.

Luxury: NZ$ 150 – NZ$ 500 and above for a double occupancy.

In general, hotels and motels are almost always clean and well-kept. Accommodations rated moderate or budget can sometimes have furnishings that are not the newest, but the hospitality and friendliness of the landlord or landlady easily outweighs this slight shortcoming. Guests often receive fresh milk upon arrival in motels.

Tea and a kettle are also provided in the rooms. The kettle, tea and milk belong to the basic provisions, because a *Kiwi* (even a traveling one) would never be satisfied without his or her morning and evening cup of tea.

Hotels in the European sense are normally only found in large cities and tourist centers, where they easily meet international standards.

Usually the visitor to New Zealand will stay in motels (room for a double occupancy between NZ$ 50 and NZ$ 110), most of which offer a completely-furnished kitchen so that you are able to prepare your own meals, which is one easy way to spare the travel budget.

There are several exclusive lodges for those travelers who like a little luxury and do not have to watch their dollars. The most well-known are: Huka Lodge at Taupo; Puka Park Lodge, Pauanui/Coromandel Peninsula; Wharekauhau Lodge near Wellington and Muriahoha Lodge near Rotorua.

Backpacker Hostels

New Zealand has become a genuine El Dorado for backpackers in the past few years. In almost all larger cities and tourist centers there are inexpensive backpacker accommodations available. Up and down the country, backpacker buses run regularly, there are backpacker newspapers, and backpackers are welcomed everywhere as guests.

Information and newspapers catering to backpackers: Kiwi Backpacker, 36 Custom Street, Box 1247, Auckland, Tel: 09-3777049; Backpackers News, 50 Somme Street, St. Albans, Christchurch, Tel: 03-3559055.

Lists of accommodations can be obtained at: Youth Hostel Association, Travel Centre, Box 436, Christchurch, Tel: 03-3799970; Backerpackers, 34 Auckland Street, Picton, Tel: 03-5736598: Budget Backpackers Hostels, Rainbow Lodge, 99 Titiraupenga Street, Taupo, Tel: 07-37885754; or Foley Towers, 208 Kilmore Street, Christchurch, Tel: 03-3669720.

Camping

New Zealand has been divided up into 14 camping zones. For more information contact the Camp and Cabin Association of New Zealand, P.O. Box 394, Paraparamu, Tel. and Fax: 04-2983283.

Farm Vacations

The visitor to New Zealand can become acquainted with the typical characteristics of the country during a stay on a farm. More than 20 organizations offer vacation stays on farms throughout the country. The prices range between NZ$ 45 – 100 per person (New Zealand Farm Holidays Ltd., Box 256, Silverdale, Auckland, Tel: 09-3072024; Rural Tours, 92 Victoria Street, Cambridge, Tel: 07-8278055; and The Friendly Kiwi Home & Farmstay Ltd., Box 5049, Port Nelson, Tel: 03-5468327).

Pub Beds

Inexpensive overnight accommodations are offered by a group of more than 40 city and country pubs. Per person, the overnight stay costs NZ$ 25 – NZ$ 30. (Information can be obtained at Pub Beds, Box 21, Auckland, Tel: 09-2742600, FAX: 09-2742755.)

Airport Fee

Even in New Zealand this is an annoying topic: Before your return flight departure overseas, an airport fee (NZ$ 20 from Auckland, Christchurch and Wellington) is charged. You should have this money available so you save yourself a last trip to the currency exchange office.

Awards

Caution: It is a common passtime in New Zealand to honor touristic enterprises and restaurants with awards. It is extremely rare not to find an award on the entrance wall, behind the bar or next to the sales sign. Do not be dazzled by these honors; New Zealand is frequently flooded with an awards boom. A genuine guarantee for actual quality is not given in many cases.

Business Hours

The "magic word" for the late or last minute shopper is dairies. These corner shops can be found throughout the country, and sell everything from your daily household needs to items for "survival."

They are generally open daily until 11 p.m. This compensates for the "normal" business hours, Monday through Thursday from 9 a.m. to 5:30 p.m., Friday until 9 p.m. and Saturday until noon. Offices are open Monday through Friday from 9 a.m. to 5 p.m., and banks Monday through Friday from 9 a.m. to 4:30 p.m.

On Good Friday and Christmas almost everything is closed. Museums and public offices are closed, transportation is shut down, and the best thing to do is to find a nice sandy beach on which to enjoy

the holiday atmosphere – just as the *Kiwis* do.

Celebrations

A bit of typical New Zealand farm life can be enjoyed at an "A&P" show. These Agricultural and Pastoral Shows offer a cross-section of the farmers' products and work, and usually take place regionally in the period from February to April.

Sailboat races in Auckland (January), Waitangi (February), Golden Shears in Masterton and the Maori Regatta Ngaruawahia in Hamilton (both in March), and the Canterbury Show Week in Christchurch (November) are celebrated nationally.

Clothing

New Zealand is very informal as far as clothing is concerned. Suits and ties are seldom required for men and the same goes for elegant womens' clothing. However, do not forget that even for summer trips a warm sweater, sturdy shoes and raingear are necessary.

Department of Conservation

Approximatley one-third of New Zealand is legally protected under nature conservation. The Department of Conservation (DOC) administrates and cares for the 12 national parks, three maritime parks and 18 forest parks. It is also responsible for the huts and cabins along the hiking tracks in the various regions. Overnight coupons can be purchased either in the regional offices or at the headquarters in Wellington. You can also obtain maps and information on all regions of New Zealand here.

Department of Conservation, Box 104230, 59 Boulcott Street, Wellington, Tel: 04-710726, FAX: 04-711082.

Electricity

The power supply in New Zealand is 230-volt alternating current (50 hertz). A flat, three-poled plug is required for the sockets. These should be purchased before your trip, but can also be found in special electrical shops in New Zealand.

Emergencies

The police, fire station and emergency rescue can be reached on the phone by dialing 111 in the cities. In rural areas, the respective number can be found on the first pages of the public telephone book.

Food and Drink

This topic is, of course, controversial. Even if the tourist authorities do not like to hear it (and one or the other New Zealand traveler would contradict it), eating out in New Zealand is still combined with a certain culinary adventurism. The quality of food in many places leaves much to be desired, the atmosphere and the service is often just average.

In the last few years, however, a new restaurant generation has established itself (especially in Auckland, Christchurch and Wellington). They are attractively furnished and serve good food. A number of these restaurants are listed in the respective *Guideposts*.

For most "normal" travelers on the road outside of big cities and centers, the solution to the question of where to eat is frequently answered with "take-away"; or they can cook for themselves, which is no problem at motels. The prerequisites are excellent. Along with the large selection of fresh fruits and vegetables comes the abundance of fish, lamb and game. In addition, a choice selection of good, even internationally distinguished wines is available.

A large portion of the restaurants have no license to serve alcohol. If you see the sign "BYO," bring your own bottle. The bottles brought in will gladly be opened and serviced. Don't be surprised if this service is charged to your bill as a small fee per person. At fully-licensed restaurants BYO is not allowed.

No matter where you dine, you should, in any case, try a specialty called *Pavlowa* for dessert. This voluptuous meringue pie is garnished with kiwi fruit, which is without a doubt something typical from the rather maligned cuisine of New Zealand.

Holidays and School Vacation

A trip to New Zealand during school vacation is often discouraged – but unjustly so. Because even when school vacation begins, traffic cannot be compared in any way to that in Europe. However, difficulties can arise with regard to accommodations and the ferry connection Wellington – Picton. Early reservations are therefore advised.

Most significant dates: Christmas vacation lasts from mid-December to the beginning of February. Winter vacation is from the end of August to the middle of September. In addition, there are one-week vacations each in May and July.

Legal holidays: January 1 (New Year), February 6 (Waitangi Day), Good Friday, Easter Monday, April 25 (ANZAC Day), 1st Monday in June (Queen's Birthday), 4th Monday in October (Labor Day), December 25 (Christmas Day) and December 26 (Boxing Day).

In addition, each province has its own anniversary, which is celebrated on a Monday in the summer between November and March.

Language

The official languages of the country are English and Maori. Maori is spoken by very few Pakeha (Caucasians). English sets the tone in everyday life. If English is not your native language, you will do just fine with European "island" English, especially since the *Kiwi* slang can easily be understood.

Nightlife

With the exception of the large cities of Auckland (Mercury Opera), Wellington

(Symphony Orchestra and Royal Ballet), and Christchurch, where numerous cultural activities provide entertainment during the week, New Zealand has much to be desired as far as nightlife is concerned. *Kiwis* seem to be happiest at home within their own four walls – unless, of course, they are getting together for a beer at a pub around the corner.

Postal Service

Post offices are open Monday through Thursday from 8:30 a.m. to 5 p.m. and Friday until 8 p.m. In rural areas, postal duties are handled by dairies or small shops. Personal mail is also picked up here.

Many addresses are marked with the letters "R. D.," meaning rural delivery. Mail so designated is delivered by private persons or courier services, usually to remote villages or farms. The various routes thus bear R. D. numbers.

Restrooms

This topic may only be of interest in times of need, yet it is still comforting to know: In hardly any other country in the world will you find such well-kept and clean public restrooms as in New Zealand. This is also true for restrooms in the national parks and at remote rest stops.

Sales Tax

For goods and services in New Zealand a 12.5 % general sales tax (GTS) is charged. This tax is often but not always (for example, in restaurants) included in the price. Always check on the final price to be sure if this tax is included or not.

Sun

The destruction of the ozone layer is primarily having a negative effect on New Zealand (and Australia). Sunglasses and headgear definitely belong in your luggage. Protective sunscreen is absolutely necessary (factor 15 plus!). This can be purchased in New Zealand more reasonably than in Europe.

After the local weather report in the evening news, the burn times are reported daily. At these times, usually between 1 and 3 p.m., you should avoid staying out in the open and having extended direct exposure to the sun. You will see most *Kiwis* on the beach in a t-shirt – not only during these times. Skin cancer has increased considerably due to the intensified ultra-violet rays. This is probably New Zealand's greatest future health problem.

Telephone

The New Zealand Telephone Company introduced a seven-digit system in 1993. This means a step-by-step change in the existing area codes and local telephone numbers. In the future, the number 03 serves all of South Island and the numbers 09, 07, 06 and 04 the North Island. When in doubt, call the Information Free Phone at the number 0155.

Telephone cards are well-established in New Zealand. The practical cards can be purchased in various stores and takeaways with card values between NZ$ 5 and NZ$ 50.

Numbers beginning with 0800 are toll-free or cost as much as a local call. 025 numbers are for cellular phones and can be expensive. The minimum rate is 1.20 NZ$.

The country codes for English-speaking countries are: Australia 0061, Canada 001, Great Britain 0044, Ireland 00353 and the USA 001. Information can be reached under the number 018 for national and under 0172 for international numbers.

Time Difference

New Zealand is 12 hours ahead of Greenwich Mean Time (London 11 a.m. = Auckland 11 p.m.). The difference is one hour less during daylight savings time in other countries, and one hour more during the New Zealand daylight savings time (October to end of March).

AUTHORS

Peter Hinze worked as editor for leading German travel magazines after studying journalism and politics. Since 1988, he has been working as a free-lance journalist and photographer based in Munich, Germany, where he also manages a news agency and publishing house. He wrote the chapters "The Secret Capital," "Across the Northland," "On Coromandel Peninsula," "Capital of New Zealand," "Magical Center of the South" and "The Wild West," and contributed to "The Southern Region."

Ainslie Talbot has been working for more than 15 years as a reporter for the news program of *Television New Zealand.* He has devoted himself above all to environmental issues and nature conservation. He co-authored "The Heart of New Zealand" and "South Island" with Marc Marger (see below), "The Southern Region" with Peter Hinze (see above), and wrote the feature on tramping.

Marc Marger traveled to New Zealand for the first time in 1979. South Island has since become a second home for the free-lance journalist. He co-authored two chapters with Ainslie Talbot (see above) and wrote "In The South" and "Highlands and Plains."

Mareen Te Rangi Rere I Waho Waaka is one of the most well-known Maori women in New Zealand. She was Miss New Zealand in 1962. In 1971, together with her husband she founded the *Rotorua Maori Entertainers.* She lives in Rotorua, where she lives with her five children and seven grandchildren. She contributed to the feature "New Zealand Today."**John Berry** has made a name for himself during his 30 years of journalistic work as a TV and show columist in Auckland. He has now retreated to Gisborne on East Cape to write books. He wrote "East Cape."

Pat Hanning worked for years as a reporter for the daily newspaper *The New Zealand Herald.* He wrote about farming and co-authored "New Zealand Today."

Peter Birkenmeier was a free-lance consultant for ten years at New Zealand's Tourist Association in Frankfurt, germany. He and Peter Linden joined forces for the chapter "Maori Mythology."

Peter Linden is a sports editor for the *Süddeutsche Zeitung* in Munich, Germany. In New Zealand, he mainly sought outdoor adventure and traced Maori culture ("Maori Mythology"). He also wrote the feature on sports.

Conrad Stein is a writer of travel guides and publisher with extensive experience in New Zealand. He updated the *Nelles Guide New Zealand* together with **Marie-Luise Tolkmit**.

PHOTOGRAPHERS

Explore the World

AVAIBLABLE TITLES

Afghanistan 1 : 1 500 000
Australia 1 : 4 000 000
Bangkok - *Greater Bangkok,*
  Bangkok City 1 : 75 000 / 1 : 15 000
Burma → *Myanmar*
Caribbean Islands 1 *Bermuda,*
  Bahamas, Greater Antilles
  1 : 2 500 000
Caribbean Islands 2 *Lesser Antilles*
  1 : 2 500 000
Central America 1 : 1 750 000
Colombia - Ecuador 1 : 2 500 000
Crete - Kreta 1 : 200 000
China 1 - *Northeastern*
  1 : 1 500 000
China 2 - *Northern* 1 : 1 500 000
China 3 - *Central* 1 : 1 500 000
China 4 - *Southern* 1 : 1 500 000
Egypt 1 : 2 500 000 / 1 : 750 000
Hawaiian Islands
  1 : 330 000 / 1 : 125 000
Hawaiian Islands 1 *Kauai*
  1 : 125 000
Hawaiian Islands 2 *Honolulu*
  - Oahu 1 : 125 000
Hawaiian Islands 3 *Maui - Molokai*
  - Lanai 1 : 125 000
Hawaiian Islands 4 *Hawaii, The*
  Big Island 1 : 330 000 / 1 : 125 000

Himalaya 1 : 1 500 000
Hong Kong 1 : 22 500
Indian Subcontinent 1 : 4 000 000
India 1 - *Northern* 1 : 1 500 000
India 2 - *Western* 1 : 1 500 000
India 3 - *Eastern* 1 : 1 500 000
India 4 - *Southern* 1 : 1 500 000
India 5 - *Northeastern - Bangladesh*
  1 : 1 500 000
Indonesia 1 : 4 000 000
Indonesia 1 *Sumatra* 1 : 1 500 000
Indonesia 2 *Java + Nusa Tenggara*
  1 : 1 500 000
Indonesia 3 *Bali* 1 : 180 000
Indonesia 4 *Kalimantan*
  1 : 1 500 000
Indonesia 5 *Java + Bali* 1 : 650 000
Indonesia 6 *Sulawesi* 1 : 1 500 000
Indonesia 7 *Irian Jaya + Maluku*
  1 : 1 500 000
Jakarta 1 : 22 500
Japan 1 : 1 500 000
Kenya 1 : 1 100 000
Korea 1 : 1 500 000
Malaysia 1 : 1 500 000
West Malaysia 1 : 650 000
Manila 1 : 17 500
Mexico 1 : 2 500 000
Myanmar (Burma) 1 : 1 500 000

Nepal 1 : 500 000 / 1 : 1 500 000
Trekking Map *Khumbu Himal /*
  Solu Khumbu 1 : 75 000
New Zealand 1 : 1 250 000
Pakistan 1 : 1 500 000
Peru - Ecuador 1 : 2 500 000
Philippines 1 : 1 500 000
Singapore 1 : 22 500
Southeast Asia 1 : 4 000 000
Sri Lanka 1 : 450 000
Tanzania - Rwanda, Burundi
  1 : 1 500 000
Thailand 1 : 1 500 000
Taiwan 1 : 400 000
Uganda 1 : 700 000
Venezuela - Guyana, Suriname,
  French Guiana 1 : 2 500 000
Vietnam, Laos, Cambodia
  1 : 1 500 000

FORTHCOMING

Dominican Republic - Haiti
  1 : 600 000
South Pacific Islands
Trekking Map *Kathmandu Valley /*
  Helambu, Langtang 1 : 75 000

Nelles Maps in european top quality!
Relief mapping, kilometer charts and tourist attractions.
Always up-to-date!

Explore the World

NELLES GUIDES

AVAILABLE TITLES

Australia
Bali / Lombok
Berlin and Potsdam
Brittany
California
   Las Vegas, Reno,
   Baja California
Cambodia / Laos
Canada
   Ontario, Québec,
   Atlantic Provinces
Caribbean
   The Greater Antilles,
   Bermuda, Bahamas
Caribbean
   The Lesser Antilles
China – Hong Kong
Corsica
Crete
Cyprus
Egypt
Florida
Greece – *The Mainland*
Hawai'i
Hungary
India
   Northern, Northeastern
   and Central India
India – *Southern India*

Indonesia
   Sumatra, Java, Bali,
   Lombok, Sulawesi
Ireland
Israel - *with Excursions*
   to Jordan
Kenya
London, England and
   Wales
Malaysia
Mexico
Morocco
Moscow / St Petersburg
Munich
   Excursions to Castels,
   Lakes & Mountains
Nepal
New York – *City and State*
New Zealand
Paris
Philippines
Portugal
Prague / Czech Republic
Provence
Rome
Scotland
South Africa
Spain – *Pyrenees, Atlantic*
   Coast, Central Spain

Spain
   Mediterranean Coast,
   Southern Spain,
   Balearic Islands
Sri Lanka
Thailand
Turkey
Tuscany
U.S.A.
   The East, Midwest and
   South
U.S.A.
   The West, Rockies and
   Texas
Vietnam

FORTHCOMING

Brazil
Croatia – *Adriatic Coast*
Canada
   The Rockies, Pacific,
   Prairie, and the Territories
Myanmar (Burma)
Norway
South Pacific Islands
Syria – Lebanon
Tanzania

Nelles Guides – authorative, informed and informative.
Always up-to-date, extensivley illustrated, and with first-rate relief maps.
256 pages, appr. 150 color photos, appr. 25 maps